Making the Move to eLearning

Putting Your Course Online

Kay Lehmann and Lisa Chamberlin

ROWMAN & LITTLEFIELD EDUCATION
Lanham • New York • Toronto • Plymouth, UK

Published in the United States of America
by Rowman & Littlefield Education
A Division of Rowman & Littlefield Publishers, Inc.
A wholly owned subsidary of The Rowman & Littlefield Publishing Group, Inc.
4501 Forbes Boulevard, Suite 200, Lanham, Maryland 20706
www.rowmaneducation.com

Estover Road
Plymouth PL6 7PY
United Kingdom

British Library Cataloguing in Publication Information Available

Library of Congress Cataloging-in-Publication Data

Lehmann, Kay Johnson, 1957–
  Making the move to eLearning : putting your course online / Kay Lehmann and
Lisa Chamberlin.
     p. cm.
  Includes bibliographical references and index.
  ISBN 978-1-60709-040-3 (cloth : alk. paper) — ISBN 978-1-60709-041-0 (pbk. :
alk. paper) — ISBN 978-1-60709-042-7 (electronic)
  1. Computer-assisted instruction 2. Internet in education. 3. Curriculum planning.
4. Teachers—Effect of technological innovations on. I. Chamberlin, Lisa, 1966–
II. Title.
  LB1028.5.L4336 2009
  371.33'44678—dc22   2009006968

∞ ™ The paper used in this publication meets the minimum requirements of American
National Standard for Information Sciences—Permanence of Paper for Printed Library
Materials, ANSI/NISO Z39.48-1992.
Manufactured in the United States of America.

Contents

Acknowledgments

We would like to thank our families for their unwavering support and patience. We would also like to acknowledge Coffee Perk: thank you for letting us use you as our second office. Thank you to Dr. Peggy Gaskill, Michigan Virtual University; Dr. Sheila Bartle, Kendall College; and Joan Vandervelde, University of Wisconsin–Stout, for donating generously of your time for interviews and e-mail exchanges. Also thank you to Dr. Stephen Ehrmann of the Teaching Learning and Technology (TLT) Group for your valuable advice; Dr. Chris Dede of Harvard University for sharing the in-press chapter of your upcoming book; and Will Richardson for your time and commentary on our work.

Our final thanks go to the thousands of online students we have had over the years. We have learned something from each and every one of you!

1

The Radical Truth: Online Education Can Be Better Than Traditional Education

Online education, also known as **eLearning** or **distance education**, can be an exceptional mode of learning when facilitated well. On the other hand, the impact on students of a poorly trained instructor can be dire, as will be illustrated. A recent student wrote the following email that illustrates, better than the authors of this book ever could, why training is an absolute necessity for online **facilitators**.

> I have taken a few online classes, and I have learned that you can tell whether or not the instructor is competent and well-organized (thereby minimizing technology problems and other issues) pretty much right away (as a general rule). I really appreciate you taking the time to engage each of us, as well as cover the netiquette piece. It bodes well for relationship-building and for the benefit of the learner.
>
> I tell you the following as an encouragement for writing this book and to illustrate the importance of the material. I began taking online graduate classes this past summer. I took an e-learning class and an instructional leadership class. I had exceptional instructors. I officially began my Master's program with my cohort group a couple of weeks ago with the kickoff of fall semester. One of my required courses began back on 9/3. The books needed were posted on 8/20 as there were multiple titles that needed to be ordered by the student. Many of the editions were incorrectly posted, making it impossible to find some of the titles. I decided to order what was close and be done with it. It worked out fine.
>
> Then, about a week and a half into the class I received a mass email from my instructor to multiple people in the class, sent as though it was from me. In other words, he sent an email to multiple colleagues in my class at one time, counseling them on their lack of involvement in class. It wouldn't have been a big deal except for the fact that he was still impersonating me when he sent it,

and he didn't sign his name. That means that upwards of 30 people in my class (he merged 2 classes into 1) received a mass email from me, schooling them about being disengaged. To make matters worse, because of his lack of skill in navigating the system . . . the information . . . was incorrect.

Consequently, I began receiving multiple angry emails from my colleagues. At first, I tried to respond to some of them stating that I didn't send the email. I contacted my instructor, and he blamed [the CMS]. I contacted [the Help Desk], and they explained what I already knew. I had been given instructor status in my e-learning class to create various components, so I knew that [the instructor] has access to my account. The rest of my colleagues, however, are new to online learning. There was no discussion on netiquette, etc. I respectfully confronted my professor, and he sent out somewhat of an apologetic email to the class. That said, he definitely left room for interpretation.

This was this past Saturday. As I glance over the class list for your class, everyone in this class is in that other class. It is uncomfortable, and to be honest, I felt like quitting. I am not a quitter; however . . . the whole situation just stinks. Besides the impact that this has had on me, the impact of the conduct and limited proficiency of the professor is impacting my colleagues as well. (e-mail communication, 2008)

When a skilled online facilitator teaches a well-written online course, the opportunities for learning are incredible, even better than **traditional learning,** also known as a **face-to-face (f2f)** class. This is the radical truth proposed here: that online education can be better than traditional classes. In a survey of online educators and administrators, Kim and Bonk (2006) came to this conclusion as well.

Clearly, respondents believe that face-to-face instruction provides a valid benchmark for teaching and learning outcomes and that online performance should at least equal its effectiveness. Such views, while politically important, seem to forget that much of the learning that occurs online could not take place in a face-to-face delivery mode (for example, **asynchronous** online discussions or online mentoring). It also assumes that face-to-face instruction is superior. What if institutions took the opposite stance and measured face-to-face courses based on whether they could accomplish all that online instruction can? (Kim & Bonk, 2006, p. 28)

Online education, *when conducted as defined throughout this book*—keep this proviso in mind while reading the following list—is better than traditional education for a host of reasons; 26 reasons are gathered here for consideration.

A. Students must be active learners. Those who sit quietly trying to avoid participating in an online class remain invisible to their instructor and colleagues. To earn a score, a student must participate (Chang & Smith, 2008).

B. Course materials remain current. Unlike textbooks or instructor's notes which are static, digital material can be updated with the newest information at any time (Gupta, Eastman, & Swift, 2005).

C. Instruction engages the learner with the content through multiple channels. **Learner-content interaction** is key. Interaction occurs through discussion, role play, **simulation**, research, and a myriad of other ways (Keeler & Horney, 2007).

D. Learners are engaged with each other and the instructor. All discussions are open to all members of the course and everyone is involved with one another's commentary (Richardson & Newby, 2006).

E. **Online learning** is **pandemic proof**. One of the first plans that will be put in motion should large-scale illness ever affect our nation or planet is to switch over to digital delivery of education (Weiss, 2008).

F. The exploration of ideas is deep; each additional comment to a discussion takes the conversation deeper (Gupta, et al., 2005).

G. All discussions are captured in perpetuity. This allows students to review or remediate content at anytime from anywhere.

H. The **anonymity** of the online environment offers more freedom to disagree and question others (Wenger, 1998).

I. Learners receive the benefits of a vibrant learning **community** where discussions build cyclically when they have time to fully evolve (Collison, Tinker, Elbaum, & Haavind, 2000).

J. Everyone can work at a time most convenient for them and in an environment they define as most conducive to their working style.

K. Using today's technology, all **learning styles** and needs/disabilities can be met in the optimal learning environment so that all learners thrive.

L. Education is not bound by geographic constraints. Students can study at any institution that meets their needs. Institutions can market their courses to anyone, anywhere. Instructors can teach from anywhere (United Nations Educational Scientific and Cultural Organization [UNESCO], 2002).

M. Potential issues of gender, race, and other physical characteristics are invisible in the online environment. In terms of physicality, learners meet in the online classroom on a level playing field.

N. Economics are less of an issue when learning online when students do not have to buy gas, parking fees, or pay for daycare (Sweeney, 2007).

O. Time is maximized for learners. Time on authentic tasks is emphasized through **course design** using scaffolding.

P. Class sizes are smaller. In online education, instructors get to know every student more thoroughly. Instructors cannot teach 700:1 classes in the environment, as it would be impossible to handle the student load of a typical on-campus Psychology 101 class.

Q. In general, students showcase their learning through application of the material rather than through tests. This leads to more authentic learning through **authentic assessment** (Baker, 2005).

R. Students can learn from the best instructors in the world no matter where the instructor lives. For that matter, students can attend the best schools in the world, no matter where the students live.

S. Online learning contributes to sustainability; it is a green industry (Viscusi, 2008).

T. All participants benefit from the global **diversity** of online learning population. Viewpoints from all over the world can be expressed in a single class open to global enrollment (Shea, 2007).

U. Technology skills for all participants are further developed.

V. Communication skills increase because every student and instructor must communicate, and communications must be clear.

W. Feedback is meaningful, timely, and expected (Tennessee Board of Regents, 2006).

X. Instructors working at a distance are not involved in typical face-to-face administrative duties and can be working for multiple institutions.

Y. Feelings of being part of a community are unlike what is experienced in traditional courses. Students in successful online **communities of practice** often remark about feeling closer to their colleagues than in campus-based courses.

Z. The successful use of **social learning theory** and communities of practice creates transference beyond the immediate course in a positive, impactful way (J. M. Lehmann, 2008).

The goal of this book is to show educators a new way of doing business and to excite them to the possibilities that can happen when online instruction is in the hands of well-trained experts. **Backward diffusion** of best practices from online learning is already being transferred to traditional education. Increased diffusion of the best of online learning will benefit all learners.

To paraphrase an old saying, when eLearning is good, it is very, very good. Yet, when it is bad, it is, as it was for the student whose email began this chapter, truly horrid. Does all online education match the characteristics listed? No. If it did, there would be no need for this book or **eCertification** courses in online teaching.

In fact, online education, like traditional education, has its problems. According to Harvard professor Dr. Chris Dede (2006), distance education is often like pouring, "old wine in new bottles" (p. 1). If 21st century educators are simply taking limited **pedagogy** and poor student interaction to a digital interface, the results will be disastrous. The cold and impersonal myth often associated with online education stems, in part, from the bad experiences of many online learners.

THE COLD, IMPERSONAL MYTH

The myth that online learning is cold and impersonal is just that, a myth. Many students, once acclimated to the online environment, find that they participate more, know their instructor and colleagues better, and discuss the content more deeply than they ever have in a traditional classroom.

Is Text Cold and Impersonal?

Why does the myth persist? One reason for the persistence is that the world of online learning is still very much text-based. While strides are being made to incorporate audio, video, and other forms of multimedia, the fact is that in many, if not most, online courses the majority of the content, the discussions, and the assignments, remain text-based. Text alone appears cold and impersonal. But is it?

Think of the first time you read a book like *Old Yeller* and felt the sadness at the end, the overwhelming grief when you received a *Dear John* type letter, or the *gut-busting* laughter caused by reading a funny story or email. Text can obviously, therefore, evoke strong emotions. This book will provide much more information on how to engender passion for the content and a sense of community to the learners through a text-based environment in future chapters.

Challenges Posed by the Lack of Physical Presence

Another reason for the cold, impersonal myth's endurance is that online learning is devoid of the communication nuances such as vocal, facial, and social cues that help students interpret the **messages** of others (K. L. Lehmann, 2008). Without the use of audio and video, the learners simply do not have access to the cues taken for granted in a face-to-face environment. Stated more directly, learners cannot hear the voice, see the face, or interpret the body language of their instructor or colleagues.

According to Dr. Sheila Bartle (personal communication, September 5, 2003), former assistant director of the Master's in Education program at Walden University, "Distance education certainly offers its challenges, the foremost of which is, of course, the absence of immediate physical presence of students to the faculty member and to classmates . . . the inability to see a face, read its meaning, and respond with all the rich possibilities of physical presence."

Instructor Skills

Since instructor communication skills are crucial to the success of a course or program, it would follow that these skills are purposefully taught to future facilitators, and instructors would be supported as they develop these skills. This is rarely the case. Most instructor training programs focus on how to use the tools of the **course management system** (**CMS**), not methodology and communication skills.

The developers of these tool-based training programs probably assume, albeit wrongly, that communication and teaching skills can be transferred directly and easily from the face-to-face environment to the online environment. This is not always the case. While there are similarities in teaching within both of these environments, there are marked differences as well. The best practices for traditional education are not necessarily the same as in eLearning. However, online learning is so new that the research base is still evolving.

HOW TO USE THIS TEXT

This textbook is organized to help online professionals, from those who have not yet taught online to veterans who would like to refresh their skills and perhaps learn some new ways of tackling old problems.

For the beginner, we suggest reading this text in order—learning about the history of online teaching, the applicable learning theory through course design, troubleshooting, and finally learning how to find and keep online teaching employment.

For the intermediate practitioner who is perhaps in the middle of their first or second course, we still suggest reading the entire book, but for your immediate needs, Chapters 3, 6, 7, 9, 10, 11, and 15 may be your highest priorities.

For the veteran online educator wanting a refresher, we continue to suggest Chapters 6, 7, 9, 10, 11, and 15. From there, the veteran facilitator may want to refer to the list of 26 Radical Truths on pages 2–4. Cherry picking among the areas listed will allow the experienced online instructor a chance to read about specific topics of interest.

Finally, readers should know that some topics, which the authors consider highly important, are referred to in more than one chapter, though they might be covered lightly in one chapter and more in depth in another. A glossary is also provided at the end to clarify unfamiliar terms.

In *Making the Move to eLearning* we've culled research and experience to help you become the best online practitioner you can be. Teachers and **course designers** who use the concepts, ideas, and skills in this book will be contributing to a better world of online education—a world where online education is very, very good; a world where traditional education is striving to match the superiority of eLearning.

The Past, Present, and Future: Development of Online Learning

DISTANCE LEARNING: THE PAST (EARLY 20TH CENTURY THROUGH THE LATE 1990s)

How did online learning develop and where is it headed? To truly understand the present as well as shape the future, facilitators need to know where distance education began. This background will help build the knowledge necessary to talk about how to appropriately and successfully teach in this new environment.

Distance education did not begin with the advent of the Internet. In fact, students have been learning in remote places far away from their instructors for quite some time now. "In 1840, Sir Isaac Pitman, the English inventor of shorthand, came up with an ingenious idea for delivering instruction to a potentially limitless audience: **correspondence courses** by mail" (Phillips, 1998). Since Pitman's time, however, correspondence courses have had a poor completion rate compared to their face-to-face counterparts. Why is it so many students never complete correspondence courses? To answer that question, we must first take a look at the nature of early correspondence courses through a typical, yet hypothetical, student.

Typical Correspondence Course

Suzy, a 19-year-old undergraduate student needed a class to complete her degree, so she decided to take the course during the summer and registered with NotAReal University for its Math 111 class taught as a correspondence course. She then headed home for the summer. Several weeks later, her course materials arrived along with directions stating she had six months in which to complete the work. No sweat! She ordered her textbook and headed for a weeklong camping trip. Suzy returned home from the trip to find her book had arrived, and she completed her first assignment, sending it off to her instructor through the U.S. postal system.

Suzy intermittently worked on her assignments while finding a job, having her usual summer fun, and spending time with friends. By the time summer was over, she was a third of the way through the coursework but half the way through her time allotted from the university. Unfortunately, Suzy now had to head back to her regular fall class schedule at school. The correspondence course was put on the back burner to be completed in her spare time, where it was promptly forgotten and replaced by the immediacy of day-to-day interactive classes. Eventually, Suzy received a letter from the university noting her failure to complete the course requirements resulted in an "F" grade on her transcript. Without the frequent contact and interaction with her course instructor, peers, and the content, Suzy did—as many correspondence students often still do—she procrastinated her way to failure.

Telecourses

Students in **telecourses** did not fare much better. Telecourses were made up of a series of TV shows either broadcast or prerecorded and given to the student for the duration of the course. They were supplemented with print materials as well. In the early days, students worked through video tapes much like correspondence courses, with the same inherent problems. Faculty were assigned to the courses, but many failed to actively interact with the students in the courses they were assigned—instead they managed the paperwork of the course. The long-term, limited success rate of these programs also seems to suggest that early distance-learning students didn't utilize the faculty for any substantial reasons. Dynamic growth in telecourses failed to occur, just as it failed to occur with correspondence courses.

With the advent of the Internet and its use by the public, online teaching and learning was born. However, those first baby steps were only marginally successful. Some institutions simply used the Internet as little more than a faster version of the post office and carried on with business as usual—just slightly faster.

Two characteristics distinguished those early online courses from traditional correspondence courses. One, students read much of the material online instead of from a textbook or another *paper-based* format; and two, assignments were emailed to the instructor instead of sending them through the traditional mail system. Other than that, most online courses were virtually identical to typical correspondence course offerings of the time. There was little-to-no interaction with other students in the class and little interaction with the professor. In addition, instructor feedback was weak and, therefore, generally not helpful in fostering the growth of the student who was on his or her own to learn the content.

Computer-Assisted Instruction

Computer-assisted instruction (**CAI**) used the Internet to create a more *interactive* course by having students read through web pages and then answer multiple choice questions at the end of each section or unit. The interactivity happened as students selected multiple choice items at the end of the reading. These self-paced, tutorial-type courses did provide the student with instantaneous feedback, but there was zero facilitator or **learner-learner** interaction, and the material was often forgotten shortly after it was completed. While students could quickly complete many small learning units, the lack of retention of learned material was certainly a downside.

Why didn't students retain the material learned through CAI? Social learning theory suggests "discourse between people is needed for deep learning to occur" (K. L. Lehmann, 2008, p. 13). The lack of discourse, learner-learner or learner-instructor, ultimately limited the software's effectiveness. "The establishment of an online community is widely held as the most important prerequisite for successful course completion and depends on an interaction between a peer group and a facilitator" (Nagel, Blignaut, & Cronjeacute, 2008). CAI programs of the past through the present day lack the discourse and community needed for true learning to occur.

No wonder so many distance education offerings became, as one former student described them, *university donations* (K. L. Lehmann, 2004). The university got the tuition dollars, but students never completed the courses, making the tuition, in essence, a donation rather than payment for credits earned. Very little of what we know about good educational practices, such as (a) the benefits of learner-learner interaction, (b) the importance of timely feedback and **assessment** by a highly qualified instructor, and (c) the opportunity to quickly clarify misunderstood or unclear concepts before building upon those concepts with new material and ideas were part of the distance education courses of the past.

K–12: Our School Is on the Web

In K–12 public education, the distance learning movement was all but non-existent until the late 1990s. Dot-com companies did attempt to breach this market at that time by providing free **portals**, websites, or web pages for schools or individual classrooms to have a presence on the Internet. These sites were little more than web page templates made simple by providing the designer, in this case usually the classroom teacher, a graphical interface in which to type text and upload pictures. The storage was small and the interactivity was usually limited to an email link. Teachers would often post an *About Our Class* web page, with announcements and homework being posted regularly by the more technically savvy. In this way, the sites became like classroom eNewsletters.

The most innovative teachers created ways to put coursework online, which students could work on independently and email or return to the teacher face-to-face. The sites, therefore, were an early example of **blended learning**, or **hybrid courses**, as they would be called today. Some of the more advanced portal systems sold to entire school districts included attendance and grading modules and were the early precursors to the large course management systems (CMS) used today, like Blackboard, ANGEL Learning, eCollege, and Desire2Learn.

ONLINE LEARNING TODAY

Course Count

According to Zandberg and Lewis (2008) "37 percent of all public U.S. school districts and 10 percent of all public schools" are currently offering some form of technology-based distance learning in K–12 education. Of these courses, 71 percent of them are delivered online. While there hasn't been a substantial growth in the number of school districts offering courses between years of the United States' Department of Education (USDOE) survey, there has been substantial growth in enrollment in the courses offered "from an estimated 317,070 enrollments in 2002–2003 to 506,950 enrollments in 2004–2005" (Zandberg & Lewis, 2008, p. iv). In other words, while the number of courses offered by the school districts in the two years between surveys only grew by approximately 1 percent, the number of students taking those courses almost doubled.

Comparably, 56 percent of all degree-granting institutions of higher education are offering distance-education courses of one form or another to their students (Wirt, Choy, Rooney, Provasnik, Sen, & Tobin, 2004). The overwhelming majority of these courses are offered online.

Online enrollment trends reflect economic hardships as well. The rapid spike in gas prices in 2007–2008 was followed by a trend in requests and enrollment spikes by students seeking to keep commuting costs down. According to Young (2008), the community colleges of Tennessee, Brevard,

Harrisburg Area, and Northampton all reported online course enrollment gains of 18 to 29 percent.

Types of Current Online Classes

Modern online courses cannot be pigeonholed into neat categories. However, some categories can be used to help define the types of courses offered online. Course types vary in: (a) level of expected facilitation, (b) level of learner-learner interactions, (c) expected outcomes, (d) start-end and assignment due dates, and (e) involvement of the sponsoring entity or institution. These categories are used to describe six generalized models of common online courses in Table 15.1.

Many online courses now depend highly on learner-learner and facilitator-learner interactions on a regular, if not daily, basis. This means there are several opportunities to clarify concepts before adding new ideas into the mix. These communication opportunities can include use of an online bulletin board or forum to elicit comments from fellow learners or the instructor and/or emailing or even phoning other learners or the instructor directly.

A good online course features opportunities to stretch thinking skills and get almost immediate feedback. Course materials can be offered through visual and auditory messages such as **podcasts** and **streaming video**, as well as the more traditional textbook, either student-purchased or web-based. These are characteristics and tools of online courses of the present time; changes in all of these features will undoubtedly occur in the future.

Natural Considerations

One serious consideration of distance learning is one mentioned in almost every K–12 emergency planning report, and yet not talked about too often, and that is the use of eLearning for its ability to answer the call of pandemic-proofing education. In 2006 when President George W. Bush released the United States' National Strategic Plan for pandemic readiness, federal and state agencies were given 12 months to comply with a list of over 300 actions to take. According to John Lange, State Department representative on the avian flu, "Infectious diseases know no borders . . . and a key aspect of our campaign to contain the spread of highly pathogenic avian influenza and to prepare for the possibility of a human pandemic is large-scale global engagement, specifically ongoing efforts by governments, international organizations and the private sector" (Pellerin, 2007).

We know that the pandemics of the past were horrific. The influenza outbreak of 1918 killed more than 675,000 Americans and the 1957 influenza pandemic took 70,000 more (United States Department of Health and Human Services, 2008). Should such an outbreak occur in modern times, a distance learning infrastructure ensures that the U.S. education system can continue with only a brief interruption as the switchover from extended (a regular classroom with a web presence) and blended classrooms to fully online classrooms takes place. This is especially true in the higher education circles where more classes have a current presence online.

The checklist offered by the United States Department of Health and Human Services (USDHHS) pandemic flu website for both higher education and K–12 includes this statement, "[d]evelop alternative procedures to assure continuity of instruction (e.g., web-based distance instruction, telephone trees, mailed lessons and assignments, instruction via local radio or television stations) in the event of district school closures" (USDHHS, 2008). As well as the need to, "[d]evelop a continuity of operations plan for essential central office functions including payroll and ongoing communication with students and parents" (USDHHS, 2008). Any competent CMS could quickly provide for both of these actions, and for schools with distance education programs currently up and running, the infrastructure is already in place, should the need arise in a larger scale.

Pandemic preparation has also boosted preparation for other types of emergencies and disasters. Consider the hurricanes Katrina and in later years Ike and Gustav. Katrina devastated the educational system in and around the New Orleans area. But, just three years later, with lessons learned about the need for preparation and planning, and despite the devastation caused by Ike and Gustav, education was able to continue.

Bret Jacobs, executive director of information technology at Loyola stated it this way, "Since Katrina, the school has also moved its course management system online and has it hosted remotely so that students can continue their classes over the Internet in the event the campus is closed during an emergency. What we're trying to do is make sure the educational process is not interrupted. We're not a distance learning campus per se, but we're using some of those technologies" (Weiss, 2008).

Sustainability of Green Technology

As the *green* movement takes hold in the United States, more and more public and private institutions, as well as business enterprises, are concerned with presenting an environmentally conscious presence to their communities and the greater public. To that end, ideas like telecommuting, web seminars (webinars), and distance education are seen as areas where businesses and schools alike can preserve energy costs and help the planet. This is what members of the Association for Information Communications Technology Professionals in Higher Education (ACUTA), as reported by Viscusi (2008), confirmed in a recent survey,

> According to the survey's findings, universities are taking these steps by launching initiatives like distance learning and online education programs to reduce the need for students and faculty to commute and to reduce the amount of energy used to run their schools. Sixty-five percent of those surveyed said their schools are buying new equipment and instituting these polices.

ONLINE LEARNING IN THE FUTURE

What does the future hold for online learning? "By all accounts, the 1990s witnessed a revolution in distance education. The growth of the Internet, coupled with a growing demand for convenient and flexible access to higher education, has brought about the greatest change in education delivery since the first correspondence courses were made available in the early nineteenth century" (American Council on Education, 2000).

The changes noted by the American Council on Education (ACE) are echoed by this statement from a *Forbes* magazine's supplement, "E-learning is the fastest-growing and most promising market in the education industry" (Hall, 2000). In 1999, Cisco Systems CEO John Chambers gave a keynote address that included this oft-quoted statement, "The next big killer application for the Internet is going to be education. Education over the Internet is going to be so big it is going to make e-mail look like a rounding error."

While Chambers may have missed the mark a bit on his predictions of education via the Internet making email seem obsolete, his analogy meant to show a change, such as what the cell phone has done to the land line; the growth of students taking coursework online has certainly been nothing short of phenomenal. According to the most recent statistics released by the United States Department of Education, more than 70 percent of K–12 public school districts currently offering technology-based distance learning are planning expansion of their offerings in the future (Zandberg & Lewis, 2008). The trend for expansion seems to fall more in the urban, larger metropolitan markets, with 86 percent expected growth, compared to suburban and rural markets expecting 70 percent increases.

Higher education expects to see growth in online learning as well. The most recently available statistics shows a

> 9.7 percent growth rate for online enrollments far exceeds the 1.5 percent growth of the overall higher education student population. Almost 3.5 million

students were taking at least one online course during the fall 2006 term; a nearly 10 percent increase over the number reported the previous year. Nearly 20 percent of all U.S. higher education students were taking at least one online course in the fall of 2006. (Allen & Seaman, 2007, p. 1)

The highest levels of growth are occurring at the community college level, which reports figures consistently in the mid-teens to low twentieth percentile ranges for online enrollment growth in the 2006–2007 years nationwide.

Correspondence Courses Never Became Ubiquitous—Will Online Learning?

Whether or not these predictions of exponential growth come to pass depends greatly on the type of courses and the quality of instruction offered. There is a reason that the whole world did not replace face-to-face secondary and postsecondary education with correspondence courses. The truth is, distance learning, like correspondence and telecourses, only filled niche markets in the past.

For online learning to become truly mainstream, it has to offer the best qualities of face-to-face learning, as well as the global focus, convenience, and flexibility that can only happen in the online educational realm. No face-to-face course offers the ability to discuss topics with colleagues in Peoria, Pyongyang, and Prague, while the learner is dressed in pajamas freed from the need to pay a babysitter or find parking. In addition, every learner can study at his or her optimum time of day for learning. These are just some of the advantages of online learning when compared to traditional educational settings.

The possibilities for online learning are clear. Seeing these possibilities blossom will require more attention to the most crucial aspect of any course: the instruction. A great instructor can make a poor course shine, whether it is delivered face-to-face or online; but a poor instructor can drag down an entire group of learners, even if he or she has the most enticing materials available. Instructors averse to distance learning may work against positive movement if forced put *their* courses online.

As one anonymous 2007 Instructional Technology Council survey respondent stated,

Vocal conservative faculty members with little computer experience can stymie efforts to change when expressing a conviction that student learning outcomes can only be achieved in a face-to-face classroom, even though they have no idea what can be accomplished in a well-designed distance education course.

That is not to say that course development and the mechanics underlying the course are not equally important, they are!

The keystone for the success of online education is an understanding, well-trained, highly communicative facilitator who pushes, challenges, praises, and excites a group of learners to their maximum level of achievement. To do this, facilitators need an understanding of the educational theories underlying online learning. These theories are discussed in the next chapter.

3

Applicable Educational Theories

What would a methods textbook be without a chapter on educational theory? There are valid reasons for including educational theory in this book. The theories discussed here underlie the practices essential in the development of excellent online facilitators. This chapter includes **constructivism**, social learning theory, **instructivism**, **adult learning theory** also known as **andragogy**, pedagogy, and Gardner's (1983) multiple intelligences.

Building and maintaining a community of learners is an essential underlying principle of this book. Building on this teaching philosophy is the idea online teachers should be a *guide on the side, versus sage on the stage*. Essentially this catchphrase identifies the difference between the educational theory of constructivism, and more traditional teaching practices, known as instructivism. Most of the best practices in this book are based on the educational theory of constructivism.

CONSTRUCTIVISM

Constructivist theories, and there are several, all have in common the need for learners to experience and work with the concepts to learn them deeply. The emphasis is on, "the learner's contribution to meaning and learning through both individual and social activity" (Bruning, Schraw, & Ronning, 1999, p. 215). In a constructivist class, learning is (a) situated in real-life experiences and **scenarios**, (b) activities are hands on, (c) **dialogue** between learners and the facilitator is emphasized, (d) learning is not prescribed—it is guided but allowed to be evolutionary, and (e) assessment is authentic.

Social Learning Theory

A subset of constructivism, known as social learning theory, underpins the reliance on rich discussions and community discussed throughout *Making the Move to eLearning*. The current understanding of social learning theory builds on the work of Jean Piaget, Lev Vygotsky, and Albert Bandura. In K. M. Lehmann (2008),

> Social learning theory in its simplest terms, states that learning occurs when people discuss the content of the lesson with others . . . interaction with others is necessary for true learning to occur. True learning is not just the basic memorization of facts, but also the reevaluation [and] . . . application of the knowledge to new situations or problems. (p. 12)

When a true community of learners is created and sustained, the community provides the interactions necessary for true learning to occur.

How did social learning theory develop? Piaget and Vygotsky each defined a major educational philosophy underlying social learning theory (Berlyne, 2001; Vygotsky, 1978). Both hypothesized that true learning happens through social interactions with others. The core of social learning theory inherently involves this interaction with others.

According to Piaget and Vygotsky, the interactions are important because they challenge students to improve thinking and deepen learning through the discussion of the curricular topic. "Piaget and Vygotsky differ in their theorizations about learning in one major respect. Piaget believed learning occurred through an *internal* dialogue that is inside each learner. However, Vygotsky believed the necessary dialogue for learning was *external*, occurring between the parties involved in discussion through their verbal give and take" (K. M. Lehmann, 2008, p. 13).

Piaget's Personal Constructivism

Piaget's theory, known as personal constructivism or psychological constructivism, hypothesizes, "When learners interact with others, they are challenged to reconsider their own understandings, see additional information on how to resolve conflicts, and reconcile differences between themselves and others" (Gillies & Ashman, 2003, p. 12). This is an internal result that occurs inside the learner, cognitively. This differs from Vygotsky's belief that the interactions *between* the learners were the key.

Vygotsky's Social Constructivism

Vygotsky theorized that learning occurs when people discuss concepts with others. This dialogue causes learners to challenge other's understandings and beliefs. Vygotsky's theory, also known as social constructivism, differs from Piaget's in that "speech acquires a synthesizing function, which in turn is instrumental in achieving more complex forms of cognitive perception" (Vygotsky, 1978, p. 32). The common theme in both philosophies is that discourse between people is required for deep learning to occur. "Individuals create or construct their own new understandings or knowledge through the interaction" (Abdal-Haqqs, 1998, p. 1).

According to Piaget and Vygotsky, learning happens through the student-student discussions. These group interactions about the curriculum are the core of social learning theory.

Citing the work of Vygotsky, J. L. Lehmann (2008) states,

> Learning does not occur within isolation but requires the type of interactivity dialogue generates. Dialogue is part of an overall process. Learners think or reflect, and then they participate in dialogue or speech, which leads to more reflection and thinking, followed again by dialogue. (p. 11)

This dialogue is a core element of nearly all online courses. In an online course all students must participate in the dialogue, unlike in a traditional discussion where students may listen but not actually participate.

Another difference in dialogue between online courses and traditional is that all students can respond to the points made by all colleagues. Moreover the dialogue is captured and available in perpetuity. These differences in critical thinking in online course dialogue versus discussions in traditional courses illustrates why social constructivism is a principal theory in *Making the Move to eLearning: Putting Your Course Online*.

One fallacy about social constructivism is that no real instruction takes place, that the instructor is in fact not necessary in the constructivist classroom. In reality, the instructor is critical in creating the constructive learning environment. The first step in creating a constructivist lesson is to identify the core knowledge a student must learn. With this end result in mind, the instructor then plans for a variety of activities from which the students can choose that will lead to the students' understanding of the underlying core knowledge.

In addition, the instructor may need to develop scaffolding to assist learners as they work to create their own understanding of the concepts. This scaffolding may include some direct instruction to build the background knowledge necessary for students to succeed in constructing their own understanding. When direct instruction is necessary, the theory of constructivism begins to blend with traditional practices known as instructivism.

INSTRUCTIVISM

Instructivism, also called guided instruction, involves traditional teaching techniques familiar to most learners of any age. The teacher or facilitator in

Table 3.1.   Characteristics of Instructivism versus Constructivism

Characteristic	Instructivism	Constructivism
Central focus	Teacher centered	Curriculum and student centered
Knowledge source	Teacher is the fount of all knowledge; the sage on the stage	Information comes from multiple authentic sources; the teacher acts as the guide on the side
Daily lessons	Lesson design: Read, discuss, homework; repeat	Each unit is different depending on the needs of the lesson and the learners
Student activities	Activities are generally simple comprehension level activities, such as essays and multiple choice quizzes	Activities can be anything from role playing to writing a script to creating a castle
Inquiry	Student questions are answered by the teacher	Students are encouraged to find their own answers to their questions
Assessment	Quizzes and tests are the norm	Authentic assessment of student learning, usually project based

an instructivist classroom is the sage on the stage. An excellent illustration of the differences between instructivist classroom practices and constructive practices can be seen in Table 3.1.

In the online classroom, instructivism is sometimes used to build the background knowledge for learners. Providing diverse groups of learners with the same background knowledge allows them to proceed in a constructivist manner while ensuring all learners have the same vocabulary and understanding of the concepts for their dialogue in the course. While instructivism may play a useful role in background building, a fully instructivist online class is boring and does not allow for the dialogue that is central to building knowledge. That said, the balance between instructivism and constructivism may depend on the age of the learners in the class. Adult learners in particular thrive in a more constructivist environment. Constructivism and adult learning theory, also known as andragogy, have many tenets in common.

ADULT LEARNING THEORY

Adults learn differently than children. While this fact seems too basic to state, "there has been relatively little thinking, investigating, and writing about adult learning" (Knowles, Holton, & Swanson, 1998, p. 35). Throughout history the greatest teachers of all time, including Confucius, Jesus, and Socrates, taught adults.

> Because their experiences were with adults, they developed a very different concept of the learning/teaching process from the one that later dominated formal education. They perceived learning to be a process of mental inquiry, not passive reception of transmitted content. Accordingly, they invented techniques for engaging learners in the content. (Knowles, et al., 1998, p. 35)

Engaging learners with the content is a hallmark of the constructivist philosophy; this makes constructivism a logical approach for the instruction of adults.

According to Knowles and colleagues (1998) adult learning theory has six major tenets. These are: (a) the need to know, (b) the learners' self-concept, (c) the role of the learners' experiences, (d) readiness to learn, (e) orientation to learning, and (f) motivation.

The first principle, the need to know, can be better stated as a question. Adult learners often ask, "Why do I need to know this?" with an emphasis on the pronoun *I*. While many K–12 students also ask this question, it is adult learners who will stop the learning process until they get a satisfactory answer about the personal benefit inherent in the concept to be learned. Real-life scenarios and experiences need to be a part of the lesson planning for adult learners. Please take note that such scenarios are also constructivist in nature.

The second principle, the learners' self-concept, honors adults' independence and the need to be responsible for their own learning. "They resent and resist situations in which they feel others are imposing their wills on them" (Knowles, et al., 1998, p. 65). Adults want to be allowed to self-direct their learning. One way to incorporate self-directedness is to offer choices for how an assignment can be completed. The ability to choose the avenue learning will take is also common to constructivism.

The role of the learners' experiences is the third principle of andragogy. Adult learners bring to the classroom a vast amount of experiences. In general, adult learners grouped in a class have more heterogeneous backgrounds from which the entire group can learn. This richness of *lived lives* can benefit everyone when lessons allow for sharing of these experiences. Adult learners expect to share their experience and expertise. When opportunities for such sharing are blocked, both the learners' self-concept and learners' experiences are devalued (Knowles, et al., 1998). Adult learners may then become resentful.

Readiness to learn is the fourth tenet of adult learning theory. The concepts to be learned need to have an application to the adult learners' lives and the direction those lives are taking. As explained by Knowles and colleagues (1998), "Bench workers are not ready for a course in supervisory training until they have mastered doing the work they will supervise and decide they are ready for more responsibility" (p. 67).

The fifth principle of andragogy is orientation to learning. As previously stated, adults are life-centered. Lessons must allow adults to apply the knowledge and skills to their own lives and interests. Adult learners want to orient their assignments to a real part of their lives. Consideration of how adults will use the knowledge to be gained is the key.

Finally, the sixth principle is motivation. Simply stated, adults are, in general, not motivated by external rewards. Intrinsic rewards and personal motivations drive adult learners to succeed. Adult learners can be quite focused on what appear to be external motivators, such as grades, but their focus is actually internal. They know they are *A* students, for example. They are less concerned with who will see their grade on a transcript. Instead they want affirmation in their own minds that the grade they received represents their image of themselves.

Many of these principles are related to constructivist philosophies. Obviously adult learners will benefit from constructivist activities. What about learners who are not yet adults? The education of children is based on the educational theory known as pedagogy.

PEDAGOGY

The term *pedagogy* has two meanings that are used interchangeably in educational literature. One definition refers to *all* educational practices, and the other refers to childhood, or K–12, educational practices. Having already defined andragogy as the educational theory related to adults, the definition for pedagogy used in this chapter will be the educational theory of school-aged children. "The pedagogical model assigns to the teacher full responsibility for making all decisions about what will be learned, how it will be learned, when it will be learned, and if it has been learned" (Knowles, et al., 1998, p. 62). This theory emphasizes that the teacher knows all that needs to be learned, and the student is dependent on the teacher for all knowledge—in other words, instructivism. This definition is the one used to develop much of our current K–12 and higher education systems.

Pedagogy has been evolving as constructivist theories have made inroads, especially in the K–12 environment. In online education involving K–12 students, there is more reliance on teacher knowledge and teacher direction of learning. Some of the recent evolution in traditional K–12 classrooms away from a strict pedagogical, instructivist environment is due to the application of neuroscientific theories of learning, such as constructivism and **multiple intelligences** (Gardner, 1983). The current mania on standardized testing has caused many districts and states to revert back to rigid instructivist environments.

Such environments are not going to develop the kind of citizens needed in our world of the future. "A crucial challenge for U.S. education is to transform children's learning processes in and out of school and to engage student interest in gaining 21st century skills and knowledge" (Dede, 2006). Development of **critical thinking** skills is necessary. Online educators must focus on how to culture thinking skills in course design and facilitation.

LEARNING STYLES

Students have different preferred methods and modes of learning. Either online or face to face, any group of students will have a variety of learning styles. Course design and instruction needs to differentiate to meet the needs of as many learning styles as possible. There is not one set of definitions for learning styles, and all people have a mix of learning styles, however, they usually have one learning style more dominant with several lesser learning styles present. Different theorists have described learning styles in different ways.

Visual Aural Read-Write Kinesthetic

An easy to understand learning style definition is visual aural read-write kinesthetic (VARK) (Fleming, 2006). The VARK website makes it clear that the following is just part of a true learning style. These definitions are based on how the senses are involved in learning. All learners take in information when learning. That information can be presented in a variety of ways, and students can work with the information using a variety of senses.

Read-write learners best take in information through written text. This text can be from web pages, discussion forums, books, handouts, and any other method of supplying text to the learner. In addition these learners process information better when they write about what they are learning (Fleming, 2006).

Students with aural learning styles need to hear the information and speak about it to best learn it. In one study it was suggested that learners use screen reading software so that the text-based web material would be read aloud to them by the computer (Simoncelli, 2005). This was an attempt to reduce the amount of reading as well as to meet the needs of aural learners. Music, chants, and rhymes are commonly used in the primary grades in face-to-face classrooms to assist aural learners with understanding. In the online world, besides the possibility of using screen readers, multimedia can be used to assist learners with this preference. Tools such as video, **vodcasts**, and **Vokis** have the advantage of combining audio for aural learners and video for the visual learners (Fleming, 2006).

Students whose dominant learning style is visual take in information best through sight. This can include still images, video, animation, and live action. People working with current K–12 learners will find this generation is, overall, very visual. They benefit from visual teaching techniques. They also can be kinesthetic (Fleming, 2006).

Kinesthetic learners take in information best through movement. This can include the use of manipulatives, physical movement, touch screens, and other tactile movements. This is a harder style to meet in online learning than the others. Course designers and instructors can suggest activities that incorporate some movement, but it would be up to the online learner to actually decide whether to perform kinesthetic actions to go with the lesson (Fleming, 2006).

Many learners blend their preference equally among two or more of the VARK modes and are known as multimodal. This is similar to the idea of having more than one intelligence.

Multiple Intelligences

VARK is a simple definition of learning styles when compared with Howard Gardner's multiple intelligences. Gardner (1983) attests the intelligences are more than learning styles. Despite this assertion, multiple intelligences are included as another view of how people learn. Gardner postulated that every learner has not one intelligence but multiple intelligences. The first version of the theory described seven intelligences, with an eighth intelligence added later.

The original seven intelligences are: (a) logical-mathematical, (b) bodily-kinesthetic, (c) interpersonal, (d) verbal-linguistic, (e) intrapersonal, (f) spatial, and (g) musical. Naturalistic was added in 1999 and an existential intelligence is under consideration. Brief definitions follow, however the most important thing to remember is that according to Gardner, everyone has a variety of intelligences in varying strengths. Some are more dominant intelligences and others less so, but no one has just one.

- Logical-mathematical: Linear thinkers who follow logical patterns well are the students with this dominant intelligence.

- Bodily-kinesthetic: Learners who are skilled at sports, dance, and other physical activities have this as their strongest intelligence. This equates strongly with the kinesthetic learning style from the VARK system.
- Interpersonal: Learners with interpersonal skills are extroverted and skilled at working with others. These are the students who love **cooperative learning** group projects.
- Verbal-linguistic: Students with verbal-linguistic as their dominant intelligence are good with words and languages. These would be the read-write learners in the VARK system.
- Intrapersonal: Learners who are strongest in the intrapersonal intelligence work best in solitude and are highly reflective. Philosophers and writers would be examples of people with this as their dominant intelligence.
- Spatial: The spatial intelligence is related to visual strengths including the ability to see things in the mind's eye. Artists would have strong spatial intelligence.
- Musical: This may be the most self-explanatory of the intelligences. Musical intelligence relates to abilities with music.
- Naturalistic: Students with this intelligence as their dominant strength are good with nature and understanding the natural order of things.

When planning instruction, it is not necessary to teach to all intelligences all the time. Lessons and instruction should keep in mind a variety of intelligences at all times with an attempt to hit all of them regularly throughout the course.

Jung's Learning Styles

Psychologist Carl Jung identified personality types that have been used to describe learning styles. The basis of Jung's theory is that all personalities fall into one of four quadrants created by two intersecting lines as shown in Figure 3.1.

One line is the definition of how people perceive the world and the second line is how they make judgments about those perceptions. The perceiving line has sensing at one end and intuition at the other. According to the theory, people at one extreme take in all their information about the world only through sensations (indicated by an *S*), at the opposite extreme they learn about the world only through intuition (indicated by an *N*). Nearly everyone falls somewhere along the line in between sensing and intuition.

The other line is how people deal with what they have learned through their sensations and intuition. This line is judgment. At one end is thinking

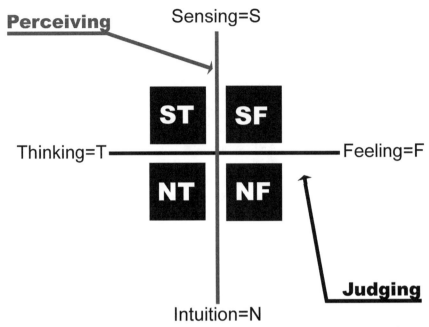

Figure 3.1.   **Illustration of Jung's theory; the intersecting lines representing judging and perception.**

(indicated with a *T*) and at the extreme opposite is feeling (indicated with an *F*). Learners fall into one of the four quadrants formed by the intersecting lines. The quadrants are labeled *ST* for sensing thinkers, *SF* for sensing feelers, *NT* for intuitive thinkers, and *NF* for thinking feelers. Like multiple intelligences, no one is exclusively ST, SF, NT or NF. Everyone has characteristics of several styles, but each person has one of the four as a dominant learning style.

- ST: "Sensing thinkers are realists. They perceive the world and then logically come to a conclusion about how to proceed" (K. M. Lehmann, 2008, p. 16). ST students do not mind drill and practice and programmed instruction, which have lost favor in the current educational realm. They do well with mastery learning and memorization as well (Silver & Hanson, 1996). In online courses, ST learners would do well using online tutorials or computer-assisted instruction (CAI).
- SF: "Sensing feelers are very interpersonal. They perceive the world and then move forward based on emotions" (K. M. Lehmann, 2008, p. 16). SF learners work well in groups and prefer activities that are in some way social such as labs, teams, and peer tutoring (Silver & Hanson,

1996). Discussion groups and cooperative projects would appeal to SF students in an online course.

- NT: "Intuitive thinkers are intellectuals. They are interested in abstractions as well as facts and prefer to be mentally challenged" (K. M. Lehmann, 2008, p. 17). NT students enjoy problem solving and inquiry (Silver & Hanson, 1996). Problem-based learning, scenarios, and action research would work well with NT personalities.
- NF: "Intuitive feelers are creative. NF personalities think out-of-the-box better than the other three personality types; they are not limited by what is known. What is known drives them to find out more" (K. M. Lehmann, 2008, p. 17). These learners do well with any online activity that allows for creative expression and open-ended responses to the curriculum.

In addition to VARK, multiple intelligences, and Jung's model, there are other learning styles that could be included here. However, the three presented here provide enough food for thought to assist course designers and instructors in differentiating the online curriculum to best meet the needs of everyone. A final reminder, learners do not have just one learning style or intelligence. All people have a mix of styles in varying strengths making up their learning preferences. One additional personality characteristic to be considered by instructors is the working style preference of students. Working style is discussed in the next section.

Working Style as a Personality Characteristic

Even simple personality traits play a role in how to work with the online learner. Some students are go-getters, **Type A personalities**, who will enter the course site the minute it is available. Such students are often the first to post discussion messages and assignments. Most of the traits they exhibit are not problematic in any way for the online instructor outside of a little patience when dealing with requests to open things early or respond more quickly to their queries.

One area where the Type A, or early bird, personality should be a concern for the online facilitator is when assigning students to small groups. These early birds work best when placed in small groups with other early birds. This type of student likes to get started as quickly as possible on a group project and want it to be completed well before the assignment deadline. These learners do not mesh well when they are forced to work in a small group with laid-back students who prefer the pressure of a deadline to get them started on a project. When forced to work together, early birds assume that the laid-back students are just lazy and refusing to do their part. Sometimes the early birds even complete the project without input from the laid-back students (K. M. Lehmann, 2008).

Students with a more laid-back style, **Type B personalities**, are not lazy at all. They prefer to spend time considering the project before beginning. They work best when a deadline looms for the project. This group of students does need interim deadlines for the project to make sure they stay on track. They will get the work done; however, it will be completed and submitted at the last minute. This last-minute attitude drives early birds crazy, while the laid-back students do not even understand why the early birds are in such a rush to get going or why they fuss so much about completing the project early.

Since the online environment lacks many of the social cues (i.e., voice inflection, body language) that can be used to mediate these conflicts in the face-to-face environment, the online instructor is wise to assess Types A and B personalities and assign them to groups accordingly (K. M. Lehmann, 2008). Two possible survey tools for assessing personalities are shared in Chapter 15.

CONCLUSION

Working styles, VARK, multiple intelligences, Jung's learning styles, and other educational theories discussed in this chapter are referred to throughout the book. These theories provide guidance for online instructors in planning their course and their instruction. Course designer and online facilitator are just two of the many hats the online instructor wears, as will be discussed in the next chapter.

4

The Many Hats of the Online Instructor

If you are reading this textbook, you must be interested in teaching online. Does it take any particular kind of person to teach online? A particular personality type? Must you possess a pocket protector and laptop from birth to want to pursue employment in this field? The answer is that anyone *can* teach online, but not everyone can do it *well*—at least not without pedagogical training and due diligence. Facilitation is a skill and like any other skill, it can be learned, but it does take practice and training.

To really begin to understand what it means to be an online instructor, it first merits taking a look at who is currently teaching in the industry—who has led the way as the field developed.

CURRENT PROFESSORS AND TEACHERS

Some of the earliest instructors in online learning were already instructors in the face-to-face realm of higher education. Remember, online education grew out of the era of correspondence and telecourses—both of these were already being sponsored by colleges across the country and around the world. With the advent of the Internet, online learning was just one more extension for higher education's reach.

Even when K–12 got on board with online education—it was teachers who were already experienced face-to-face educators (albeit the more computer-oriented ones)—driving the transition. Even now, it does not take long for technically savvy instructors with teaching experience and subject matter expertise to become successful online instructors.

PROFESSIONAL DEVELOPERS

When computer and Internet technology began to rapidly spread, those who needed to use the technology naturally needed to be trained to keep their skills updated. Again, online learning came to the rescue with self-paced tutorials easing the way through ever-increasingly complicated versions of software upgrades, networking protocols, and operating system platforms. Moreover, instructional technology professionals, whose job it was to keep these systems running, needed to keep their own skills up to date, and online certification programs run by professional developers were born.

SUBJECT MATTER EXPERTS

Subject matter experts (SME) often came to online learning to fill a niche for businesses that created "canned" curriculums or modules that could be purchased by educational or corporate entities. They knew their content and worked as part of a team alongside a pedagogical expert to figure out how to best deliver the content inside a course management system (CMS).

In higher education, the term *SME* was, and still is, sometimes used to refer to instructors, or course designers, who are degreed (or have considerable successful work experience) in their content area and are therefore qualified to teach at the college or university level but may lack the pedagogical experience on the ground desired for course construction in an online setting.

EDUCATION FREELANCERS OR ADJUNCTS BY CHOICE

In the age of four-dollar gas and second, or even third, career changes, many technologically savvy teachers took their work schedule into their own hands and opted to become their own boss by becoming educational freelancers. In the same way that freelance writers and reporters do piecework and work-for-hire by multiple institutions, educational freelancers contracted out their instructional services to multiple institutions on a per-class or per-term basis and have been making a living that is not bound by the standard school day or school year rules ever since. While this sort of lifestyle can be very appealing for some, it is not without its risk (or lack of health benefits).

CORPORATE TRAINERS

Educational institutions and information technology departments were not the only place where instructors had shifted to the online classroom. In the old days of corporate training, staff would gather in a room once a year for the obligatory training regarding one policy or another. These days—everything from training on sexual harassment policy to avoiding repetitive stress injury—now takes place online. Corporate trainers have moved their curriculum online to save time, space, and money for their corporation.

WHY DO THEY TEACH ONLINE?

With an understanding of the current establishment of instructors in the online realm, you now need to ask what drives an individual to spend hours sitting at a keyboard interacting with individuals digitally instead of doing it live and in person. It is important not only to understand the motivations of these instructors, but to also understand your own motivations for choosing this method of instruction. The reasons can be as many as they are varied.

Early Adopters

Many experienced online educators, veterans with more than five years teaching online, are undoubtedly early adopters of Internet technology for education, also called eLearning. These same instructors also tend to be early adopters of Internet tools such as email, search engines, web page software, and such. As these tools become easier to use, veteran online educators incorporate them into their CMS—even before the tools are standard parts of the course shell environments.

According to the Pew Research Center's study for the American Life Project: *A Portrait of Early Internet Adopters: Why People First Went Online—and Why They Stayed* (Wells, 2008), "The responses of these early Internet adopters suggest they saw themselves more as co-creators of the online environment than, say, car owners felt about the auto environment" (p. 4). Online educators continue this cocreation of the online learning environment today as we are still on the frontier of online learning.

Educators' use of **Web 2.0** social technologies, like blogging, webcasting, photo sharing, streaming video, and tagging, has created a change in the industry requiring software developers to incorporate these **social networking** tools inside the CMS as well. The technically savvy online educator does not just work online; he or she thrives in the online environment. As Wells (2008) states, "These early adopters are quite proud of these contributions. They see themselves as doing more than manipulating the exterior of the Internet. They argue they are crafting the interior by, in part, bringing along older social technologies" (p. 4).

Telecommuters

For some online educators, the appeal to the virtual world has not so much to do with content or environment as it has to do with the environment from which the educator works. The same asynchronous environment, attend-class-in-your-pajamas, no-commuting rules that apply for online students also apply to their online instructors who teach fully online. It is the rare educator who is able to work his or her daily teaching schedule around caring for a young child at home, attending a business meeting or civic meeting downtown during the public school day, or perhaps doing some research at a nearby museum or art gallery. The online educator could do all three.

Virtual educators can stop in at a local **wi-fi**-enabled coffee shop, laptop in hand, check in online with one of his or her classes, and look in his or her email for student questions at 10:00 a.m. Then, after his or her meeting and gallery stop, he or she could check in with the second class at 2:00 p.m. He or she could then finish correcting the coursework for the remaining courses in the evening during some spare time. The amount of hours are the same, but as an online instructor, he or she can determine when to put the time in his or her day to best meet the courses' and his or her personal needs. This flexibility is what often leads interested individuals to becoming educational freelancers.

Travel

The ability to travel while continuing as a teacher is another big draw to the online educational field. We both travel extensively between the Pacific Northwest and the East Coast. With the availability of mobile broadband access, public libraries, and Internet cafes, instructors have Internet access, and consequently, course access, no matter where they are traveling. The tools of the trade demand that an online educator know how to stay in contact with his or her course no matter if he or she is across town or across the country (or traveling internationally); so being untethered from a desk and cubicle should almost be a given perk that comes with the job.

While the flexibility seems a standard practice of the job for now, there does seem to be a concern among some veteran online educators that as online learning becomes more institutionalized and mainstream, flexibility for both the instructors and students may begin to fade a bit. For now, this issue does not seem to be speaking to time in as much as responsiveness to change. "As online programs mature, they are increasingly viewed as mainstream, have become a part of the campus bureaucracy, and are losing several of the program characteristics that made them stand out initially" (Lokken, Womer, & Mullins, 2008, p. 7). Keeping eLearning flexible and responsive to needs and changes in technologies and society for both students and instructors should be a high priority for institutions who value the added dynamic it brings to the learning environment.

Expanded Teaching Opportunities

Peter Shea's (2007) study, "Bridges and Barriers to Teaching Online College Courses," exposes some exciting reasons for educators to pursue online learning as a path for both experienced faculty and those new to online teaching. Shea's research shows that working with a diverse student body, which is, quite literally, geographically far flung, is highly appealing and educationally rewarding. His faculty was able to see how online learning provided "opportunities to reach new students with different cultural backgrounds, more mature students, and students in different geographical locations" (p. 82).

The more successfully experienced a faculty member becomes, and the more they experience the kind of diversity of student body in their online courses that is possible through a class roster, which may include students from around the globe for an eight-week session on business management, the more committed to the online experience they become.

The Gender Factor

Women make up a higher majority of students in online learning—this trend results from a variety of reasons including, high among them, the flexibility it provides for student mothers and those who must juggle work, school, and families. As with commuting and other factors, what is good for the students generally is also good for the faculty in online learning. "Results hinted that female faculty may be more attracted to online teaching for the flexibility and convenience it affords . . . results suggest that these advantages may appeal to female online instructors as well as online learners" (Shea, 2007, p. 82).

Forced into Online

Not everyone embraces online learning, and rightfully, those who do not, should be allowed to proceed with caution when it comes to teaching online. However, some institutions who have invested heavily in technology infrastructures do not quite see it this way. The institutions, instead, create policies forcing face-to-face instructors to move some of their coursework online to increase online class offerings in the course catalog. This is a well-intentioned goal to meet student demand for online learning on the surface, but the fallout can be quite detrimental to that very goal in the long run.

Of institutions *fully engaged* in online learning, 62 percent of faculty value and accept "the legitimacy of online education" (Allen & Seaman, 2007, p. 10). This sounds like an enthusiastic acceptance toward the trend of increasing online learning offerings. Unfortunately, it is only speaking of schools who are already fully engaged, meaning the faculty has already bought into the idea. When you dig a little deeper into Allen and Seaman's study and average the statistic across all institutions surveyed, academic leaders report that only one in three faculty members (32.9 percent) valued online learning. The danger here is that instructors who neither accept nor value the medium of eLearning are being forced to educate students using this same medium. This is a recipe for educational disaster.

Resistance, Anger, and Fear

Shea (2007) cites a faculty member's *opportunity to volunteer* to teach online as one of the key factors in whether the instructor is motivated or not.

> Faculty who felt they had been required to teach online were more de-motivated by perceptions that the technology was confusing, the absence of face-to-face interaction, perceptions that students might lack access, lack of opportunity to experiment with technology, inadequate time to learn about online teaching and inadequate time to develop online courses. (p. 80)

When compelled to teach courses online, these nonvolunteers continued to have negative feelings toward others areas of their online programs, including course quality, compensation for course development, and concerns over their teaching efforts "not being recognized by campus administration," which was amplified by those who were in part-time or nontenure track positions.

CHALLENGES FACING THE NONVOLUNTEER FACULTY AND THEIR SCHOOLS

Once administration has made the decision that an entire department or college will, by mandatory edict, move a percentage of their coursework online, the challenges begin almost immediately. In survey after survey of administrators and other leaders of online learning, both in public high schools and higher education, these individuals reported the difficulty of getting faculty to commit to training as a highly rated problem area. Faculty training involved not only the demonstrations of the CMS itself, but also new tools for interactivity.

Ironically, concerns over adequacy of pedagogical skills have begun to surface lately, with equal if not higher importance than that of the need for the SME or the technological expert in online learning. According to Kim and Bonk (2006), there is a distinct separation between what online educators are doing online, and what they know they should be doing online for the best outcome for their students.

> [O]nly 23–45 percent of online instructors surveyed actually used online activities related to critical and creative thinking, hands-on performances, interactive labs, data analysis, and scientific simulations, although 40 percent of the participants said those activities were highly important in online learning environments. In effect, a significant gap separated preferred and actual online instructional practices. (Kim & Bonk, 2006, p. 23)

Statistically, we know that the students are most successful in online courses taught by faculty who are pedagogically sound, SME, and who have sound technology skills. It begs the question then of those in charge of growth in online faculty—why continue creating policies requiring courses be taught online by those who are not ready pedagogically, who may lack the technical training, and certainly lack the intrinsic motivation to teach in the online environment? In other words, why set up both the students and the faculty member for failure? Instead just the opposite should be happening—the most pedagogically qualified, technically sound, and intrinsically motivated faculty members should be teaching online courses to ensure student success. And they should be well compensated for their efforts.

Compensation

Those who are nonvolunteers to the online teaching faculty often cite, at times rightly so, the concern over being adequately compensated for the time spent developing, teaching, and revising courses. Because compensation is often at different rates than traditional face-to-face courses, faculty have concerns over online learning being viewed as *marginalized* or on the *periphery* to that of the real institution and do not wish to have their reputation *stigmatized* by teaching the lesser courses (Shea, 2007). "If the goals of increased access and quality are to be achieved we need policies that enable full-time faculty to make online education a higher priority" (p. 84).

THE HATS OF THE ONLINE EDUCATOR

Either by choice or by mandatory teaching assignment, once in the online classroom the online educator is a busy, multifaceted individual. To teach effectively online requires a skill set like no other, and you will wear the hat of many different disciplines. Will you be an online teacher or an online facilitator? Which is the true role of the instructor in the online classroom? The answer is both and more! Online instructors often find themselves playing multiple roles far beyond that of a face-to-face teacher. These roles may include course designer, **instructional technologist**, SME, **counselor**, and **advisor**—not to mention writer, copy editor, and proofreader. What exactly are some of these roles in relationship to eLearning, and why does the online instructor wear all of these hats?

Teacher

Just as in the regular classroom, much of the important work for instruction occurs before class begins. Preparation for the lesson may include setting objectives, gathering materials, determining the elements of the lesson, and deciding how students will be assessed. Even when teaching a course designed by someone else, whether online or face to face, the teacher must prepare for the lessons in advance, become familiar with the content and determine how student success will be defined. These are traditional teacher duties in all settings and they apply in the online world as well. The role of facilitator is also part of being a face-to-face teacher, but in the online world there are some nuances of being a facilitator that need defining.

Facilitator

The facilitator hat differs from the teacher in one key shift of the pedagogical **paradigm**: online facilitators step away from the front of the room. Where teachers often see themselves as the leaders in charge of the learning and the course—facilitators, quite purposely, help the learners arrive at the intended objects using guiding questions rather than lectures, provide interactive activities rather than passive ones, and have more Socratic-style discussion rather than tests. Assignments are authentic and real world more often than they are not.

Facilitation is as much art as it is science, just like classroom teaching. In fact, many good classroom teachers will quickly develop into fine online facilitators. Helping students understand the course materials, drawing out their thinking with carefully constructed questions, and providing a scaffold of support when needed as students work to show competency with the material are all a part of both face-to-face and virtual classroom environments.

The major differences between teaching in the face-to-face classroom and the virtual classroom are how messages are communicated and the need to troubleshoot technical problems. Currently, in online courses, the majority of the communication will occur through text-based mediums. Communication through email, **instant messaging (IM)**, **threaded discussion**, and **chat** is written communication. Though with the increase in broadband technologies, **streaming audio** and video are becoming more frequent in appearance in the online classroom; good technical writing skills are still a big plus for the online instructor. However, it is not enough to just be able to guide someone using step-by-step directions, it is also important to connect with students to give the online classroom warmth and a human touch. Adding a touch of humanity and even humor through text is not always easy but it can be done!

Instructional Technologist

The online facilitator has to be prepared to help troubleshoot technical problems. Often the problem is not the tool; it is the students' unfamiliarity with the tool. In other words, they just do not know how to use it. This unfamiliarity might be anything from not knowing how to attach a document to an email to not knowing how to capture a screen shot to put into an assignment. The instructor needs to know not only how to use all course tools, but also to be adept at describing the procedures to fix the problem. In this way, the facilitator wears the hat of the **instructional technologist**—or a person whose job it is to provide instruction in the current use of technology. Having several good resources to which students can be directed or that the instructor can utilize to help solve a problem dramatically increases student satisfaction with a course.

Some institutions provide technical support services for both online students and the instructors. These support people can be invaluable. Good technical support takes much of the troubleshooting burden off of the back of the instructor, but even so, it is likely that the online teacher will still need the technical skills to troubleshoot basic computer-related problems within the course shell. When technical support is poor, or completely absent from the institution's infrastructure, the burden of troubleshooting falls heavily on the course facilitator. Effective methods for troubleshooting with students will be shared in Chapter 13.

Much of the need for troubleshooting can be eliminated if a course is well-designed with clear, consistent navigation and visual design. Often the online instructor can help him- or herself out with this as he or she adds the hat of being the own course designer.

Course Designer

In some cases instructors wear the hat of course designer, meaning they write and prepare their own online courses rather than teaching from an already prepared curriculum. We have each taught courses designed by others as well as designed our own. There are some distinct advantages to teaching a self-designed course. There are also some disadvantages. An important consideration is who owns the intellectual property rights to the course materials. Course design will be discussed in more detail in Chapter 7.

Writer, Editor, and Proofreader

You may be asked to write a course at some point in your online teaching career. In fact, you may be hired to write a course you will never actually teach. This is actually a quite lucrative supplemental industry for experienced online educators. Generally, to be hired as a freelance course designer or writer, companies and institutions look for people with degrees in education, experience in the subject matter, and experience teaching online. It does not hurt to have some writing credentials or an English minor in your background either.

Proofreading and editing the courses that you teach requires certain permissions and access to the course shell. If you were the course designer, you would already have the right to proofread and edit the course as you are working through it. If you were not the course designer and find an error or wish to make a change, you will need the permission of the writer or copyright holder.

Depending on the institution and CMS, you may be able to make the edits to the course pages yourself, or you may need to request the changes be made by information technology support personnel. As an instructor, if a module starts going badly and you notice errors leading to student confusion, it is terribly frustrating to be unable to edit or revise the directions in a timely manner. This is why we encourage high quality review of course design prior to publishing any courses that will be taught by anyone other than the course writer.

Counselor and Mediator

Whether by **synchronous** chat, asynchronous discussion board, IM, or email, even in the best of online classes, community can break down, or a student can suffer a personal tragedy that requires a faculty member to remove the teacher hat and put on the counselor or mediator hat.

Despite perceptions to the contrary, online students reveal quite a bit of personal information about themselves. At times, they feel so close to their classmates and facilitators they will reveal issues of marital strife, abuse, health crises, and other such things. When this happens, the instructor needs to leave the public realm of the discussion boards for the private realm of email or the immediacy of the telephone—depending upon what is revealed—or both. If you do make a personal telephone call, avoid giving advice—simply make sure the student is doing okay, that they have the necessary services available to them, and ask if there is anything that you can do for them. You may wish to follow up with an email, thanking them for speaking with you by phone about the issue, as a way of documentation. This is certainly a time to notify a program coordinator if the issue warrants further concern.

Because online learners and facilitators cannot see each other, the medium is ripe for misinterpretation. The discussion boards, if not watched carefully by a skilled facilitator, can lead from misinterpretation to full-scale flame, which is when one or more students attack each other personally and lose sight of the topic they were discussing.

This is when the facilitator needs to grab his or her mediator hat and figure out how to extinguish the flame while still maintaining the dignity of the learners and helping them to learn something about the discussion process as well. We will discuss more about the specific techniques for this in future chapters.

Advisor and Registrar

One of the final hats you may wear in your collection as an online instructor is that of the institution's advisor and registrar. While you may not physically register students for classes, you more than likely will be responsible for passing on information about where students can get their transcripts at the end of the course, who they contact regarding technical problems, degree programs, degree audits, and adds or drops.

Be sure you only promise what you can deliver. If you are not in charge of withdrawing students, avoid making promises about course refunds. If you are not in charge of transcripts, avoid making promises of the date of delivery. This will eliminate frustration on your part and on the part of students who will forward your email promises up and down administrative lines. Remember, the chancellor or president of your institution has an email address as available to the student body as yours is. Students who get frustrated over failed promises think nothing of firing off an angry email to the highest echelons of power.

Lastly, as the advisor or registrar of your online program, you may be asked to provide a link for your students to complete a survey evaluating the effectiveness of your course. In face-to-face courses, these kinds of surveys are often conducted by impartial department personnel. Online, you provide the link or email directly to your own students.

The variety of people who have come to teach online is vast and the reasons they do it are as varied as the people. Yet, they seem to share a passion for teaching and an enjoyment of the flexibility and maverick nature that the online realm still provides. As you shall see in the next chapter, the online learner is just as diverse.

5

Who Are Our Online Learners?

People take online classes. This may seem like too basic a statement to make here, but many students in online courses feel they are treated like numbers, or worse, nonentities. In the virtual realm when only text-based tools are used, students have no gender, race, or other distinguishing physical characteristics unless they choose to share them with you. If images or video are used, then students are less anonymous to all. Some people, however, prefer the anonymity of the online realm. Many students opt not to share a photo of themselves for a variety of reasons including Internet security fears. But one reason may be that they favor remaining physically anonymous. Whether they seem anonymous or not, there are often clues as to who they are, or they share enough information that gender and race are evident.

In this chapter we discuss the people who make up the clientele in online courses. These people vary in a couple of different ways. First they vary by sophistication with the technology in general, and specifically the technology of online learning. Their needs vary and this variance is often defined by their age. For example, adult learners are generally training or retraining for work, and K–12 students are working toward graduation requirements. Finally they vary by other characteristics that are much harder to *see* in the online world including gender, **learning disabilities**, and other ways that impact how an instructor may need to interact with the student.

SOPHISTICATION

As an instructor the first thing that will become clear about a new group of students is how sophisticated, or to be more blunt, how unsophisticated they are. Motteram and Forrester (2005) state it this way, "Students fall into two types—those who are information and communication technologies adept and have previous experience of online learning, and those who are complete novices" (p. 292). The complete novices, the unsophisticated folks who are new to technology in general (or at least the technology associated with on-line learning) are often referred to as **newbies**.

Extreme Newbies

Since online courses do require some level of technological expertise, it would seem logical that those who do not like, or are unfamiliar with, tech-nology in general, would not choose to take such courses. For a variety of reasons such students do, in fact, take online courses. The instructor will quickly learn who these students are because they will be in nearly constant contact with the instructor asking for help early in the course. Providing that help is part of the instructor's job.

Extreme newbies are those folks for whom any computer-based task is un-familiar and challenging. This may include skills as basic as sending an email with attachments. In one of Lehmann's classes, a group of students worked together on their online course at a computer lab so they could help one an-other with all aspects of the technology involved in taking the course. This group of extreme newbies even needed help with entering email addresses into the *To:* field of an email.

Most instructors will run across such extreme newbies who need an ex-traordinary amount of help. Later some tips will be shared for creating tip sheets that can be sent to guide newbies through unfamiliar territory. Another solution is to ask the newbie to find a tech tutor in their home, school, office, or neighborhood to whom they can turn for help before contacting the instruc-tor. These folks will be in frequent contact and lots of patience is needed as they develop their skills. The payoff for this time and effort is the effusive thank yous from the student's when they successfully complete their course.

Newbies

Newbies are one step up from extreme newbies. Newbies have some com-puter experience but are still easily flummoxed by the technology involved with online courses. Most first-time online learners are extremely nervous prior to starting the class. Instructors need to remember that online courses are not night-and-day different from traditional classes, they are night-and-apple different. There is almost nothing that is familiar to the learner when taking an online course, leaving these students filled with anxiety.

Virtually everyone has been to school. Students know what to expect from a traditional classroom environment. Even if someone is unsure about what to expect from a particular face-to-face course, they at least have some general idea how a class operates. In the online world, nothing is familiar. There is no classroom. Students may not see their instructor or fellow students. Turning in assignments is completely different; the student does not even need a new binder that they might have clutched as a security blanket. Good instructors use best practices for reassuring first-time online learners. These techniques are discussed further in Chapter 11.

More Sophisticated Learners

Student sophistication can be seen as a continuum that begins with extreme newbies and varies upward from there. More sophisticated learners require less hand-holding from instructors when it comes to daily tasks; however, they provide their own challenges. Sophisticated students may need: (a) enhancements of course projects to provide additional challenge, (b) reining in if their use of tools or computer jargon is confusing to other learners, and (c) guidance about the appropriate use of their technology skills, especially when it comes to locating, then properly quoting or citing, material from other sources. Sophisticated students can serve as models and helpers for newbies. Furthermore, they are often finding great resources to share with the entire class.

An argument could be made that sophistication with technology is inversely proportional to the age of the learner. There is no doubt most of the current generation, dubbed **millennials** by some, are **digital natives** (Prensky, 2001) and in general, have very good technology skills. However, many older learners are equally adept with technology and some younger students are not digital natives as illustrated in this story.

> I'd assigned my students to read [a blog post] and post a reaction to promote their digital literacy skills. To my great surprise (Prensky didn't prepare me for this), about 40 percent of my students in this class, while liking the subject matter, have not liked going out on the Internet. Most of the students in my classes were students who were in remedial or "basic" courses all through their public education and some did not graduate at all. The highest form of technology they use regularly is a cell phone or mp3 player. Even at their young age they are digital immigrants and are resistant to the technology. (Chamberlin, 2006a)

Whether native or immigrant, learners may have some technology skills, but they can still be akin to newbies in online classes because the environment is unfamiliar to them. Digital natives do pick up skills quickly and will require less assistance from the instructor than digital immigrants. The age at which students may begin to take online courses is falling and the spectrum of ages in certain types of classes may vary widely.

AGE

Number of Online Learners in K–12 Education

According to the National Center for Educational Statistics there were 506,950 enrollments in distance-education courses among elementary and secondary students in the 2004–2005 school year. This was an increase from the 317,070 during the 2002–2003 school year. "If a student was enrolled in multiple distance education courses, districts were instructed to count the student once for each course in which he or she was enrolled. Thus, distance education enrollments may include duplicated counts of students" (Zandberg & Lewis, 2008, p. 15). The definition of enrollment was consistent in both the 2002–2003 and 2004–2005 statistics, therefore the rise in enrollments is accurately described as 60 percent in just two years. The majority were secondary students, with only 11 percent identified as junior high age or younger (Zandberg & Lewis, 2008, p. 14).

Whether primary or secondary, one can assume these learners are not yet adults. Their learning needs are different from adults, as was seen in the discussion of pedagogy versus andragogy in Chapter 3. Pedagogically this age group may require more structure in online classes than adults. Stating expectations clearly, in writing, is important as these learners, unlike adults, have no real agenda for learning. Their motivations are to complete the work to graduate from high school. What they learn and how they learn it are secondary, and when compared with adult learning motivations, relatively unimportant to most young people. This age group, however, has one huge advantage as online learners when compared with adults, they are extremely proficient with technology.

"Our students today are all *native speakers* of the digital language of computers, video games and the Internet" (Prensky, 2001, p. 1). "They have spent their entire lives surrounded by and using computers, video games, digital music players, video cams, cell phones, and all the other toys and tools of the digital age. Today's average college grads have spent less than 5,000 hours of their lives reading, but over 10,000 hours playing video games (not to mention 20,000 hours watching TV). Computer games, email, the Internet, cell phones, and instant messaging (IM) are integral parts of their lives" (p. 1).

Online course designers and instructors need to keep in mind the capabilities of this group and use the tools with which they are already familiar. Online courses by virtue of being online are digital. We need to make sure we do not lose that small advantage by mimicking the mistakes being made in traditional classrooms.

> Schools have decided that all the light that surrounds kids—that is, their electronic connections to the world—is somehow detrimental to their education. So systematically, as kids enter our school buildings, we make them shut off all their connections. No cell phones. No music players. No game machines. No open Internet. (Prensky, 2008, p. 4)

Prensky (2008) summarizes discussions with the natives to illustrate the kinds of opportunities for learning that need to be a part of K–12 education and by extension K–12 online education, "Students like having goals they want to reach, doing rather than listening, getting involved with the real world, having teachers ask them about their ideas and opinions, creating products that are important to them, and thinking seriously about their futures" (p. 44).

Many of the digital natives have completed their secondary education and have gone on to college. College course enrollments, however, may include not only digital natives but also adults returning to school; many of them are older adults. Online course designers and instructors must balance the needs of digital natives, with the **digital immigrants**, while adjusting the course structures toward the tenets of andragogy. This is a big task because the highest numbers of online course enrollments are in the undergraduate courses offered by colleges and universities.

Online Learners in Higher Education

The number of student enrollments in distance education in the elementary and secondary range pales in comparison with the number of enrollments in higher education (Allen & Seaman, 2007). In the fall of 2006, nearly 3.5 million students were enrolled in online courses. The majority of these learners were taking a class from a campus within 75 miles of their home, in other words, from their local college or university. As illustrated in Figure 5.1, the projected enrollment increases for the future range from 9.5 to 16 percent. This is far above the enrollment growth of less than 2 percent for traditional courses. Allen and Seaman report more than 70 percent of respondent state a demand for online courses consistently above the growth in available courses.

The numbers cited are for all courses taught by colleges and universities, including those for two-year and four-year undergraduate degrees. According to Allen and Seaman (2007), 86 percent of online learners in higher education are taking undergraduate level courses. The majority of this

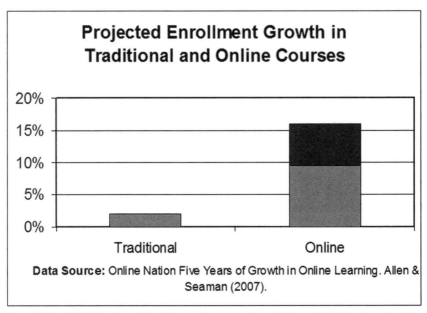

Figure 5.1.   **Projected enrollment growth comparison between traditional and online courses.**

population is in the 18- to 25-year-old range. These are the *grownup* digital natives. It is not surprising that they have embraced online courses since much of their time is already spent online. Online education is a natural fit for these students, but courses must be designed in ways that utilize all the capabilities of the digital environment.

As stated previously, 86 percent of online higher education students are taking undergraduate classes. The remaining 14 percent of postsecondary students are split between masters or doctoral programs and specialized courses such as professional development. A solid argument can be made that those who are in masters or doctoral online courses or who are taking professional development courses are older adults. At a minimum they are old enough to have completed their undergraduate degree or to be working adults in need of professional development. Very likely most of these adults are digital immigrants. They have a need for their courses to follow all the tenets of andragogy, and many of them also need a lot of help with the technical aspects of online learning.

Adult Learners Outside of Higher Education

Another type of adult professional development, outside the realm of college-based courses, is corporate-led training programs. Many businesses are moving their trainings online in either a fully online or hybrid format. These range along the entire spectrum of online course types from computer-based tutorials with no interaction to fully online, interactive courses. Whatever the type, online learning is a growing endeavor in the business world.

"eLearning is expected to remain the fastest-growing segment of the corporate training market," according to Simba Information Inc. (2007, p. 1). The same report stated that the top ten eLearning vendors would generate $660 million, a growth rate of 48 percent over the previous year. This astronomical growth for companies that provide learning management systems, Internet conferencing, and live instruction is due to, "the growing need for training programs that can be delivered to geographically dispersed personnel" (Simba Information Inc., 2007, p. 1).

Costs for delivering training face-to-face have skyrocketed, most recently due to energy costs associated with travel. Sweeney (2007) reports on one unnamed company, which has gone from a ratio of 1:9 eLearning to face-to-face training in 2001 to a current mix of 1:1. The company believed it costs $1,000 per person per day for live training when all costs, including travel and hotel bills are included. Their homegrown online training costs $150,000 per six-hour program. While that seems steep, "The Web-based program can be archived . . . transferred to a CD-Rom or DVD . . . whether it's shown to one person, or 10,000, the cost is $150,000" (Sweeney, 2007, p. 20). Cost is just one of the issues driving the corporate training market toward eLearning.

Many businesses allow employees to complete the courses during their work day. In addition, in a slow economy paycheck-conscious adults may be more motivated to complete the course, regardless of the quality of course design or instruction. Online courses allow workers to be trained no matter their location or work shift. Depending on the type of course, workers could begin and end the course whenever the need for the material arose. For example, individual new hires may be able to be trained immediately rather than waiting until a group of new hires have joined a company.

There may be disadvantages to consider. Corporate courses require design and facilitation that reflect adult learning theory just as higher education courses do. Workers required to complete a poorly designed workshop may struggle to learn the intended concepts. They, therefore, may not fully learn the skills and ideas needed for their continued employment. Moreover, workers trying to complete course work during their workday often find interruptions from coworkers are a serious issue.

According to Galagan (2001), reporting on Cisco Systems efforts at eLearning, "If you're sitting at your desk going through an interactive exercise or watching a video or, God forbid, reading a book, people think you're

Figure 5.2.   Illustration of a cubicle decorated with yellow caution tape illustrating the Cisco story.

not really working. You're open to Anyone Who Comes Along With a Problem" (p. 56). Cisco resolved this issue to some degree by allowing those who were working on eLearning courses to put up yellow caution tape alerting coworkers they were busy. This is illustrated in Figure 5.2.

CHARACTERISTICS DEFINING THE LEARNER POPULATION

Besides sophistication of the learners and the various age groups represented in the online learning population, there are some other characteristics that should be noted. These range from demographics to disabilities and beyond.

Gender

No matter the age of the population, all students can, of course, be classified as male or female. One of the most interesting things about online teaching is the instructor sometimes has no idea whether a student is a man or a woman. Try to determine the gender of the following first names (which is sometimes the only information available to an instructor when trying to figure out gender) from recent courses:

> Loren, Pat, Callon, Teri, Jordan, Kelly, Daniel, Anjli, Corey, Jamie, Chris, Jodee, Ka, Carey, Shannon.

From the list, the following were male students: Loren, Pat, Jordan, Kelly, Corey, Ka, Carey, Shannon; and female students were: Callon, Teri, Daniel (pronounced Da-kneel), Anjli, Jamie, Chris, and Jodee. How many of the 15 did you get right? Does it matter? The answer is yes and no.

In adult education, specifically higher education, the numbers consistently show that the majority of online learners are women. These numbers may not hold true for corporate training. The reasons women are in the majority are complicated, but they all relate to the flexibility of online learning. Women who interrupted their education for any reason whether it was marriage, child rearing, or another issue, appreciate the flexibility online learning offers in completing that education.

Many of these learners work on assignments late at night or early in the morning when the household is still asleep. The flexibility of working at home at 3 a.m. without having to worry about parking, travel, getting a baby-sitter, or any of the other complications that would be involved in a traditional course makes online learning a great choice. While these reasons could certainly also be applied to households with single fathers, in most families women are still responsible for a majority of the chores and child-rearing tasks and are most in need of flexibility when considering how to complete their education.

One study (Herman & Kirkup, 2008) of women in science, engineering, and technology helped those returning from a career break create an **ePortfolio** that could be used when searching for employment. The study gathered data from 47 women in an online course in which the ePortfolio was created. The reasons for aiming this course at women returning after a break in their work career were stated as follows,

> Women returners to the workforce face a particular set of problems, and difficulties . . . personal issues such as lack of confidence and out-of-date skills, structural factors, and cultural norms within these industries can make it more difficult for women, especially those with dependent children, to find suitable work. (Herman & Kirkup, 2008, p. 68)

Certainly it is not only women in the scientific fields that face these issues when they want to return to work after a protracted absence. Many women find their skills do need updating, and they are, therefore, in the market for online courses to prepare them for new fields. Online education provides women with opportunities to take courses in almost any field while they are preparing to return to the workforce.

Many women are in the workforce but in low-level jobs. They also need to update their skills and knowledge and not all of them live near a college. "Women studying online valued the convenience of being online given that many of them were studying in remote locations" (Price, 2006, p. 357). Women in Third World countries particularly are in need of skills allowing for advancement out of low-paying jobs.

In a study by Loh-Ludher (2007) based in Malaysia, women who worked from home creating items for low wages were offered a chance to take online classes to become eHomeworkers, doing computer-based tasks for better wages. Cultural and socioeconomic issues kept many women from taking advantage of this opportunity. "Gaining access to training programs and materials is frustrated by socioeconomic and gender-related factors that completely undermine the viability of distance-based delivery at this time" (Loh-Ludher, 2007, p. 190).

While not all female online learners are from Third World countries with male-dominant cultures, many female students have some type of disadvantage. Like the women from Malaysia, other women also have competing interests for their time and energy. "Females often felt like they did not have enough time to complete everything they wanted, not only in coursework, but also in all aspects of life" (Chang & Smith, 2008, p. 419). Some researchers have noted that female students may not only be stressed for time, but they may also be less confident.

In one study, women's self-efficacy, or self-confidence, improved from the beginning of the semester to the end, just by taking part in the online course (Chyung, 2007). This improvement was not related to the number of **postings** made by the women, "The degree of online participation and the improvement of self-efficacy are not in parallel relationship" (Chyung, 2007, p. 221). Chyung theorized that it was merely taking part in the course and completing it that improved self-confidence of these students. Price (2006) suggests self-confidence is not an issue at all however. "Women studying online are confident independent learners who may outperform their male counterparts" (p. 349). Since research is mixed in this area, online instructors should be aware that female learners may have issues of confidence.

Not only has self-confidence been noted as a possible area in need of development among female students, but some researchers point to a lower level of technology skills and even access to technology (Loh-Ludher, 2007; Royal, 2005). This point is disputed by Price (2006), "They do not have reduced computer and Internet access compared with men, nor are they disinclined to enrol [sic] on online courses" (p. 349). For the online instructor these mixed messages are presented here as an opportunity to be aware that women in online courses may need additional assistance with technical skills. The issue may not be gender so much as age or naiveté about online learning. In other words, the students may simply be newbies. There are noted differences, however, in the way women communicate online, which may be impacting enrollment.

Several researchers note women have particular communication styles online. Chyung (2007) states "Women tend to exhibit more social behavior online" (p. 214). Price (2006) too finds differences in the way genders approach communication. "Women tended to attach more importance to the affective" (p. 356) aspects of online dialogue. In particular, the research seems to show that women prefer social environments in which they can communicate in depth with a few colleagues. Since more and more online classes are becoming interactive and collaborative, womens' preferred communication styles may be matching up with current trends in course design, therefore resulting in more females enrolling in online courses.

Multicultural Student Populations

Race and culture are generally invisible to the instructor except for surnames, which are not always a true indicator of race or culture. The colorblind nature of online learning can be beneficial, but the online instructor needs to be aware of possible cultural issues that may arise. The global nature of online learning means a variety of cultures may be represented in a single eLearning course. When students are geographically disparate, even simple things such as scheduling a synchronous chat, where all learners must be online at the same time, can become challenging. When it is daytime in the United States, it is dark in Asian countries. While timing can be an issue, the bigger issues for online instructors have to do with honoring the learning patterns and needs of various cultures.

Instructors and course designers have to keep an ear to the ground for issues relating to culture. We have each recently had students from Korea, Japan, and China. Most of these students were practicing teachers working to maintain teacher certification by taking online professional development classes. These teachers offered insights about online learning and traditional education for students raised in Asia.

Many Asian cultures honor teacher knowledge and presentation of knowledge very highly. These students are used to the teacher being the sage on the stage and presenting everything the student needs to know. In a constructivist environment, where students are expected to develop the knowledge on their own through the learning activities, Asian students can be befuddled by the lack of teacher direction. This is one of the ways that culture may impact instruction in an eLearning course.

Students in developing countries are also increasingly enrolled in online courses. As stated by the United Nations Educational, Scientific, and Cultural Organization (UNESCO), "As a force contributing to social and economic development, open and distance learning is fast becoming an accepted and indispensable part of the mainstream of educational systems in both developed and developing countries, with particular emphasis for the latter" (2002, p. 3). The globalization of distance education provides many opportunities for developing countries for the realization of their education system-wide goals.

"Two main factors have led to an explosion of interest in distance learning: the growing need for continual skills upgrading and retraining and the technological advances that have made it possible to teach more and more subjects at a distance" (UNESCO, 2002, p. 3). Students in developing countries may often experience outages of service. Lehmann's husband, also an online teacher, spends part of each year on the coast of Ecuador. Outages of Internet service and power are common occurrences in that area. Instructors may need to be more flexible with due dates when students from developing countries are enrolled in an eLearning course.

As noted in the discussion of gender and the home-based workers in Malaysia (Loh-Ludher, 2007), culture may impact the ability of certain parts of a population to fully participate in online courses. In the research by Loh-Ludher, the male-dominated Muslim society didn't fully allow some women to participate. In addition, many women put themselves last in the priority list, "The computer . . . is kept in her son's room, so that he will have ease of access to play games with friends. Many homeworking mothers indulge their sons in this way, sacrificing their own needs and wants because they feel guilty . . . and also in the hope that he will be her support in old age" (p. 189).

To maintain the enrollment of these women in a course may require flexibility and understanding on the instructor's part. Culture and race may be only one part of the equation however when incorporating a geographically diverse population into an online course.

English as a Second Language Students

When an online course attracts students from a diversity of populations including different cultural groups there may be language difficulties for **English as a Second Language (ESL)** students. Students may believe their language skills are strong enough to take a course in something other than their primary language (Language 1, or L1). However, students may find that they have overestimated their abilities in the second language (Language 2, or L2). Students may struggle to understand the vocabulary of a class in L2, or they may lack the ability to write well in L2. Since most online courses are still text-based, writing is a critical part of online course work. All communication and most assignments are text-based, and students who cannot write well in L2, will be frustrated. In addition, colleagues may be frustrated with the incorrect grammar and syntax of the second-language student.

Online instructors can assist ESL students in several ways. First, they can suggest the student access services provided by a school or university such as a writing center. While school or university services have, in many cases, been slow to keep up with the online nature of eLearning, there are more and more examples of student assistance, including assistance with writing, that are available to the fully online student. Obviously if the student lives near a campus, they can be encouraged to utilize the traditional services available on campus as well. Such services are not always available, however, especially if the learners are in nonacademic settings such as business trainings.

Providing materials in a way that meets many learning styles, including the use of visuals and audio components, may help the second-language learner understand the content of the course more fully. The eLearning instructor's willingness to use the phone can be helpful to ESL learners. A final suggestion is for the second-language learner to seek out local help that can assist with translation of materials or edit writing before it is submitted for the course. There is another population of students who will be well served by additional help from the community at large and the online instructor, these are **remedial learners**.

Remedial Learners

Students in need of remediation, in other words, those retaking a class or course of study will benefit from many of the techniques used to help ESL learners. Use of visuals, such as screen shots or animations, and the use of audio often benefits students who struggle with coursework. Unfortunately too many learners find that the use of audio and visuals are lacking in online education just as much as they are in traditional courses. "Too often distance education courses offered over the Web are nothing more than electronic textbooks, which force students to navigate through a plethora of content, and thereby fail to utilize the medium effectively" (Simoncelli, 2005, p. 102). Simoncelli adds that it is important to adjust, "traditional teaching and practices when conducting courses and communicating in cyberspace" (p. 102).

One of us (Chamberlin) has had considerable experience with remedial learners in online courses at the community college level. Remedial students are similar in their lack of technological expertise to the newbies described previously in the chapter. This lack of technological know-how adds to their difficulties. They need lots of reassurance from the instructor about all phases of the course. Students are so technologically nervous that Chamberlin spends as much time answering emails about whether assignments are visible in the **dropbox**, for example, as about the content of the course.

Remedial students need lots of support from the instructor to build their confidence that they can use the CMS and learn the material. Low self-efficacy is much of the issue with this population, and this leads to them overlooking tools and instructions that will assist them.

In Simoncelli's study (2005) students were encouraged to use text-to-speech tools, such as the free software Read Please, so that students had audio delivery of reading materials. This was supposed to decrease the time and frustration related to the reading assignments. However, students failed to use the tools, and they failed to even notice the instructions about using the tools.

"None of the participants attempted to use any of these text reading programs and never gave it much thought. Kathy, who did not recall reading information on how to obtain the CD of the audio lectures, also failed to notice the section on the course Website concerning the text-to-speech software" (Simoncelli, 2005, p. 116). Simoncelli goes on to say that one student, "noted that she did not remember hearing about screen readers even after being asked about them in subsequent interviews" (p. 116). Any online instructors working with this population of students will need to be prepared for a good deal of virtual hand-holding.

Learning Disabilities

Additional populations that may require extra attention from an instructor are learners with disabilities of various types. These can range from minor learning disabilities to more serious conditions. The online environment may be the perfect solution for learners whose disabilities have made place-bound learning, such as on a college campus, very difficult.

Those with physical disabilities may be example students. "The use of computer technology and the asynchronous nature of the Internet have provided an independent outlet for these students" (Simoncelli, 2005, p. 93). eLearning may be so freeing to the individuals that they do not disclose any **disability** to the agency sponsoring the course or the instructor. We have both had the experience of a learner disclosing a disability well into the term of a course, which echoes the findings of Simoncelli. Conditions disclosed to us have included blindness, deafness, autism, attention deficit/hyperactivity disorder (ADHD), and learning disabilities such as dyslexia.

According to U.S. government policy, specifically a policy known as **Section 508** of the Rehabilitation Act last amended by the U.S. Congress in 1998,

> While people with disabilities may seem to be the greatest beneficiaries of this new ubiquitous technology, they are often shut out of government services and employment because the technology was not designed to be accessible. For instance, just as a set of stairs may be a barrier to a person who uses a wheelchair, a computer program or web site that does not include basic programming needed by a screen reader (a computer program that reads out text on a computer screen using voice) will be useless to a person who is blind. Worse yet, designing EIT to accommodate a wide-range of disabilities is usually easy-to-do and "invisible" to non-disabled users demanding the most interactive and compelling interfaces. (United States Access Board, 2008)

Since implementation of Section 508 for eLearning began in 2000, much of eLearning should be fully accessible to all learners. Unfortunately this is still not happening.

Course designers and online instructors need to be aware of how to make the course fully accessible to all learners. The law states that this is not to be done in an ad hoc approach. In other words, the designer shouldn't *fix* things when they know a student with a disability will be taking a class. As noted previously, such learners do not always self-disclose their disability. They often disclose it to the instructor when a problem with the interface arises. For example, one of us (Lehmann) had a student who was blind and used a screen reader for her coursework. She did not self-disclose this condition until she tried to use the synchronous chat tool for a course assignment and her screen reading software could not keep up with the flow of text. This issue occurred years ago. Hopefully the chat tool in that CMS is now fully compliant with Section 508.

Whether tools or the course materials are compliant with Section 508 and accessible to all learners is often not something the online instructor controls. Therefore, learning some ways to assist students when they do disclose an **accessibility** issue will be useful to eLearning instructors. Tips on accessibility will be shared in Chapter 7.

WHO SHOULD NOT BE AN ONLINE LEARNER?

A lot of different characteristics of online learners have been described here, but no consideration of who should be an online learner has taken place so

far. Are there people who should not take online courses at all? We believe
the answer to this question is *yes*. Online courses do not have enough structure and face-to-face style authority for the most extreme laid-back learners.
These are learners who think the online world will be a panacea for them, a
world where they can work at their own pace endlessly. Unfortunately such
learners often fail to be self-motivated enough to complete the course work.

Online learning does require the learner to be self-motivated. Type "Is
online learning for me?" into any search engine and scads of surveys from
a variety of educational entities will arise; every one of which includes self-
motivation questions. Of all the characteristics an online learner or facilitator
must have, it is the ability to regularly work in isolation and stay on task.

CONCLUSION

Our learners in online courses are complicated individuals just as they are
in the traditional classroom. However the anonymous environment of online
learning makes it more challenging for the instructor to figure out the various
characteristics of each person and how to adjust instruction for the individuals. For those designers and instructors who have been working in traditional
classrooms and are used to seeing and hearing their students, the online
classroom will be different. Making that paradigm shift from face-to-face to
eLearning is the subject of the next chapter.

6

The Paradigm Shift from Traditional to Online Learning

In 1987, Chickering and Gamson's now widely distributed research article the "Seven Principles for Good Practice in Undergraduate Education" was published. In it, Chickering and Gamson declared seven common factors for good teaching, gleaned from 50 years of research on the subject. The statements were simple, yet powerful, and applied across the campus curriculum. Good practice:

- encourages contacts between students and faculty.
- develops reciprocity and cooperation among students.
- uses active learning techniques.
- gives prompt feedback.
- emphasizes time on task.
- communicates high expectations.
- respects diverse talents and ways of learning.

Following on his work with Gamson (1987), Chickering and Ehrmann (1996) updated the classic article as technology began to take a foothold in the classroom. *Implementing the Seven Principles: Technology as Lever* made the principles of good teaching more relevant to the current technology-driven classroom. Chickering and Ehrmann were certainly heading in the right direction as they worked to create standards for technology use. Ehrmann and Zuniga (1997) developed the Flashlight project, which is a set of evaluation tools to measure the effectiveness of the technology on learning.

Educators relying on this background knowledge from Chickering and Gamson (1987), Chickering and Ehrmann (1996), and Ehrmann and Zuniga

(1997) continue to find and refine the right tools for each job. "But for any given instructional strategy, some technologies are better than others: Better to turn a screw with a screwdriver than a hammer—a dime may also do the trick, but a screwdriver is usually better" (Chickering & Ehrmann, 1996, p. 3).

Now, distance learning is asserting its place in the educational pantheon. It is time to take Chickering, Gamson, and Ehrmann online, from the *high touch* classroom to the *high tech* one. How might their good practices in teaching transform the digital classroom to a *high teach* course?

GOOD PRACTICE ENCOURAGES CONTACTS BETWEEN STUDENTS AND FACULTY

Facilitator-learner contact needs to occur not only during the course, but also before the course even begins. We will discuss precourse communication in Chapter 11, but for now it is important to know that the tone and climate between students and their instructor is set from this first communication.

Online facilitators need to be *seen* often by their students through posting of announcements, a proper discussion board presence, timely email replies, and multiple forms of feedback. Students need to be encouraged to ask questions both by email and through question-and-answer (Q&A) forums. Facilitators must answer these questions within a 24-hour time frame to limit student tension. The longer simple questions go unanswered, the higher student dissatisfaction and frustration rises. Good facilitators will interact with students regularly, which will help build community and put students at ease.

GOOD PRACTICE DEVELOPS RECIPROCITY AND COOPERATION AMONG STUDENTS

In an online course built on constructivist principles, students not only *can* learn from each other, but they *must* also learn from each other. It is built into the very fabric of the course. As Marsha, an online graduate student in eLearning recently realized:

> Aha! The key to a successful learning community is good facilitation. After reflecting on what we have learned thus far, I see collaborative learning as a circle model: good facilitation, good collaboration among learners, knowledge gained, knowledge shared, and back around to good facilitation. This has made me curious about ways that I can better my facilitation without being too involved and backing off enough to foster collaborative communities—finding

my individual balance as a facilitator. (Marsha Tweedy, personal communication, July 3, 2008)

Good facilitators find ways through their course design and discussion questions for students to work together. This is not for the social aspect but to help deepen the learning that occurs when students are able to bounce ideas off one another, share life experiences that enrich the topic, role-play scenarios, and otherwise engage in a more fruitful discussion than the one-dimensional lecture mode of old. As students add their experiences and inquiry to the discussion, it evolves. When this happens, the facilitator truly becomes a guide to learning rather than the fountain of all knowledge.

GOOD PRACTICE USES ACTIVE LEARNING TECHNIQUES

Active learning has been characterized in many ways, but essentially it can be defined by its opposite: passive learning. Those unfamiliar with good distance learning usually picture it as a low **engagement** endeavor: a student sits passively, reading screen after screen of scanned lecture notes and then clicks his or her way through a series of multiple choice recall-level questions. Best practices in online teaching are the opposite of this.

Today's course management systems (CMSs) can be dynamic—filled with audio, streaming video, simulations, **blogs**, **wikis**, podcasts, synchronous and asynchronous discussions, individual and group projects. Walla Walla Community College has an award-winning online yoga class, which teaches the principles of health and fitness alongside streaming video of yoga positions.

Students are dissecting digital frogs, performing stress tests in digitally designed bridges, collaboratively writing books, and learning to edit digital photographs and sharing them with their fellow students halfway across the world in real time. Students are using real time chat to discuss the merits of the current economic policies of the government for high school political science classes and using asynchronous discussion boards to deliver peer feedback on curriculum plans for master's degree programs. The ability to provide authentic activities is only limited by the technology available and the scope and imagination of the course designer.

GOOD PRACTICE GIVES PROMPT FEEDBACK

A key element in online assessment is the use of feedback, both **formative assessment** and **summative assessment**, for student improvement. One program called Quality Matters, developed from a U.S. Department of Education grant, uses extensive research to provide a peer review process to certify the quality of online courses. Quality Matters research found that:

> Students learn more effectively if they receive frequent, meaningful, and rapid feedback. This feedback may come from the instructor directly, from assignments and assessments that have feedback built into them, or even from other students. Examples of good feedback include:
>
> - Instructor participation in a discussion assignment.
> - Writing assignments that require submission of a draft for instructor comment and suggestions for improvement.
> - Self-mastery tests and quizzes that include informative feedback with each answer choice.
> - Interactive games and simulation that have feedback built in. (Tennessee Board of Regents, 2006)

In addition, instructors should indicate the turn-around time students can expect grading, email, and other communication or feedback to take. This time frame should be clearly spelled out in the syllabus, the grading expectations, and in other course procedural areas. Instructors need to abide by the time frame as it is part of the community contract held between the instructor and the student.

A general rule of thumb is to answer emails within 24 hours. Even if you cannot resolve the problem within the email, simply acknowledge its receipt and let the student know you are working on the problem. Student work should be graded and returned within the week it is received with feedback comments attached. Also, the instructor can provide *self-check* quizzes or learner-learner feedback, which takes some of the feedback burden off of him or her, but still provides information to the learners about their progress.

GOOD PRACTICE EMPHASIZES TIME ON TASK

Online practitioners who exemplify best practices in teaching in their online courses know that students hate having their time wasted. One way to do this is to proofread the course from the perspective of the student. Where are the potential distractions leading students off topic? What directions need to be clarified or broken down into smaller steps? Where will a screen shot clarify a difficult concept? Eliminating potential trouble spots before they occur saves the student frustration and the instructor from having to re-explain, refocus, and redirect any lesson gone awry.

To help students be more efficient, instructors should provide consistent, predictable scaffolding for student success. When it comes to helping students spend more of their time on tasks, that scaffolding includes providing a course calendar with due dates listed, checklists of assignments per module, links to outside reading rather than just the titles (or better yet, PDF copies of the articles made available inside the CMS), and limiting or redirecting off topic discussions in content-based forums.

Instructors should provide appropriate tool choices for students depending on the task required—this saves time from students emailing instructors with questions about which tools can or should be used or having students spend their assignment time simply looking for the appropriate tool to use. Instructors should consider **teachable moments**—separate mini-modules or insert boxes providing extra instruction with an unfamiliar tool or skill necessary to complete an assignment.

Finally, instructors need to consider the efficiency with which they provide feedback for student use. Feedback should be in a predictable format, always located in the same place (i.e., sent by email weekly, placed in the weekly module grade book comments, etc.). Feedback needs to be delivered in a timely enough fashion that students can use the comments to improve performance in the next module. Online students need to feel connected to their instructor and their work. By providing timely feedback and allowing revisions, instructors can fill this need for students and raise the quality of learning in the course.

GOOD PRACTICE COMMUNICATES HIGH EXPECTATIONS

True collaborative experiences require that learners be stretched beyond what they could do alone. This stretching comes through the types of questions that are asked, the expectations for the assignments or products to be created through **collaboration**, and the materials to be used. As you will soon see however, encouraging critical thinking is **EASy**! EASy is an acronym for evaluate, analyze, and synthesize (discussed more in Chapter 7).

Learning communities require critical thinking by all members of the team. The facilitator is the key element in fostering an environment that encourages both collaboration and critical thinking. The facilitator is first and foremost a role model for critical thinking. According to the Foundation for Critical Thinking, "We must become active, daily, practitioners of critical thought. We must regularly model for our students what it is to reflectively examine, critically assess, and effectively improve the way we live" (Criticalthinking.org, 2008).

Facilitators model critical thinking in their own postings, as well as through the questions they ask of students. An online instructor should not hesitate to ask tough questions once the course is underway. Such hard questions can be directed at specific students as long as the student will not feel undue pressure, or the question can be based on an individual's posting but directed to the entire group. Practitioners can increase critical thinking in their own courses by remembering the acronym EASy. The acronym includes terms from the highest levels of Bloom's revised taxonomy. Readers unfamiliar with the revised version of Bloom's may want to investigate this new interpretation meant to incorporate standards-based teaching and performance-based assessment.

Encouraging critical thinking is EASy in the online course as well. While critical thinking will be discussed in more depth in Chapter 7, some brief examples follow:

- writing open-ended prompts with no right or wrong answer.
- providing a variety of course materials showcasing several points of view even those contrary to the course designer.
- using scenarios or case studies that allow for multiple students to construct meaning.

Another way to encourage high performance in distance learning is through the use of **rubrics**, examples, and sample student feedback. Rubrics explicitly define what a student needs to do to reach an exemplary or top score, examples of quality work demonstrate visually what the instructor meant in the directions, and sample student feedback helps learners understand where other students may have faltered in their own efforts.

Giving students a good look at the target helps them hit it more accurately. This is no different from a traditional course. The unique element provided for in the online course is that the exemplars are available to students from the first day of the course to the last—by the simple click of a mouse. The student does not have to wait for the instructor to copy and distribute (or in some cases, to write) the rubrics. Nor do they have to try to remember what a teacher said or showed in class as an example—they always have it available as a reference.

GOOD PRACTICE RESPECTS DIVERSE TALENTS
AND WAYS OF LEARNING

By its very nature of existing on the world wide web, eLearning both encourages diversity and is blind to it. As discussed in Chapter 5, diversity abounds in our online courses. Not only do students stem from every country, but class rosters also include the young and old, male and female, middle school through postdoctoral students, and everything in between.

While an instructor may have a grade level or course level defined, unless pictures are included in the course roster, all are blind to a student's gender, race, physical size, or any other distinguishing feature. In essence, a student is what he or she posts. As long as instructors are careful to remind students to be respectful of differing ideas, alternate viewpoints can flourish in this diversity.

Another type of variety needs to be considered in online learning: learning styles. Some students are more visually oriented, some more aurally, and others a blend. Instinctively, instructors tend to teach to their own preferred learning style. With this in mind, instructors need to consciously differentiate or construct the learning experience to appeal to a variety of learners. For instance, visual learners are put off by web pages densely filled with text. Try breaking up long paragraphs into short ones and provide extra white space. Take concepts and use bulleted lists where possible. Consider creating a diagram or providing some other graphic.

For the auditory learner, a link to an audio clip explaining a complex concept is greatly appreciated. Using screen capture software with audio capabilities allows the more technically savvy instructor to provide variety for both these learners.

Differentiation can also be provided for by creating a range of tasks allowing for individual, group, and a mixture between the two for those who are more independent learners and those who are more socially driven.

Finally, when an online instructor considers best practices in meeting the needs for all learners, he or she needs to remember that some online students are **differently abled**. Some online students are visually impaired and use screen reading software such as **JAWS**, or they may adjust the text size to its largest viewing capacity, while deaf or hard-of-hearing students need less visual accommodation but require scripts of any recorded messages, videos, and such. To be compliant with the **Americans with Disabilities Act (ADA)**, courses need to be accessible for students with these kinds of disabilities.

There is some differing interpretation among institutions between the intent and the letter of the law when it comes to ADA compliance in online classrooms. Some simply put a compliance notice in each course and then retrofit the course and assignments on an *as needed* basis. Other institutions align themselves more with the spirit of the law by requiring courses to meet with minimum standards of accessibility as they are being designed and written. This includes providing alternate text titles for all graphics and captions, written scripts for all audio and video, and checking to see that enlarged font views will not obscure alignment of information on any given page. Because it is easy to design with compliance in mind right from the start rather than retrofit on the fly while teaching a course, upfront ADA compliance is certainly a best practice for the top-notch facilitator. Chapter 7 will go into designing with disability in mind in more detail.

GOOD TEACHING

The shift from the traditional classroom to the digital one is exciting for the instructor who is engaged in the learning process. The seven principles have evolved in their application as the environment to which they are being applied has evolved. But at its core, good teaching is good teaching. And no amount of content expertise or gadgets and gizmos can make up for the teacher lacking pedagogical training and practice.

Chapter 7 will explore the process of good instructional course design for distance learning. Both the principle of backward design and social learning theory are utilized in this process.

7

Basics of Course Design

Designing an online course is a complex endeavor requiring knowledge of lesson planning, teaching strategies, technologies, and the population for whom the course is intended. There is a clear need to pay attention to course design as noted by Shea, Fredericksen, and Pickett (2001), "In our experience of working with more than 1,000 faculty we discovered that given complete freedom to design a course, faculty often leave out components that students need in order to feel well oriented, to participate actively and to experience high levels of learning and satisfaction" (p. 8). This chapter will give a brief overview of these areas; however, it should be noted that anyone designing an online course without any prior experience in course design (face-to-face or online) will need more information than shared here. This is a starting point, an appetizer, but not the full meal.

PLANNING THE COURSE

Once a need for a course and the general topic is established, deeper planning for the course can begin. **Instructional design** begins at the end. According to McTighe and Wiggins (1999),

> The most effective curricular designs are backward. Backward design may be thought of as purposeful task analysis: Given a task to be accomplished, how does one get there? Or one might call it planned coaching: What kinds of lessons and practices are needed to master key performances? The approach to curricular design we recommend is logically forward and commonsensical, but backward by conventional habits, whereby many teachers typically *begin* with

textbooks, favored lessons, and time-honored activities rather than deriving them from targeted goals or standards. We are advocating the reverse: One starts with the end . . . and then derives the curriculum. (p. 37)

In backward design, the course designer or instructor must first identify the core knowledge and skills to be learned by the end of the course. Beginning with this in mind, you as the course designer next determine the order in which these elements should be presented. Common sense, when invoked, would mean the most basic skills and knowledge must be learned before more complex items.

Plenty of courses exist where such a commonsense arrangement has not been followed. A well-planned class scaffolds the skills, presenting the basic building foundation, upon which the learner must rest more complicated structures. In other words, a course designer must first know what the whole house will look like before he or she can plan for the construction of the house. The foundation is first, followed by the building of a simple skeletal framework, leading eventually to the more complicated details.

Once a general list of learning outcomes and an order of basic skills through more complicated ones has been determined, you must figure out the types of assessments that will establish whether students learned what they were supposed to learn. McTighe and Wiggins (1999) state this in the form of a question, "What evidence would I accept that students have attained the desired understandings and proficiencies" (p. 38)? By first defining the **acceptable evidence** of learning prior to planning the teaching activities the course designer is beginning with the end in mind.

It is important to know how the student will be assessed and how the acceptable evidence will be gathered at the end of the lesson so the learning activities can be designed to lead to success (McTighe & Wiggins, 1999). Let's consider two examples. Which one leads to the observer being able to assess if students learned the required information?

Example One: The Multiple-Choice Test for a Learner's Permit

Young people who want a driver's license must first earn their learner's permit. In many states all a student has to do is pass a multiple-choice test to get the permit. There is no authentic performance involving driving skills before the permit is granted. Students who are good at multiple-choice or *multiple-guess* tests could earn a permit without really knowing much about laws or driving skills. Permit in hand, they are allowed behind the wheel with a worried parent at their side. Such a test only assesses low-level recall and the ability to analyze multiple-choice questions and answers.

Example Two: The Driving Test

After a certain amount of coursework and driving practice, the young person is ready to take the road test. With an objective official in the car, the student must now perform all the best practices of driving, while also following the law.

It should be clear that Example Two is the authentic assessment and is the better choice for assessing driver's skills. Even if the young person passes the multiple-choice learner's permit exam, it is not clear they really mastered the required outcomes before heading out on the road. When taking the road test, the objective observer is analyzing if the young person has mastered the required outcomes as defined by the state. The driver's coursework and practice sessions were assigned with the driving test in mind. Whoever taught the driver's course was preparing students with success in mind. In this case, it was passing their road test. The class would have been taught in such a way that the skills and knowledge were developed over time, building up to the final assessment. The desired results are that students would be successful when taking the driving test and the observer can see they have met all the required outcomes.

The **instructional designer** needs to design assessments, both for the end of the course and for the various course segments, which clearly show the required outcomes have been met. The listed outcomes should include critical thinking and need practice to achieve them. The assessment should therefore require critical thinking as well. Low-level tests and quizzes are poor ways to really assess critical thinking. In a constructivist environment, where students are creating their own understanding there is no substitute for authentic assessments. There is more information on authentic assessment in Chapter 8.

Up to this point, the course designer has determined the required objectives for the course, put them in a commonsense order from simple to complex, and determined what assessments would show student mastery of the objectives. You are now ready to determine how to chunk the course content into segments that are manageable for the learners.

Chunking

Chunking the content means that the designer divides the work into modules, weeks, or units, having enough material to keep students engaged during the timeline for the segment. The segments should not have so much work that students are overwhelmed trying to complete the tasks in the given amount of time. There are often natural breakpoints in a curriculum where it is appropriate to stop providing background information and have the learners do something with the material.

You need to make sure the planned activities have a balanced workload from one segment to the next. This can be difficult to gauge since you must consider that some learners will be newbies who struggle with even the simplest of technological tasks. In addition many learners may be extremely busy and have little time to spend on the coursework, while others may have lots of time to devote to the course. Student reading level and speed can also impact how quickly or slowly the student may take in the background information or discussion postings. You will want to make sure the very first unit has a somewhat lighter workload. Many students will still be acclimating to the new online learning environment. This acclimation takes time and energy, therefore the amount of work needs to be adjusted to not lose students during the first week. There is more information about planning for the first week in Chapter 11.

Student workload is one area where feedback at the end of the course is critical in helping you revise the course and provide a more balanced workload. Every course will go through several revisions before the final version is reached. Revisions include consideration of the student workload. Revisions should be expected; more about the feedback and revision process will be discussed later in the chapter.

GENERAL COURSE STRUCTURE AND INTERACTIVITY LEVEL

In Table 15.1, the various ways that an online course can be structured were shared. The interactivity of a course was a part of Table 15.1. Interactivity plays an important role in an online course. However, the level of interactivity varies from institution to institution and from course to course. In general, a high level of interactivity would include daily interactions from instructor to student and from student to student. The lowest level of interactivity would be a self-paced online course where there is a little, if any, interaction between instructor and students. Research has shown that interactivity is a key element in student satisfaction with online courses.

Interactions in a class occur between the learner and: (a) facilitator, if there is one, (b) fellow students, and (c) content. Online courses range from computer-automated learning systems, in which the student has no interaction with the instructor or other students, to instructor-facilitated courses using a cohort model, where groups of students move through a series of courses together.

Facilitation

Will there be a facilitator for the course or not? This is a basic, but important, question. Without a facilitator it is very unlikely that there would be fellow students in the course. Therefore, the only interaction will be between the learner and the content. The possibilities without facilitation are limited to self-assessed content and computer-assessed work. Examples of appropriate content for this type of course are yearly required trainings where a simple certificate of completion is all that is necessary for company record-keeping purposes. In other words, if the student is taking an online course without anyone to guide their study, answer questions, and assess the work, then the student is in either an online tutorial or some type of computer-automated learning system.

If it is an online tutorial, the student determines if they have learned what they wanted to know through self-assessment and determines if he or she needs to go over the material again or move on to something else. In computer-automated systems, the software assesses student work, usually through multiple-choice questions and allows the student to move on to the next topic based on a predetermined mastery level. These types of courses do not provide a rich, learning environment. They are often used as a supplemental drill, skill, or textbook enhancement. An example is MyReadingLab.com

If there is a facilitator, a wide range of possible levels of interaction between the student and the facilitator still exists. You will want to think about how much facilitation will be needed when choosing learning activities for the course. For example, if students read materials, take an online quiz, and submit a paper at the end of the week, the workload for a facilitator is minimal. If, instead, there will be threaded discussions, the facilitator will need to check in several times a week to read and respond to the postings.

The workload for the instructor is based on the interactivity level of the course and the number of students enrolled. Instructional designers need to have some idea of the expected enrollment in each course section as they consider which level of interactivity and learning activities will best serve the content and the learners' needs. Selecting a threaded discussion activity would not work if the enrollment will be 50 students per course section. The facilitator would not be able to keep up and the students would be overwhelmed.

Learner-Learner Interactivity

Social isolation has been a reported flaw in online education for quite some time. Interactions with the instructor and fellow students will not only resolve this issue, but in many instances also leave learners feeling more connected to those in their online courses than in face-to-face ones. The level of learner-learner interactivity is dependent on a couple of course design choices. If you choose a self-paced course, which students can enter at any time and proceed through at their own pace, there will be few learner-learner interactions in the class. If a cohort-style design is used, students have an opportunity to work together on the coursework depending on the choice of learning activities.

Consider this hypothetical example from a self-paced course. Student A does all the work for modules one through five in the first week while most others are still on module one, and several students have not even opened the course site. Student A will not be working with the other students on projects. Student A is not in the same point in the curriculum as the other students and working together on projects would be pointless for student A.

Designing a course where learners proceed together through the segments offers a much greater possibility of learner-learner interactions. According to social learning theory, people learn more when they work together with others to understand the content. Cooperative learning, a specific teaching strategy in which students are expected to work together, will be discussed further. In addition to the learning benefits, working with others reduces feelings of isolation. This means that you need to offer opportunities for learner-learner interaction throughout the course despite whether it is a self-paced or cohort design.

Learner-Content Interactivity

Students can interact with the content in many ways. Confucius summed up learner-content interactions very well: *Tell me and I will forget, Show me and I will remember, Involve me and I will understand.* Involving students with the curriculum has obviously been important for thousands of years if the ancient Chinese philosopher gave it thought, yet much of traditional education involves very passive activities. Reading is one of the most common learner-content interactions and it is passive.

The next step is to develop the learning activities students will be doing during each segment. However before a discussion of those activities takes place, some background about incorporating critical thinking needs to take place.

CRITICAL THINKING IS EASY

Teachers are often taught to incorporate critical thinking in the design of lessons, tests, and discussion questions by applying **Bloom's Taxonomy** (Bloom, 1956). According to the taxonomy, learning activities start with low-level thinking at the base of Bloom's Pyramid of Cognitive Learning and work their way toward the highest point to help demonstrate students thinking at the highest cognitive levels.

According to Benjamin Bloom (1956), the lowest level of learning in the cognitive domain is referred to as *knowledge* (i.e., label, list). Moving up the pyramid, the next level of thinking is *comprehension* (i.e., restate, paraphrase); followed by *application* (i.e., apply, solve); *analysis* (i.e., classify, infer); then *synthesis* (i.e., construct, design); and finally *evaluation* (i.e., critique, persuade), which Bloom suggests is the highest order of critical thinking behaviors.

Upgrading Bloom's Is EASy

The taxonomy can be used in a slightly revised way when teaching critical thinking. This new view is a process for the steps through which student's progress while working at the upper levels of critical thinking. This process can be remembered utilizing the acronym *EASy*. EASy stands for evaluate, analyze, and synthesize. In the original Bloom's hierarchy (1956), the top three levels are not in the EASy order; Bloom's arrangement of the topmost terms is analyze, synthesize, and evaluate. The difference may seem negligible at first, but there are real differences and a definite rationale for repurposing them into the EASy order. The differences should become clearer when the levels are defined.

Evaluation is to gather information from a variety of sources and then determine the validity, usefulness, and significance of the information. Or, as stated in the Merriam-Webster online dictionary (2007), it is "to determine the significance, worth, or condition of usually by careful appraisal and study." Evaluation establishes the current knowledge base about a topic or idea.

Analysis is to examine the information that has been gathered, comparing the various sources to pull out the most salient points. "Separation of a whole into its component parts, an examination of a complex, its elements, and their relations" (*Merriam-Webster*, 2007). In the analysis phase, fact is separated from opinion, theories are differentiated from laws, and students choose only that which is relevant to their assigned task.

To *synthesize* is to impart a new outlook or a new voice based on evaluation and analysis of other resources. When students synthesize, they look at "the composition or combination of parts or elements so as to form a whole, combining of often diverse conceptions into a coherent whole" (*Merriam-Webster*, 2007). Ballenger (2007) defines synthesizing this way, "Extend the conversation, change it, and take it in a new and original direction" (p. 16).

In developing the EASy process, there is an acknowledgement that the upper level of Bloom's pyramid, especially evaluation, has come to represent testing. This is as much a by-product of our assessment-driven mandates like No Child Left Behind as it is the misuse of Bloom's, which was never meant to be used in such a linear fashion as it is employed most often these days. Even Dr. Lorin Anderson, a former student of Bloom's and now a distinguished professor of education at the University of South Carolina, saw the need for a change in the way Bloom's Taxonomy has been utilized. In partnership with Dr. David Krathwhol, a Bloom's researcher, Anderson set about revising the taxonomy to better meet today's educational environment. Interestingly enough, Anderson and Krathwhol (2001) also shifted synthesis, now renamed "creating," to the top of the pyramid.

In simpler terms, the EASy critical thinking process begins with (a) gathering information, then (b) determining what pieces of the information are valid, useful, and how they relate to one another, and the final step is (c) taking that information to a new and original level—new, at least, to the student. What might this look like in the classroom at various grade levels and in a variety of curricular areas? Here are some specific fully detailed examples of lessons that incorporate EASy thinking skills.

Examples of EASy Lessons

Secondary Level History: Roman News Project

Student groups are assigned a specific aspect of Roman history to turn into a newspaper web page complete with advertisements or a live-from-the-scene news report posted to YouTube. Since web pages about historical topics, as well as books and encyclopedias, are not written in a news style of writing, students have to evaluate the information about their topic, analyze the information that is gathered from a variety of resources, and then produce news articles or scripts containing historical facts. Synthesis, the process of creating something new and original is the final step, not the first step for students.

Elementary Science: Create a New Animal

After a study of habitats and how animals are adapted to or suited for the habitat in which they live, students create a new animal using a video game called Spore and describe the habitat in which it would live. Students must first evaluate how animals adapt to their habitat, they then analyze the characteristics of different animals and different habitats, and finally they create an original animal suited for the habitat they have described.

Secondary Language Arts: Research Project

The research process in preparation for writing an essay is all about critical thinking. First students need to evaluate what sources are available on their topic, then analyze what material from those sources is valid and viable, and finally, in the synthesis step, students write their research where they add their ideas and perspective to the research that has been done before. For example, if a student is curious as to why someone his or her age might start smoking, he or she would need to find the available material on teen smoking, look to the theories and statements of those who report on addiction (and those who argue that nicotine is not addictive), decide what he or she believes and the validity of those sources, perhaps do an interview or two, and then synthesize it all together to post to their blog for comments from other teens.

Secondary Humanities: Ethics

After teaching a unit of ethics, philosophy, or critical thinking itself, students are asked to decide who, among a given set of individuals with both good and bad credentials each, should be taken to populate a new space station, placed in a fallout shelter, placed in a lifeboat, or some other survival situation. After discussion in a forum or blog, student groups use a wiki to create a persuasive writing piece explaining who they picked, why they picked them, and more importantly, the thought processes used in choosing this group of survivors.

Secondary Math: Coordinate Planes

After a unit on plotting algebraic equations, have students create a small group mapping experience for each other where the equation must first be solved, then plotted, and then the coordinate overlaid to a corresponding spot on Google Earth.

Moving to the Next Step

So far you have determined the learner outcomes for the course and the assessments that will measure those outcomes. In addition you've considered how to incorporate critical thinking the EASy way into units and activities. The next step is to align activities with the assessments. The possible choices of learning activities are virtually limitless whether face-to-face or online. Again it needs to be noted that this one chapter is no substitute textbooks or coursework on instructional planning. Only space limits the number of instructional activities shared here.

INSTRUCTIONAL ACTIVITIES

There are myriad ways to present knowledge and skills as well as have learners work with the content for learning to occur. Some strategies work particularly well in the online environment and will be presented here. For clarity, the same terms used previously in the chapter, that is learner-learner and learner-content interactions, have been used here to organize the discussion of eLearning activities.

Learner-Learner

Learner-learner activities are at the heart of constructivist online courses. For those new to eLearning, the idea that collaboration and discussion can take place even when students are temporally and geographically disparate can be difficult to envision. Instructors can look to business, which has learned to use web-based tools for collaboration and conversation among members of distant workgroups and provides great models from which K–20 educators can learn.

The first set of communication tools used in online learning are the ones still used most heavily in eLearning. These are all text-based tools including email, threaded discussions, and submission of documents for peer or instructor review. Most online courses rely heavily on these tools.

Email

Email is mostly used for answering questions about the content or further guiding students in the learning activities. This is a support tool for the learning activities rather than a **learning activity** in itself. There are some possibilities for email as a tool for learning, including having students interview one another early in the class as part of an **icebreaker** activity or interview people outside the course and presenting the information back to the class members.

Threaded Discussions

If email had been used for either of the activities mentioned, the results would likely have been communicated via a threaded discussion forum. Threaded discussions are a primary tool used in online learning. The most common use, beyond community building, is to have an open-ended discussion question about the readings or concepts to which everyone must respond. Such responses take the place of oral classroom discussions in traditional education but with an important difference. Everyone must participate. In the online classroom using a threaded discussion, the student who does not post to the discussion forum does not exist. They are invisible.

Researchers have studied participation in traditional classroom discussions for several decades and consistently come to the conclusion that the discussion is dominated by four or five individuals (Barnes, 1980; Gupta, et al., 2005; Karp & Yoels, 1987; Shea, et al., 2001). When only a few individuals do the majority of the talking in a traditional classroom, the benefits that accrue from discussion are not equally shared by everyone in the class. However, since all students must participate in the online classroom lest they be invisible, all students benefit from the discussion. Discussion participation guidelines are shared in Chapter 15.

Studies have shown that discussions increase student critical thinking. Howard (2002) summarizes the work of several researchers when stating, "Critical thinking is fostered by students' active participation in learning . . . instructors can use classroom discussion to lead students through different levels of learning" (p. 764). These benefits regarding critical thinking are true no matter whether the classroom is face to face or online. When every online student actually responds to each discussion question, versus only four or five students responding while all others listen passively in a traditional environment, the learning benefits confer more equally to online students.

Participation in the threaded discussions must be required to ensure students do not remain invisible. *Required* is synonymous with *graded*. Without a point value attached to a required element, the student has no incentive to meet the requirement. Deenen (2005) states the importance of required participation this way, "While student participation is not a direct measure of learning, it is necessary in order for a discussion activity to be successful and result in learning. Should student messages be lacking in sufficient quantity, quality, timing, and purpose then it is less likely that the learning objectives will be met through that activity" (p. 128).

Gupta and colleagues (2005) echo the critical thinking benefit and add,

> The quality of online discussions tends to be of a high level, since students have the opportunity to reflect on and edit their comments before posting them for other students to see. Moreover, since all class discussions can be logged, note taking becomes unnecessary and students can devote their energies to participating constructively on class assignments and discussions rather than taking notes. It also permits students who may have been inactive for a certain period of time to catch up (p. 83).

The key element in the use of threaded discussions to promote critical thinking is the questions or prompts to which students respond. Deenen (2005) explains how a group responds to different levels of questions or prompts,

> If an instructor were to post a question with one clear, expected answer on a discussion board, there would be little use for multiple students to reply once the correct answer was given. Additionally, there would be little reason for students

to discuss this topic further. On the other hand, if a discussion question allowed for multiple perspectives to be presented, supported, and argued, there is greater opportunity for students to engage in the activity (p. 129).

Discussion Questions

A well-written discussion question will engage every student in the course. Students will be able to respond with a unique and insightful answer based on their own knowledge and experiences as well as incorporate newly learned content. Others will be compelled to respond to these unique answers with questions, commentary, and suggestions taking the discussion deeper. This can be an exhilarating experience for students and teacher alike.

A good discussion question does not have a yes or no answer. In fact, there should be no one right answer to the question. If there is only one possible answer then after it is posted, every other answer will be the equivalent of "I agree." Boring! This is not a good discussion result in any educational environment.

One of the benefits of discussion questions, as noted with asynchronous threaded discussions, is students have time to consider their responses and colleagues can reply to one another whenever they have time. However, one of the issues with online learning that leads to social isolation is the learner having to wait for responses to posts. This wait time lacks the immediacy of the classroom discussion environment.

In a study of nine online courses, Deenen (2005) noted,

Long discussion periods resulted in threads with messages that seemed to be in dialogic response in terms of content, but they were so spread out over weeks that one must wonder whether the original author ever read any of the responses. In other words, students were going through the motions of participating in a conversation, but all parties necessary for the discussion to take place were not necessarily present (p. 136).

Tools that are synchronous, where all members of the group are online and communicating at the same time, can provide some of that immediacy.

Synchronous Chat, Instant Messaging, and Voice over Internet Protocol

Two synchronous tools, chat and instant messaging (IM), are very similar and will be considered as one for course design purposes. Both are primarily text based, although some newer versions of the tools have voice and even video capabilities. Another synchronous tool, **Voice over Internet Protocol** (VoIP), essentially uses the Internet to provide telephone conversations online. This section will not go any further into a discussion of the mechanics of these tools as that will occur more fully in a later chapter. These tools are addressed here in terms of presenting synchronous discussion capabilities for learning activities.

Synchronous tools add a live element to online courses that more closely mimics classroom discussions or instructor office hours where questions are asked and answered immediately. In a study by J. M. Lehmann (2008) about the use of VoIP in online classes, one student stated it this way, "Interaction makes you think on your feet and not merely restating what was read. Verbally stating what you are learning and being questioned about it is very effective. Hearing others speak makes it more real" (p. 149). The immediacy of synchronous tools puts more burden on the facilitator than the course designer. If you are not going to teach the course you are designing, you should provide good open-ended questions and perhaps a protocol for instructors to use during the live sessions.

J. M. Lehmann (2008) noted the work of prior researchers who showed that a student's natural tendency in discussions was to respond at the lower levels of critical thinking. Lehmann suggests,

> To encourage maximum learning from students, instructors need to be aware of this natural tendency and provide questioning that guides learners into critical thought. VoIP sessions can be successful and can promote a high degree of thinking among students. Instructors need to prepare for each VoIP session by creating a scaffolding of questions or protocol (p. 144).

The course designer can, and very likely should, prepare the discussion protocol and provide it to the instructor. However, even with the most well-designed list of questions, the actual session will be up to the instructor's skills and capabilities at questioning and keeping live discussions on track. Of course this is true with threaded discussions as well. One strategy that relies less on the instructor and more on learner-learner input is peer review.

Peer Review

One excellent strategy that honors the experience and wisdom of all learners, but especially adult learners, is peer review. In peer review, students provide comments and feedback on work produced by their colleagues in the class. Peer review of assignments can be informal or formal. Informal peer reviews occur when students post draft assignments and ask for comments from others. While you might suggest that this take place in the course, it would not be a graded learning activity. Most likely informal peer review will occur spontaneously or with instructor encouragement rather than as part of the course design.

You may choose to incorporate formal peer review into a course. Formalizing it generally means a rubric or checklist or other assessment tool would be used and some grade would be attached to peer reviewing. As noted with threaded discussions, if something is required but not graded, students will not feel compelled to participate. Peer review should occur after students have built a learning community. A certain amount of trust has to be established between students if the review is to go beyond, "Great job! Looks good!" Getting students to provide good constructive critiques of the work of others is dependent on a feeling of safety in the group.

Peer review can be a planned learning activity, but it is actually more of an assessment technique. More information on peer review will be shared in Chapter 8 where assessment is discussed. Peer review expects learners to work in collaboration with their colleagues. Collaboration, like peer review, can be informal or formal.

COLLABORATION OR COOPERATIVE LEARNING

Asking students to work together informally or formally may not, at first, make sense to you. "Intellectually it may seem that cooperative learning . . . would not be feasible in online environments since the participants are geographically diverse. However just as businesses have learned how to have work teams collaborate across great distances using electronic tools, so too has education" (K. L. Lehmann, 2008, p. 20). Collaboration and cooperative learning are both possible in online learning.

There is a difference between these two terms, and they are often, and erroneously, used synonymously in educational literature. A down and dirty way to differentiate between the two is to think of them as informal or formal. Collaboration can occur informally at any point in a course. Students might ask others for input on an assignment, or they might begin adding comments to another student's wiki or blog. Or they may just reach out to one another for support. "Many students reiterated the importance of the group process in keeping them going when the course became difficult and in providing them with an ongoing network of support" (Stacey, 1999, p. 2).

Collaboration

Informal collaboration may be planned and suggested but is usually not graded. For example, having students post challenging vocabulary terms to a wiki and encouraging everyone to add definitions as they begin to understand the terms is informal collaboration. This is a preplanned activity but the participation is informal, ungraded, and everyone has a choice whether to participate. According to social learning theory, working with others is important if learners are to gain the deepest understandings. When collaboration is a choice, some students will be left out and will therefore not learn as much as possible. "While working and talking with other students about the content may occur spontaneously between students, it may not be universally spontaneous" (K. L. Lehmann, 2008, p. 18). To include all learners teachers plan formal cooperative learning projects.

Cooperative Learning

Cooperative learning is a formal method of having students work together. "Cooperative group work ensures that students will discuss the content with others, thereby benefiting from increased understanding of the content" (K. L. Lehmann, 2008, p. 18). Students are in defined groups creating a defined product or completing a defined task. The product (what the group creates) and the process (how the group works together to create the product) are usually both graded.

When planning for a cooperative project in the course design phase, the most important thing is to determine a product that will not only showcase the important knowledge and skills but is also a task that would be difficult, if not impossible, to complete alone. This compels the group to work together to accomplish the task.

A long enough timeline needs to be allowed that the groups can legitimately contact one another while working at a distance to complete the work. However, too long a timeline will encourage procrastination. In addition, the group projects should be shared publicly. Presenting the work to others validates the efforts of the group and increases the knowledge gained by everyone in the course. As will be discussed in the assignments and assessment chapter, you should provide rubrics for all elements of the group work including process and product. A rubric that assesses both product and process in a cooperative project is shared in Chapter 15.

LEARNER-CONTENT INTERACTIVITY

The need for interactivity in eLearning has already been established and the strategies in the learner-learner section will help meet that need. Not all work in any class, traditional or online, should be completed while working with others. Some assignments should be solitary endeavors for a variety of reasons including but not limited to (a) a need for differentiating the curriculum, (b) meeting the learning style of those students who are intrapersonal learners, and (c) being able to adequately assess each individual's understanding of the content. Good course design *mixes it up* by incorporating a good variety of assignment types. Learner-content strategies help to create that mix.

Traditional Papers and Their Technological Counterparts

In K–12 and higher education one of the most traditional learner-content strategies is to have students author a paper of some type. Whether it is a report, an essay, a letter to the editor, or some other form of writing, students are familiar with such assignments. Using the strategy of asking students to write can be a valuable way of assessing student knowledge *if* critical thinking is incorporated into the assignment. Students should be expected to take information, synthesize it, and use it in some new way so that they are required to show critical thinking about the topic. In addition, this helps to avoid the problem of plagiarized work. Well-designed writing prompts allow for student synthesis and creativity. They create less opportunity to *find* a paper that meets the prompt while surfing the Internet.

The Internet also provides new ground for posting student writing. For example, a student can post their original piece on a blog rather than submitting a paper to the instructor. When the work is published in this way, students are more motivated to do a good job. This echoes several educational theorists who consistently state that work needs to be authentic. What could be more authentic than publishing writing for the entire world to read? Learning that requires writing as the product is the most problematic area in terms of plagiarism however. Much attention needs to be paid to how the prompt is written so the product is truly original. Asking for writing other than an essay may be a better way to guarantee the work is original to the student.

Created Documents

Students can create documents and products other than traditional essays. In many cases these types of assignments are more motivating because students can be more creative with them, and they are often more authentic tasks associated with real-world issues or needs. For example, having teachers create a PowerPoint that can be used to present content in their own classroom is more motivating than writing a paper about the same knowledge and skills. Having marketing personnel create a brochure is more directly tied to their day-to-day work and will result in a unique application of the knowledge.

Instructors should consider planning for critical thinking the EASy way for ideas on creating authentic, real-world tasks that result in documents that can be attached to a threaded discussion or uploaded to a course dropbox. The best way to keep things authentic is to not specify the exact kind of product that needs to be created, allowing the learners some choice in how to apply the knowledge and skills to their own life. Writing the rubric to assess such an open-ended assignment prompt is tricky but can be done. Another way to both confirm the work is original and begin the assessment process for such assignments is to ask students to reflect on their learning.

Personal Reflections and Journaling

Reflection is an important part of the learning process particularly for adult learners. Research (Knowles, et al., 1988) has shown that adults need to reflect on the concepts and how they apply to their own lives before they can fully learn the ideas in the course. There are a variety of ways to have students reflect on their learning in a formal way. One way is through the use of an online journal. Many CMSs have such a tool. Another is through surveys that allow for open-ended responses. In general, such reflections are not open for other students to read. If you want to have these shared, then the reflections can be posted in a threaded discussion.

In order to make sure that students fully reflect on the course and what they have learned, the expectations for reflections and a rubric for grading these items should be developed in advance. In addition there should be specific prompts to which the learners are responding. Without expectations, a grading rubric and prompts, many learners will write one- to two-sentence paragraphs summarizing the module activities instead of showing real critical thinking about what they have learned. One way to do this is by using a course-based survey that specifically asks about each of the module's activities. An example of this type of survey is shared in Chapter 15.

Since reflections are, in general, not shared with anyone but the instructor, this is a learner-content and **learner-facilitator** strategy. There are other strategies that similarly cross over this arbitrary division.

STRATEGIES THAT CROSS BETWEEN
LEARNER-LEARNER AND LEARNER-CONTENT

Some strategies, like reflective journals, can be learner-content or learner-instructor when kept private, and learner-learner when shared with the whole group. Case studies and scenarios likewise can be used either way. Case studies and scenarios are very similar. Both share real-life events with students and ask them to analyze and respond to the situation. Case studies are usually more in depth, while scenarios can be as short as one sentence.

Case studies and scenarios both offer students a chance to work with authentic events. Names and locations might be changed, but the facts are true, making case studies and scenarios a compelling and motivating assignment. Students, when they are done posting their own thoughts on the event, invariably ask, "Now tell us what really happened."

Case studies, in particular, are used in online medical and psychology classes. They are useful in any situation where professionals have to make real judgments about what to do. We use them heavily when training future online instructors. The reason these strategies cross over between learner-learner and learner-content is that they can be solitary assignments with a written response submitted to the instructor; or the responses can be shared and analyzed by the whole class. Sharing them with the whole class allows everyone to analyze all responses. This provides each learner with multiple eyes offering them suggestions on their own response, and conversely it provides every learner with multiple perspectives and solutions to each case. Case studies and scenario assignments should be shared with the whole group because of these advantages.

There are many other teaching strategies that can be used. These were some of the most common, and the best, for the online environment. You are urged to continue seeking out additional ideas from courses, textbooks, and research articles. This is not a comprehensive list of teaching strategies by any means.

Learning Objects

One way to quickly develop learning activities is to use learning objects. The definition of learning objects varies, but in a nutshell, these are course elements that are stored online and available to be *popped* into a course. Polsani (2003), after critiquing definitions created by others, formulated this definition, "A Learning Object is an independent and self-standing unit of learning content that is predisposed to reuse in multiple instructional contexts" (p. 5). There are repositories of learning objects online that you can use when writing a course. The best way to access several repositories at once is to use the Global Learning Objects Brokered Exchange (GLOBE, 2008) site that allows the searcher to access objects from many of the largest repositories.

Instructor Design

So far in this chapter, it has been assumed the instructional designer is creating a course from scratch. In many cases, a **course conversion**, that is, changing face-to-face course materials into an online format, is done instead of writing a course from scratch. Care must be taken in determining whether the face-to-face materials and activities are appropriate for an online course. Slapping lecture notes online is not good course design. Whether converting an existing traditional course or creating an online course from scratch, the instructor encounters several advantages and disadvantages as the course author.

ADVANTAGES OF TEACHING A SELF-DESIGNED COURSE

Teaching a self-designed course means the instructor is familiar with all materials, the course navigation, the assignments, and assessments. Obviously understanding all elements of the course makes it easier to troubleshoot for the students. The students may be confused about some aspect of the course but the instructor/designer is familiar with the whole course and can assist students with the source of the confusion. This is often not the case when teaching a course designed by someone else.

Designing the course also means that the instructor has an opportunity to balance instructor tasks so that the workload is reasonable at all times. Planning for assignment submissions, methods of communicating, and grading of the course can be considered during the design of the course. An additional benefit is that the instructor may own the intellectual property rights for the course.

DISADVANTAGES OF TEACHING A SELF-DESIGNED COURSE

Much of the preparation work for an online course takes place months in advance. If the instructor is paid for course design, this timeline for development is not problematic. However, if the instructor wants to own the intellectual property rights for their own course, then there is a lot of work done before any reimbursement for this time will be seen. "One of the greatest impediments to teaching online courses is the significant start-up time required to either develop a new course or transform an existing course to an online course" (Gupta, et al., 2005, p. 85). It has been estimated that writing an online course takes substantially longer than the same face-to-face course (Cavanaugh, 2005). At the University of Wisconsin–Stout, the distance learning faculty has estimated it takes between 300 and 600 hours to author an online course (Joan Vandervelde, personal communication, 2008).

Writing an online course includes finding web-based resources, writing lectures or explanations, and designing media to fully utilize the power of online learning. Finding or writing all these resources can be a disadvantage.

Locating or creating resources can be time consuming and frustrating. However, this aspect of course design can also be an advantage. It is a creative endeavor to find or write these elements and mesh them together in a way that creates the best opportunity for learning. And if the instructor ultimately owns their own course materials, they can be used in publications or moved to a different institution. What does it mean to *own the course*? What are intellectual property rights?

Intellectual Property

Designing and writing a course means intellectual property is being created. Defining the ownership of the rights to this creative work is an important consideration for the author of it. Simplistically put, if the author is paid to create the course, the course belongs to whoever paid for the work to be done. Conversely if the author writes the course without being reimbursed, the author owns the intellectual property. This distinction can be a bit murky but no matter whether the course is designed as part of the regular workload at an institution or if the instructor is paid on a contract basis, the author does not own the rights to their own course unless the contract explicitly states the author retains ownership of the intellectual property.

According to Gupta and colleagues (2005)

> Although faculty have property rights to their own research, it is less clear who has property rights to course design . . . particularly if the University provided resources such as release time, equipment, and training to develop the course. Some institutions believe that instructional materials produced for a specific course belong to the institution. In fact, it has been suggested that in the future, institutions will require faculty to assign all copyrights on course material to the university as a condition of employment. (p. 86)

This book contains some material from a course we coauthored. Since we own the intellectual property rights to the course material, it can be used in other forms, such as this book. Going without payment for writing a course may be beneficial in the long run. Readers should consult a lawyer for more information on intellectual property and ownership of copyrighted materials. Another area where it is wise to get advice from professionals is accessibility.

ACCESSIBILITY

Web page accessibility means that people with any disability can use the site. Both the Americans with Disabilities Act and the Rehabilitation Act have sections that have been interpreted to include web page accessibility, however, it is not entirely clear if these laws apply to all online courses and all course web pages.

According to Edmonds (2004), "No single law or court decision requires educators to provide online courses in a format that is accessible to students with disabilities. Instead, there is a patchwork of federal and state laws—some of them passed before the advent of the Internet—that apply to online education in various ways" (p. 52). For example, the laws apply if courses are among programs and services of the federal government. This would include a course that is part of a federal grant.

Presence of Student with a Disabling Condition

Courses must also be made accessible if a student with a disabling condition is enrolled. However, it just makes sense to begin with a course design and CMS that are already accessible. Starting with accessible design and tools means the course is ready for any students, or instructors, who have a disabling condition without retrofitting. This is known as **universal design**, which is design that is available to all learners regardless of ability. Revising an entire course when a student with a disability enrolls is highly challenging, time consuming, and unnecessary work during the middle of a course. In addition, universal design "results in courses that are easier to use and understand for everyone" (Edmonds, 2004, p. 52).

Blindness, deafness, neurological and cognitive ailments, and physical disabilities are some of the disabling conditions that make it difficult to navigate websites and get information. Students who are blind (or color-blind) obviously will face challenges using a medium that is highly visual and text based. Deaf and hard-of-hearing students will not be able to access podcasts or audio commentary or hear the audio track of a video. Some forms of epileptic seizures can be triggered by screen flicker or animations. Those with physical disabilities may have trouble selecting navigation links and using drop-down menus. For instructors and course designers who have not yet encountered students with these disabilities in your classes here are more specific examples of how web pages can be inaccessible to those with disabilities.

Blindness or Low Vision

Students who are blind or have low vision often use screen reading software, such as JAWS, which reads all the text on the page. Such software also may be used by students with dyslexia or other disabilities that impair the ability to read and comprehend information. For the screen-reading software to work properly, the information must be formatted in a way that will make sense when the screen reader makes it audible.

Since this course is online and email never	therefore problems with home technology
closes for bad weather, illness, etc., there is	will not be accepted as an excuse for late
always a way to get the assignment in.	work. Seek out alternate locations you can
Computers are available on campuses as	use to access the course just in case.
well as public libraries, internet cafes, etc..	

Figure 7.1. Two columns of text that screen-reading software may, or may not, read correctly.

Imagine a page that has text set up in two columns such as in Figure 7.1. If the design of the web page is done incorrectly, the software could read each line straight across instead of reading down one column, and then down the next column. In this case, the software would read the passage in the screenshot as follows:

Since this course is online and email never therefore problems with home technology closes for bad weather, illness, etc., there is will not be accepted as an excuse for late always a way to get an assignment in. work. Seek out alternate locations you can Computers are available on campuses as use to access the course just in case. well as public libraries, internet cafes, etc.

Obviously this passage does not make sense. If the software continued to read across the width of the page instead of down each column, none of the information would be comprehensible. Web pages with tables in the background or frames can also cause issues with screen-reading software. These are just a few examples of how the formatting can confuse the screen-reading software rendering the information useless to the user.

Images and colors are additional components of web pages that are often problematic when using a screen reader. Images need to have alternate text embedded in the code of the page. The alternate text is a description of what is in the image. If the image was a turkey the alternate text might read, "Photo of turkey symbolizing the upcoming Thanksgiving holiday." Screen readers do not state the color of the text being read. Therefore if the instructions state, click on the red text to go to the next page and click on the blue text to go back, the user will not know which text has been colored red or blue because the screen reader does not identify the colored text.

Offering a text-only version of pages is an easy solution to many screen reader issues. Pop-up windows and moving graphics are particularly troublesome for screen-reading software and should be avoided if at all possible.

Placing a link to the text-only page near the top of any web page allows the student with vision problems to quickly find it with their screen reader. Use of consistent page formats or layouts will also benefit those using screen-reading software.

Deaf or Hard-of-Hearing

Students who are deaf or hard-of-hearing, or those with technical difficulties with sound on their computers, will not be able to access any information shared only with an audible stream. This includes sound effects, voices, and music in all forms of media, including, but not limited to, videos, podcasts, PowerPoint presentations, audio comments from the instructor embedded into documents, and Web 2.0 tools, such as VoiceThread. This problem is easily remedied by providing a link to a transcript of the audio segments of the material. The transcript can also be helpful to students whose native language is not the language of the course.

Cognitive Disabilities

Cognitive disabilities are more common than all other forms of disability according to Keeler and Horney (2007). Cognitive disabilities include learning disabilities and attention deficit disorders. Web pages that lack white space may impair the comprehension of the material on the page for those with learning disabilities, since many such learners use the "white space as a form of scaffolding" (Keeler & Horney, 2007, p. 66). "Individuals with attention deficit disorders may find overstimulating backgrounds distracting, causing them to not focus on the primary content appearing in the foreground" (p. 66). Web page animations or screen flicker have been known to trigger seizures in some people with epilepsy. All of the design issues mentioned here are easily resolved, and removal of these problems will create cleaner pages benefiting all learners. Good navigation and easy-to-use menus will also benefit all learners, including those with physical disabilities.

Physical Disabilities

Learners with physical disabilities often use voice commands or keystrokes instead of mouse clicks to navigate web pages. Designing with clean navigation that can be activated with keystrokes will benefit elderly learners with slow physical responses as well as those with physical disabilities. This includes using drop-down menus that have a separate button to activate the choice on the menu. Course web pages are not the only consideration when considering accessible design.

Inaccessibility in the Design

According to Keeler and Horney (2007), there are a variety of ways that online courses can be inaccessible in addition to the web pages themselves. The downloaded item is not accessible to screen readers and other **assistive technologies**. In addition to course elements, Keeler and Horney found that of the online high school courses surveyed more than half required additional materials.

> Fifty nine percent [had] requirements including needs for textbooks (27%), lab kits (14%), videocassettes (14%), software (14%), telephones (9%), microphones (9%), speakers (9%), or audiocassettes (5%). It is the responsibility of the course designer to ensure that both required and optional materials are available in accessible formats and to provide directions for accessing those equivalent resources. In the case that equivalent materials are not available or possible, the designer must consider ways to provide an equivalent educational experience for individuals with disabilities. The same is true for any optional materials (p. 68).

Obviously this section did not fully cover the laws and guidelines for making online courses accessible. Nor is this a full treatment of all the disabilities that may be encountered. Since more than 13 percent of the population has some type of disability according to the National Center for Educational Statistics (2004), designers need to work on creating accessible online courses for both learners and instructors with disabilities at the start of the design process. For many course designers and instructors, this means that a currently running course must be revised to make it more accessible.

REVISING

No matter how well designed a course developer believes the product is, the truth is, every course goes through revisions. In most cases, it will take a couple of iterations before the course runs smoothly, the instructions are fully understood by the majority of learners, and the workload for students and instructors is balanced. And none of that deals with the issue of web page content that disappears overnight. Link rot, as it is known, is a continual problem with online courses. Every course designer should expect that the first iteration of the course is a pilot, and feedback should be gathered from students and faculty. There must be a plan in place to assess each course and revise it. This is one small part of assessment discussed in the next chapter.

8

Learning Activity Design
Assessment and Assignments

Chapter 7 was devoted to course design, including some information about learning strategies and the assignments that are inexorably tied to the strategies. In this chapter, designing assessments of various types along with creating the assignments to be assessed will be covered. The term *learning activities* will be used to denote the combination of assessment and assignments. In the old days, before backward design was developed, assignments and units came first in the planning process. Assessment was often an afterthought and consisted of arbitrarily assigning a point value to the work without consideration of any specific criteria. As discussed in Chapter 7, well-planned lessons now begin with outcomes, and then the acceptable evidence showing mastery of the outcomes is defined. Only then are the learning strategies and the accompanying assignments designed.

LEARNING ACTIVITY DESIGN

Learning activities need to be designed with several things in mind. The acceptable evidence for the outcomes must be kept firmly in mind, then opportunities for critical thinking and creativity should be considered, finally differentiation to address varying needs of learners should be taken into account. Differentiation means that learning activities are designed in such a way that they are adaptable to the talents and limitations of students. For example, extensions of a lesson can be listed that would challenge gifted students and those who already know something about the topic.

In addition, remediation ideas can be shared so the assignment does not overwhelm learners who have special needs or who are not ready for the challenge of the assignment as originally designed. Tomlinson (1999) states it this way, "Struggling learners focus on essential understandings and skills; they do not drown in a pool of disjointed facts. Similarly . . . advanced learners spend their time grappling with important complexities rather than repeating work on what they already know" (p. 10). For more on differentiation, the works of Carol Ann Tomlinson are suggested reading. While it may sound like differentiation means changing the outcomes and acceptable evidence to meet the needs of the students, this is not at all the case.

Outcomes and Acceptable Evidence

Chapter 7 stated that backward design of lessons begins with the outcomes and acceptable evidence showing the outcomes have been met. The outcomes are the resulting end knowledge and skills that students will gain from a lesson. These are overarching ideas, not specific bits of knowledge. Some examples may help to make the concept clearer.

- *K–12*—In a course on world history, students would study various civilizations. The important outcomes are the elements of culture and the fact that all cultures share these elements, not the specific date the Roman Empire collapsed or where the Mesopotamians lived.
- *Higher Education*—In a psychology course, students study various early psychologists and their contributions to the field. The important outcomes would be the general ideas and how these theories of psychology have been built on by more recent psychologists, not when Freud lived or whether Pavlov had household pets.
- *Corporate*—In a marketing course, students study consumerism. The important concepts are how consumer demands change with age and how to target marketing to those demands, not whether acid-wash jeans are preferable to stone-washed jeans.

The outcomes are the major themes and skills students need to take away from the course and will be applicable in other settings and in other disciplines. In *The Understanding by Design Handbook* (McTighe & Wiggins, 1999) these are referred to as enduring understandings. "Understandings of this type are important ideas or core processes that are transferable to new situations" (p. 39). Once these are identified, the designer determines the acceptable evidence. In other words, how will it be clear that students do, in fact, understand the important ideas and concepts and can they apply them.

Acceptable evidence is the proof that can be gathered and evaluated. Such proof may be able to be gathered through traditional tests and essays, although in many cases more authentic assessments, performance tasks, and portfolio items may be clearer proof of such understandings. Common sense should make it clear that producing actual items or performing skills, rather than marking a multiple-choice test, would be a better way to see if the acceptable evidence shows mastery of the outcome. The next step is to determine the assessment tool that will best show the acceptable evidence.

ASSESSMENT IN THE ONLINE ENVIRONMENT

In educational terms there are two types of assessment, formative and summative. The assessment tool needed to show the evidence of learning for the outcomes for a unit or the entire course would be called summative assessment. Formative assessment guides the student in fixing his or her own mistakes and helps the student grow as he or she progress through the course. In an online course, this would include all instructor commentary about assignments, participation, and any other type of student work. Summative assessment is a more holistic look at the student's work in the course.

TYPES OF SUMMATIVE ASSESSMENT

Before assignments can be developed to teach the knowledge and skills leading to enduring understandings, the instructional designer must know how the student will be assessed. There are a variety of ways that this can be done, including final exams, end-of-unit or course paper, or more preferably, authentic assessments, performance tasks, and portfolios.

Exams and Final Exam

Many people designing online education come from a more traditional educational environment and bring with them the practices common in traditional settings whether they make sense in an online environment or not. One of these pervasive practices is that of the exam. Whether or not exams are a good indicator of student mastery of the outcomes in a traditional setting is an argument for others to consider. However, traditional practitioners are encouraged to think about more authentic ways of assessing learning. In an online class, exams and quizzes are, quite frankly, problematic. Even in traditional education, rethinking this approach is suggested as evidenced by this teacher reflection related by McTighe and Wiggins (1999),

> I give one or two quizzes; have a project, which I grade; and conclude with a unit test, generally multiple choice or matching. Although this approach to assessment makes grading and justifying the grades fairly easy, I have come to realize that these assessments do not always reflect the most important understandings of the unit. To be honest, I tend to test what is easy to test instead of assessing what is most important. (p. 42)

This teacher went on to say, "One thing that has always disturbed me is that the kids tend to focus on their grades rather than the learning. Perhaps the way I've used assessments—more for grading than for documenting learning—has contributed somewhat to their attitude" (p. 42). When students are more focused on grades than learning, they are much more apt to cheat. Cheating is an issue in all educational areas, including online learning.

Exam security, or verifying who is actually taking an exam, is a real problem in eLearning. At least with a written assignment or project, the instructor has some assurance the person who submitted the item is the same one who has been performing other tasks in class. Individuals have distinct writing voices. When an assignment has a different tone or syntax, the instructor can quickly spot this change and investigate. It is always a question whether the person who is completing the work is the one who is on the course rolls. But honestly, cheating is also problematic in traditional classes.

Unless a face-to-face instructor asks for identification, they have to assume the person who answers to Jonas Smythe *is* Jonas Smythe. Likewise in an online class, the instructor has to assume the person completing the work *is* the person enrolled in the class. Regardless, whoever it is doing the work in the online course, the instructor can easily spot a change in writing style. They would have no idea if the person who was completing the online coursework is the same person marking an online exam. Exams offer much less evidence of individual writing style than an essay or project, making it harder to match the exam taker with the person posting regularly to the discussion board. Even if the instructor mails the test to a local proctoring site, it will be difficult to know if the person who shows up to take the test is the person who has been working in the course.

Cheating is not the only issue with online exams. Writing a test that adequately gauges the enduring understandings of the course is always difficult. This is more difficult online, however, because the exam writer cannot answer student questions as they are taking the test to clarify any misunderstandings in the exam instructions or test questions. In a traditional environment, the instructor can answer questions during the testing period, when necessary, if the items are not well worded.

Wording is not the final issue either. Technical issues can arise when a student is taking an online exam. If the computer freezes or loses the Internet connection in the middle of an exam, the student may be locked out of the test by the course management system (CMS). The instructor must then decide whether to (a) unlock the test and allow the student to complete the test after they have seen some or all of the questions and had time to review the materials or (b) deny them the opportunity to finish the test, perhaps dooming them to failure depending on weighting of the exam in the total points for the course because the power blinked off in their locale.

Quizzes worth a small number of points can be helpful in focusing student attention on certain readings. Lehmann has even instigated a quiz on the course syllabus in some classes to focus student attention on key points in that document they might otherwise overlook.

Low-stakes quizzes, worth so few points that performing poorly on them will not affect the final course grade, allow students to check their own reading comprehension. Allowing quiz retakes, so that students know which material to reread will allow students to use this tool for self-checks of comprehension. Students will be less likely to contact the instructor with arguments about the *right* answer if the quiz is worth, at most, just a few points. The higher the stakes in taking the quiz or test in terms of the final course grade, the more likely the instructor will receive emails arguing about the wording of questions or the validity of the answers. And, as noted, since the students can be using the text and other materials while taking the quiz or test, it makes sense that this tool is used to check for reading comprehension.

End-of-Course Essay

Another common practice at the end of many courses is submission of a comprehensive essay. Such a paper is usually worth a substantial number of points and is supposed to show student comprehension of the skills and knowledge. If the assignment is well designed, the final paper can show student comprehension of the learning outcomes; unfortunately, in many courses, the directions create an environment ripe for cheating. This situation is epidemic in traditional courses and is equally problematic in online courses.

There are tons of online sites where term papers can be purchased and then turned in by students. In other cases, former students from the class will share their successful works with the current learners. Catching this plagiarism is not hard using formal tools like TurnItIn.com or informal tools such as pasting a particularly suspicious passage from a paper into a search engine to look for copied source material. If students can easily recycle papers to meet the requirements of the assignment, the assignment was not well designed from the beginning. A well-planned assessment that results in a written essay needs to have the students use the skills and knowledge in unique and individual ways so that mastery of the learning outcomes can be assessed.

How might a well-designed prompt for a final paper differ from a poorly designed set of instructions? Previously in this chapter there were three examples of learning outcomes listed, one each for K–12, higher education, and corporate courses. These same course concepts will be used to illustrate the differences in prompt quality.

- **K–12 World History**

  Well-designed prompt: Select a culture of your choice that is included in the textbook but that we did not study. Apply the elements of culture that we have discussed during the course to this culture and how this culture exhibited these elements.

  Poorly designed prompt: Write a report on the Roman Empire's rise and fall.

- **Higher Education, Psychology**

  Well-designed prompt: Select one of the early psychological theorists (list of early psychologists here) and show how his or her theories are being applied today in the treatment of inpatients suffering from addiction.

  Poorly designed prompt: Explain Freud's theories.

- **Corporate, Marketing**

  Well-designed prompt: Choose a product that is currently being marketed to just one segment of consumers and describe how the marketing strategies would need to be changed to appeal to a completely different consumer segment.

  Poorly designed prompt: Describe the characteristics of one segment of consumers (list of possibilities here) and what products are currently marketed to them.

In the well-designed prompts, the skills and knowledge have to be applied in a new way. The poorly designed prompts all involve regurgitating something discussed in the course or the course materials. There is no new application, no synthesis. Course designers need to use well-designed prompts. Concurrently, the prompts need to change regularly. Otherwise groups of former students can still share final papers, even those responding to well-written prompts, with current students who will recycle and submit these final assignments.

AUTHENTIC ASSESSMENT

In traditional classrooms, essays, quizzes, and exams are assessment staples. If, as advocated here, these tools are not be used for assessment of the learning outcomes online, what tools might better take their place in eLearning? More authentic methods of assessment are described next. Authentic methods are those asking students to utilize the skills and knowledge by performing or creating something. In particular, students should be using the skills and knowledge in new ways or in new situations in order to show mastery of the outcomes. Examples of authentic assessments are performance tasks and portfolios of collected work.

Performance Tasks

Performance tasks are complex challenges based on real-world situations addressed to a specific audience and require application of the skills and knowledge learned in the course (McTighe & Wiggins, 1999). Performance tasks occurring at the end of a unit or course should be complex, completed in multiple stages, and could be done by individuals or small groups.

If done in small groups, you need to create a rubric to help the instructor assess whether all members of the group show understanding of the skills and knowledge being demonstrated by the performance task. In other words, if only one student completed the entire group's project with little or no help from the others, the instructor needs to be able to assess who has and who has not shown their understanding of the course outcomes. Examples of such performance tasks might be helpful and will be related to the content areas used previously in this chapter. These are written as the student would see them.

- *K–12*—Create your own culture. Make sure you address all elements of culture, including designing your own writing system, developing a system of laws, defining who will rule the culture and how they gained power. You may use any medium you want to showcase your culture including, but not limited to, creating an advertising campaign for your culture via a wiki, developing a website, producing a PowerPoint presentation, and so on.
- *Higher education*—Create a script that relates the ideas of the early psychologists to modern practices. The script can be for any visual or auditory medium you choose including TV talk show, radio broadcast, documentary, and so on.
- *Corporate*—Invent a new product that you believe will appeal across multiple age groups of the consumer population and develop a marketing

campaign for your product. Prepare a marketing proposal to show the differences in targeting the various age groups. Your proposal may include storyboards, print ads, or a PowerPoint presentation to show how you would market your product to this consumer segment and why you would use the marketing approaches you have chosen.

Such performance tasks, like the well-designed writing prompts, allow for individual creativity as well as application of the knowledge and skills. These tasks are complex and are meant to be end-of-course or end-of-unit assessments. Performance tasks can take a lot of time to develop and cannot be done until all skills and knowledge have been assimilated. Another way to conduct a final assessment without taking as much time at the end of the unit or course is to have students develop a portfolio of work, gathering examples to put in their portfolio throughout the unit or course.

ePortfolios

Paper portfolios of work have been in vogue for some time now allowing learners to showcase their growth over time. "Paper portfolios got learners more implicitly involved in the evaluation phase as they would select which work items they would submit" (Baker, 2005, p. 2). These repositories of student work could not, however, capture one very important component of the portfolio-building process: reflection. "Reflection is part of the process when using paper based portfolio but they do not allow for this reflection process to be captured in any tangible manner" (p. 2).

Electronic portfolios, known as ePortfolios, allow for the reflective process to be captured in a variety of forms. ePortfolios therefore serve to show not only the skills and knowledge, but the development of them throughout the course with the reflective thoughts of the learner as part of the documentation. The compilation of assignments can be highly beneficial to the student and used in job interviews or with clients long after the course ends to showcase their abilities and knowledge. There are a variety of tools that can be used to electronically house ePortfolios. This can be as simple as a web page with links to documents or as elaborate as using a site specifically designed for ePortfolios.

The way the ePortfolio is housed online is not as important as the choice of documents and the reflective process that accompanies these documents. You should identify assignments throughout the course as ePortfolio items. The compilation should show mastery of all important skills and knowledge for the course. Instructors or peers should offer feedback on the assignments at the time they are submitted, and learners should be expected to revise these assignments and reflect on the changes in preparation for submitting the entire ePortfolio at the end of the course. Instructions need to clearly state that assignments should be revised based on feedback and that the reflective process should be captured and submitted as part of the ePortfolio. Without a clear statement of the expectations for revisions and reflections, students often do not follow through. ePortfolios will, in general, include a variety of assignments completed throughout a course or training. The feedback given on ePortfolio items needing revision is one form of formative assessment.

FORMATIVE ASSESSMENT

The preceding section was concerned with major assessments that are done at the end of a unit or course. That type of assessment is known as summative assessment. Throughout a course, however, there are a variety of types of formative assessment prior to the summative assessment. Formative assessments allow both instructor and learner to check that the skills and knowledge to be gained in the course are being developed. Formative assessments usually gauge just one or two concepts at a time, unlike summative assessments, which assess all the concepts for the unit or course.

Many formative assessments are more often referred to as assignments. Assignments allow learners to practice skills and show their understanding of the knowledge in the course. In order for students to know they are correctly performing the skills and that they are understanding the concepts, they must receive feedback promptly and regularly on assignments. Prompt, substantive feedback is a hallmark of online instructional excellence. Types of assignments and how they would be assessed follows.

ASSIGNMENTS

Assignments are the smaller elements of assessment that form the bulk of the work in any educational setting. Well-designed assignments are as important as well-designed summative assessments, and many of the same principles apply. Assignments should require critical thinking and practice with the new skills and knowledge but in smaller bites. Opportunities for differentiation should be included, especially if the learner population will be adults. Adult learning theory suggests opportunities to use the new information or skills directly in their own life are a key element of course design. In addition, social learning theory and adult learning theory hold that learners need to discuss ideas with peers in order to fully grasp the new concepts.

Discussions

One of the most commonly used assignments in online learning is the threaded discussion forum. Some information about threaded discussions has already been shared. Prompts for threaded discussions need to be open ended and general enough that a variety of answers are possible. If a prompt has just one answer, there is nowhere for the rest of the group to go once that singular answer has been shared. The **original response** to the prompt from the students is only half of the discussion that should take place in the threaded discussion forum. Many learners think they are *done* once they have posted their original response. However, just like in a face-to-face discussion, replies are needed to any response to create a true discussion. Expectations for the replies must be as clearly stated as they should be for the original response to the prompt.

Students should be expected to reply to at least one original response posted by a colleague. That reply should add depth to the discussion in some way. This can be done by asking questions or requesting clarification, suggesting a related concept, sharing a resource, analyzing how the response is similar to or different from another student's original message, and so on. Replies need to invite further discussion, and everyone should be encouraged to answer the replies received by their original response to the prompt. For a true discussion to take place students must post their original response early in a unit.

If the student waits until the 11th hour of the final day of a unit to post an original message, this allows little time for colleagues to reply to them, and even less opportunity for the originator of the response to reply back. Requiring the original response to be posted by midunit is a fairly common practice and one that works well. In addition, requiring a certain number of replies to colleagues is another effective practice. These requirements need to be stated clearly in the syllabus with reminders in the course materials. The discussion rubric should incorporate these requirements as well. Examples of rubrics for discussion participation explanations are shared in Chapter 15.

Documents Shared in Threaded Discussions

In addition to messages that contain the student's original response, learners can be required to post documents or other forms of assignments as attachments to their threaded discussion messages. This practice encourages peer review and also allows others to see different ways of approaching the assignment. For example, in online professional development courses for K–12 teachers, sharing of documents has been a valuable way for the teachers to get new ideas for their own classrooms. For these professional development students, seeing how other teachers whose specialties are science, English, music, and kindergarten all approach a PowerPoint assignment inspires new ideas.

Sharing ideas among colleagues at any level should be encouraged, and posting documents or assignments is one way to do this. Few students will overtly copy the work of others when assignments are shared, but instructors do need to be on the lookout for plagiarism of posted work.

Documents and Draft Papers

Another common online practice is to submit work to a dropbox for the instructor to download and view. This practice limits the chance students will plagiarize the work of others but also prevents the sharing of ideas contained in the documents. The design of these assignments needs to follow the same principles of design as the end-of-course papers discussed previously. Differentiation for a variety of levels and needs, as well as opportunities for critical thinking, needs to be incorporated. Expectations for the assignment must be spelled out clearly in the directions and in the rubric.

Formative papers should showcase just one or two concepts or skill sets since the purpose of formative assignments is to practice using these newly learned elements of the course. Instructor feedback on these assignments is an important aspect since students need to know if their practice was correct or not. Another way to let students know if they are correct or not is to use self-grading quizzes.

Quizzes

As mentioned previously, major exams are problematic in online courses, yet low-stakes quizzes are an effective tool in eLearning. This is especially true if the quizzes are set up to provide immediate feedback to the learner. Learners can take the quiz and immediately find out if they correctly applied the new knowledge or skills. Writing good quiz questions can be challenging. The question, or question stem, and answer choices need to be exceptionally clear, yet still assess the knowledge and skills from the current unit of the course. Web-based quizzes offer some real advantages over paper-based quizzes in traditional classrooms.

Web-based quizzing tools can be set up with several features. One of these features is the ability to draw questions from a bank of items. If, for example, the instructor wanted a five-question quiz, and he or she wanted to ensure that students were less likely to cheat by sharing questions and answers with one another, the 5 questions could be drawn from a bank of 10 to 15 questions. This way each student would get a different set of questions. Using a bank of questions is also a good idea if students can retake a quiz. Students will have to know the material well enough to answer the varying set of questions rather than relying on memory of the correct answers. A bank of questions is also needed if a branching question design is used.

Branching quizzes use intelligent technology to do one of two things. The quiz can return students to the content materials when they miss a question so they can study the appropriate information and retake the quiz. This is a pretty straightforward technology and easy to understand. The other option is a bit more complex. Branching quizzes can also be set to intelligently analyze the pattern of student answers and then lead the student into higher or lower (depending on how the student is doing) levels of questioning to determine the reaches of their knowledge.

The first type of branching, returning the student to the appropriate spot in the course materials, was used in a study by Green, Eppler, Ironsmith, and Wuensch (2007) to determine if students learned more when a branching quiz, rather than a standard linear quiz design, was used. Their results showed that students did perform better when their review quiz was the branching style, but students disliked the branching quizzes because of technology glitches. Technology issues are always a potential consideration when using more advanced technical tools such as intelligent quizzes.

Designers need to weigh the benefits against the possible issues that will arise. Technical issues with quizzes will increase instructor workload. Students who have a problem with a quiz will inevitably contact the instructor for help. Reducing instructor workload issues should be one consideration for all designers. One area where instructors often get overloaded with student cries for help is when there is a cooperative group project in an online course.

COOPERATIVE LEARNING PROJECTS

Information on cooperative learning was shared in Chapter 7. More specifics about setting up such assignments are needed, however, since these can be a source of great frustration for instructors and learners alike, whether in face-to-face or online settings. In fact, the potential for problems is exacerbated in eLearning. The lack of physical and vocal cues such as voice inflection and body language in online settings means that communication is more difficult (Papastergiou, 2006).

The course designer should set out the expectations for student participation clearly in the directions and in the grading rubric. The rubric needs to assess both participation and the final product to prevent the *free-rider effect* from developing. Free riders are those who do little or no work on the project but earn full credit. "The free-rider problem, also known as *social loafing*, is the focus of many complaints voiced by students regarding unsatisfactory group-work experiences" (Brooks & Ammons, 2003, p. 268). A rubric that assesses student participation in the group process helps to prevent free riders since they cannot earn full credit without participating. The real key in preventing group discord, however, is creating equity in the overall workload.

The project needs to be meaty enough that all group members will need to be involved if the group is to complete it within the required time frame. Groups of students can be encouraged to define roles for each member of the group early in the process. This will help ensure that all members have something to do and they know what it is that the group expects from them. Knowing the role and completing the work in a timely manner sounds easy to define but, in actuality, this depends on student working styles.

As discussed previously, Type A learners, or early birds, have difficulty working harmoniously with Type B, late riser personalities. When developing small groups it is best to assign early birds to one set of groups and late risers to other groups (K. L. Lehmann, 2008; Keinan & Koren, 2002). Using a simple survey, have students self-identify as Type A or B, and use this information to create the groups for cooperative projects. A sample identification survey is available in Chapter 15. Paying attention to how the groups are formed will help create equity in the workload; therefore, participation should be equitable. Nonetheless, participation and the final product created by the group should be assessed.

TYPES OF ASSESSMENT

Keep in mind assessment of student work is more than grading a paper and assigning a score. Assignment scores and grades are the tangible assessment element. In the online classroom, intangible assessment is an important part of the communication process that helps students build their skills and knowledge base, and more importantly, aids their personal and professional growth. When assessment is done well, it can guide students to find their own answers, improve their performance, and fix their mistakes. Creating a high-quality assessment system begins before the course starts.

Beginning at the Beginning with Tangible Assessment

The instructor, or sometimes the institution or entity, will define in advance how the course will be graded. This is usually contained in a syllabus or course outline and should include the grading scale, objectives to be met and standards to be assessed, expectations for student work in all parts of the course, and rubrics to guide student work as well as instructor grading. In the kind of constructivist environment where learning for mastery of the skills and knowledge is the goal, grades are not very meaningful. The objective is that all students successfully master the skills and knowledge. However, in K–12 and higher education, grades are usually a necessary evil.

There is no doubt that grades are an important element for many students. For some, it is much too important. They stress about every lost point and how it will impact their final grade. These students have lost the focus on learning for the knowledge gained and are, instead, focused on a letter grade. There are some ways to minimize the impact of grades and put the focus back on learning.

Woolfolk (2004) advocates the following guidelines for minimizing the detrimental effects of grades:

- Avoid reserving high grades and high praise for answers that conform to just your ideas or to those in the textbook.
- Make sure each student has a reasonable chance to be successful, especially at the beginning of a new task.
- Balance written and oral feedback (in online learning there may not be oral feedback, but there are a variety of types of feedback which will be discussed).
- When grades are necessary, make them as meaningful as possible.
- Base grades on more than just one criterion (p. 542).

Grades should definitely be based on multiple criteria. The real trick is finding the right balance for all the elements of the course. There is no right or wrong balance, but there are some things to consider when weighting the various elements for the grading scheme. The most important parts of the course, the elements in which the majority of learning takes place, should be weighted the most heavily. In a constructivist course, this may be the assignments and projects. That said, depending on the learning goals, the construction of knowledge may occur in the threaded discussions, in which case, the discussions should be weighted heavily in the grading scheme.

As noted previously, when quizzes are used, they should be low stakes, meaning they would be weighted much less heavily than other categories. In many case, it may take one or two iterations of the course before the proper weighting of the grade becomes settled. This is one area where feedback from instructors and students to the course designer can be valuable and is an area that should be open to revision after feedback has been received. More important than the weighting in the grade scheme is how grades for the various elements of the course will be determined by the instructor. Clearly stated expectations need to be provided to the students in advance. One place these expectations should be outlined is in the grading rubrics being used to evaluate different elements of the course.

Rubrics

Rubrics are commonly used tools in K–12 classrooms and are becoming more common in higher education. Rubrics offer both structure and objectivity to students and the instructor as they complete the course elements. According to Andrade (2005) a rubric is, "An assessment tool that list the criteria for a piece of work . . . and articulates gradations of quality for each criterion, from excellent to poor" (p. 27). There are examples of rubrics in Chapter 15. Andrade goes on to explain that a rubric used just for grading purposes is a *scoring rubric.*

An *instructional rubric* is used to guide student completion of the assignment as well as to encourage peer and instructor evaluation while the assignment is being created. It may be used for scoring after assignment submission also. The course designer can suggest the rubrics for a course be used in an instructional manner, but it will be up to the instructor whether that actually takes place. Therefore rubrics will not be referred to here as scoring or instructional. The assumption will be that all rubrics will be, at a minimum, the scoring rubric.

A well-written rubric guides the student to create a high-quality assignment or performance that meets the outcomes to be assessed. Rubrics also help instructors quickly and objectively grade student projects. As stated previously, the rubric should be provided to the student before the assignment or project begins. This transparency allows the learner to competently meet all the criteria for successful completion of a project. A great resource to help teachers build rubrics is Rubistar (http://rubistar.4teachers.org/). Rubrics should be provided for all elements of a course including discussion participation, assignments, projects, group work participation, and reflections. Rubrics state the expectations for performance, but these expectations need to be stated in other ways as well.

Communicating Expectations

Before assessing any work, the instructor should communicate his or her expectations to students. Putting these expectations in the syllabus, including the consequences for turning in late work, is suggested. Keep in mind that some students never read the syllabus. Stating the expectations in announcements or postings is another good way to reach everyone. It is also a good idea to revisit expectations via all-class emails or forum postings as problems crop up, or even better, before they crop up. In particular, expectations for student participation need to be clearly spelled out.

ASSESSING PARTICIPATION

What is participation? In the face-to-face environment, many teachers expect students to participate in class discussions and do cooperative group projects. The online environment is no different. Most facilitated online courses also have a peer group with whom each student should communicate. If the course has a learner-learner aspect, there are usually expectations for participation in discussions or projects. How to define participation is the challenge.

Discussion Participation

At a minimum, most instructors expect each student to post an original response to every discussion question and respond substantively to the postings of others. Some instructors want the original response posted by midweek; others do not care when it is posted as long as it occurs during the week. The harder point to assess is whether the responses to others are substantive. A colleague at Walden University, Ossil Macavinta, developed a system that helped to define substantive participation.

Here are the categories Macavinta (personal communication, 2003) developed to assess the quality of discussion responses: (a) referred to course materials, (b) referred to colleagues' comments, (c) provided constructive feedback, (d) enhanced the quality of the discussion, (e) met minimum requirements of the discussion question, and (f) posted response by due date. These criteria are certainly not the only ones that could be used, but this list offers a starting point for development of a rubric that incorporates not only participation in the discussion, but also substantive participation. Students may need to be shown examples of postings that are substantive.

It is important to point out what the student is doing right as well as where improvement is needed. The most important thing about assessing discussion participation is for the instructor comments and grading to lead to improvement. All feedback, whether from the instructor or peers, should be constructive and lead to improvements.

FEEDBACK

One of the most common forms of formative assessment is offering feedback to students. This may come in the form of comments in: (a) threaded discussion forum messages, (b) the gradebook or assignment document, or (c) a personal communication such as email, phone call, or chat session. A fourth opportunity for feedback is inside reflective journal entries when a student self-evaluates their work. Most course feedback is from the instructor to the learner.

Instructor Feedback

The instructor should provide prompt, substantive feedback to students on their work. In a constructivist environment it is particularly important to let the students know if they are showing improvement and, ultimately, mastery of the skills and knowledge to be learned in the course. There are two categories of instructor feedback, public and private. In eLearning, when the instructor cannot see the learner's body language or hear their voice, feedback to a specific student should never be given publicly. There is too much danger of wounding a student when giving feedback publicly and in the online world, the instructor will never know that a student's feelings were hurt unless he or she says something.

Many students are afraid that being critical of an instructor will impact their final grade, which would be completely unethical. Whether it would be unethical or not, this is a real fear among many students, therefore many instructors never are told when someone has been deeply hurt by a public comment. All-class comments, posted as an announcement, a new thread on a discussion board or sent by email, should redirect all students without naming names. If there are students who have exhibited a positive behavior that can be trumpeted, then names may be used. If the comment is meant to redirect a negative behavior, names of those who are *doing it wrong* should never be used. Private feedback from the instructor is the only way to go if an action or piece of work needs correction. Such correction should be sandwiched, when possible, with positive comments.

The Sandwich Method

An astute principal once shared that the best way to begin a parent-teacher conference was for the teacher to say something nice about the child. Every parent wants to hear something good about his or her child, and it softens the bad news the teacher may need to impart when parents have already heard something positive. This same method, known as the sandwich method, works well when providing assessment comments about discussions, assignments, or anything else.

Begin the assessment comments by mentioning something good in the work. This is the first layer of bread in the sandwich. Then state the things needing improvement. This is the meat or filling in the sandwich. End with another positive comment. That is the final layer of bread in the sandwich.

This method really works. Here is a comment from a former student comparing this assessment method with another online instructor:

> My other class is over now and I got a perfect score, but it does not feel as good as getting a high score in your class. Please remind teachers that when they do not have face-to-face contact, they ought to be very specific and detailed in their feedback, as you were. In this class it seemed as though there were a boilerplate evaluation, "Dear , I have just reviewed your assignment. You did an outstanding job and have been awarded 50 points." I do not know what was outstanding and what needed work. (Joan Chu, personal communication, 2003)

Assessing Assignments

Students who are given clear expectations and well-written assignment objectives, and who possess the rubric that will be used to grade the assignment, should produce a high-quality product. Assigning a letter or numerical score to those high-quality products is generally easy. The instructor is then free to comment on the content of the assignment, to ask thought-provoking questions, and offer suggestions for extending the student's learning.

Unfortunately, a lot of instructors seem to feel that assigning the letter or numerical grade is all that is needed. Students in the online classroom, perhaps more so than in the face-to-face classroom, crave feedback about their work. Online students are isolated in their homes, schools, or offices with no teacher handy to whom questions can be addressed. As instructors this is our opportunity to help them extend their learning. Students need substantive feedback and that feedback needs to occur in a timely manner.

For changes in practice or thinking to occur, feedback needs to follow the completion of an assignment as quickly as possible. The next example is from a student who is grateful for timely feedback about her participation in a new online course:

> Your comments about the discussions were very helpful. I like to know how things are going and what is expected of me before new assignments. One thing that I have found somewhat difficult with an online course is not knowing if

I'm doing the things expected of me. I have read the criteria of the discussions. Your comments make those clearer. Thanks again. (Kathy Bishop, personal communication, 2003)

Offering personalized, timely feedback may need to be adjusted according to the personality of the learner. Some students take offense easily or become overly worried about any criticism. This is true face-to-face as well as online. Instructors have to word their feedback in such a way that students learn from it without becoming overly tense. A little tension is good. This edge of uneasiness is what Vygotsky (1978) spoke about when discussing the zone of proximal development. Students who are asked to learn way above their state of readiness feel so much tension, they shut down. If the student already knows the concept, they become bored. Finding the balance is key.

Only when the student is on the edge of their readiness to learn, feeling pushed just a little by the content, will learning be able to occur. Tension can interfere with learning and communication, and so the instructor's feedback needs to take into account the student's readiness to learn and their personality style to give personalized feedback that will be heard and acted upon. Personalized feedback often brings another plus. It opens the door to more communication opportunities with the student. When students feel they can talk openly with the instructor, it is easier to smooth over temporary rough spots and perhaps prevent the underground rumble. The instructor is not the only one who can provide feedback. In a constructivist setting, there should be other forms of feedback including student self-evaluation and peer feedback.

ALTERNATIVES TO INSTRUCTOR FEEDBACK

Student Self-Evaluation

One way to lessen the burden of providing feedback to students and encourage empowerment at the same time is to, occasionally, have students self-assess their work. This can be done using a rubric or a reflective journal entry. The student self-assessment can form part of the assignment grade along with instructor scoring, or this could be an assignment that is not scored at all except to note that it was completed.

Peer Evaluations

Another method of assessment is learner-learner evaluation. This can be done through informal comments in the discussion forum or in a more formalized manner using a rubric and commentary. When done informally in a discussion thread, students will usually post their assignment as an attachment for all to see. Colleagues are then encouraged to offer substantial comments. If done too early in a class, the learner-learner communication may be too sugary, filled with unearned attaboys without offering anything that could remotely be seen as constructive criticisms. It is a good idea to wait to try this until the group shows they are able to have discussions that include **argumentative dialogue**.

Disagreement, done correctly, is healthy for a discussion. Evaluating peer assignments with constructive criticism requires the ability to point out errors. This is a form of disagreeing with someone. It is critical that the instructor makes sure that everyone has received peer commentary on the posted assignment. If peers do not comment on the assignment within one to two days, the instructor should comment on the assignment and include a message that encourages peers to join in the dialogue.

The more formal learner-learner assessments involve each student determining all or part of a score for his or her colleague. These should not be attempted until after the small groups have developed a sense of community. Peers will find it difficult to offer a genuine critique with both positive and formative feedback if they have not yet formed a true community. Even then, they have to be encouraged overtly to offer feedback that is more than *great job, way to go*.

Student Evan Sveum spoke up, a bit loudly, in asking peers for genuine feedback recently. His subject line and message were as follows:

Evan Would Like Some FEEDBACK please!

I would like to share something with all of you that I am feeling. I feel isolated. I give 100 percent effort in my initial postings, and oftentimes I get no responses. I raise questions to strike up a discussion on a different point, and no one touches it! It makes me wonder what's wrong with what I'm doing. Is it me? Did I offend somebody?

One of the areas I have self-identified as being weak in is discussion facilitation. Why am I not getting any feedback on my postings? I know they're not perfect. . . . Is somebody in this community willing to actually help me? Give me some honest feedback? Instructors in this course have; how about the rest of the educational professionals in this room?

Feedback in an environment that is not entirely representative of the human communication process is vital! I am depending on you folks! I don't give a damn about 'being nice or politically correct!' I want feedback because I am a teacher and I care to do the best for my students!! That's the bottom line!!

This course was for online instructors-in-training and the posting was made well into the course after everyone had gotten to know each other. Such a bold posting was possible because of the community of practice that had developed. He received several replies with genuine feedback that included areas in need of improvement. Later Evan noted in his reflections the group had not become a *true* community of practice, willing to state both the positive and the negative, until the moment he posted this message.

CONCLUSION

This scenario illustrates the importance of online interactions in the learning environment. Such interactions are the topic of the next chapter.

9

Online Interaction: Facilitator, Learners, and the Tools Used to Connect Them

Connecting with others is what differentiates high-quality online learning from traditional independent study. Unfortunately, many online courses have no person-to-person interactions. Such courses are glorified tutorials or electronic correspondence courses. Is connecting with others something that happens automatically?

Think back to a time when you participated in an event where you felt alone even though you had a crowd of people around you. Online courses can feel lonely and isolated like that as well. One online student in a study by Stodel, Thompson, and MacDonald (2006) said, "I just want to have the feeling that the communication is real and that I [am] talking with a real person in real time" (p. 13).

Now, think of a different time when everyone joined in the conversations, and the experience was very enjoyable, as well as enlightening or thought provoking.

What differentiated the experiences? Why were connections made in one situation, but not in the other? The job of a facilitator is to help all students connect with one another, creating an enjoyable and fruitful learning experience.

Critics of online learning often state that a lack of human contact is a major drawback of online learning when compared to traditional face-to-face classrooms. Often students new to online learning cite this as one of their fears when resisting online learning. The following student stated as much in part of his week one summary to a prompt asking for the highs and lows of distance learning:

The disadvantage of distance learning is that it can be easy to feel isolated. You can lose that peer-to-peer response and instructor-to-peer response. The Coffee Cafe and the discussion boards really help to alleviate that but it is still possible for someone to feel out of the loop as you may not get a quick answer that is needed on a question. Although the questions are answered in a reasonable timeframe, for people who wait until the last minute to do things, that can be a troubling thing. I am used to being able to look up information on the computer and to have to wait from an answer that I posed can at times be mind boggling. — Rick. (personal communication, 2008)

To open the eyes of those who doubt the connectedness users feel through online interaction, one only has to recall an email that caused the recipient to laugh out loud, or LOL as email users often abbreviate. The proliferation of social networking sites, such as MySpace and Facebook, is further proof that it is very possible to connect deeply with others through electronic communication. To create these important human connections in the online classroom requires two elements: good facilitation by the instructor and selection of the proper communication tools for each particular course.

SPECIFIC TECHNIQUES FOR POSITIVE ONLINE INTERACTIONS

People

It is important to remember the humanity of our students. This may seem an odd thing to say, but many students in online courses feel they are treated like statistical groups or worse, nonentities. Establishing warm, human connections is key to retaining students in classes, getting repeat business, and generating positive word of mouth from the current students to future ones. In short, it's the way to build programs. The skills to create connectedness are not often taught to online instructors and may not come naturally to those whose teaching instincts are from the face-to-face teaching world.

This Is a Business

The fact is, online courses are a business for most institutions. This is especially true for those organizations hiring instructors. While it is not the specific job of most instructors in online courses to worry about retaining students, generating positive word of mouth, or other facets of marketing, they should have a basic knowledge of how the system works in their institution—be it the K–12 public school setting or higher education. Student **retention** online is something that administrators of eLearning do worry about. Stable, growing programs are good for both employers and the instructors.

The alternative is inconsistent employment, possible reduction in force, or pay cuts when programs fail to thrive.

Feeling Good

Good facilitators will set a positive tone for connecting with students from the very start in their online classroom. How do they do this? How will the facilitator know if he or she is successful?

Students who feel positively toward an instructor will often state their pleasure directly to the instructor. People rarely relate their displeasure to an online teacher unless a great deal of trust has been established or if they are really ticked off! Satisfied online students will recommend the teacher's classes to other potential students. They will discuss with colleagues in the class their good experiences in private student-student communications.

DIALOGUE AND DISCUSSION BOARDS

An online community does not exist without dialogue and messages. These are two different ideas, although they are sometimes used synonymously. Dialogue is the whole set of communications. They can be **social dialogue**, argumentative dialogue, and **pragmatic dialogue**. The introductions used in the first week of an online course are an example of a social dialogue. Social dialogues will spring up in a variety of ways throughout an online course if a sense of community pervades the course.

One sign that there is no sense of community among the participants is the lack of social dialogue. When learners get online just long enough to post their message and make their required responses, they are missing that community impact. Social dialogues are important to a constructivist course. The wise move is to provide a forum just for social dialogue. Then, when a social dialogue begins to take over a content-based discussion, the instructor can suggest that it be moved to the social forum.

Dialogues can also be argumentative. Wenger (1998) in *Communities of practice: Learning, meaning, and identity* suggests that true learning cannot happen until there is some level of disagreement among participants over the content. If everyone agrees with everyone else, the dialogue lacks real depth. Consider the following exchange. Is anything really learned by the students from the discussion?

Lisa@Cali: Wiggins and McTighe's *Understanding by Design* should be used to design every online course.

Kay@NY: I agree! I use them a lot.

Jim@Quito: Me too! W and T are the best!

Constructive disagreements help students challenge their beliefs and understanding. This is tricky, however, especially in a two-dimensional world. Text comes across emotionless and can be cold, so an argumentative dialogue can quickly turn ugly. Even audio and video discussion boards can be misinterpreted since clips are often short due to bandwidth and storage issues. This is one place a teachable moment or "just in time" mini-module could be used with a short explanation and example of how to properly deepen a conversation or challenge a statement without coming across offensively. Consider how our previous dialogue changes with a bit of a challenge by the responding students:

> Lisa@Cali: Wiggins and McTighe's *Understanding by Design* should be used to design every online course.

> Kay@NY: While I use W and McT, I'm not sure they are the only answer to course design. Have you considered designing by multiple intelligences or other learning styles?

> Jim@Quito: I do use UbD, but I also incorporate learning styles in my overall course design consideration. What about EASy based around critical thinking?

In this case, both Kay and Jim were able to challenge Lisa's initial statement without coming across offensively, and they were able to broaden the discussion to include other theories on learning and course design. Argumentative dialogue is powerful if managed well; however instructors need to aggressively monitor discussion boards to make sure that ideas are being challenged, but people are not.

Pragmatic dialogues are discussions where the sharing of ideas and resources that may be helpful to others. Collison and colleagues (2000) in *Facilitating Online Learning: Effective Strategies for Moderators* believes that pragmatic dialogues work because the foundation has been laid previously through its three basic goals of community building, maintaining a culture of respect, and fostering dialogue, which deepens the reasoning on the forum. This can be done in a social dialogue, but often pragmatic dialogues have a more topic-directed tone.

Dialogues are made up of messages. Individual messages can also be categorized. The following descriptions are based on instructor messages.

Messages can be content related, technical, procedural, and evaluative.

Content-related messages are those that help explain the curriculum. Posts that clarify content, further explain it, or add details are all examples.

Technical messages are explanations of how to do something, like how to attach a document to an email, for example.

Procedural messages explain how the curriculum is to be carried out. This would include how long a paper should be or what elements should be included in a group project. These messages may be posted as part of the course management system (CMS) course pages or as clarifications in a question-and-answer (Q&A) forum.

Evaluative messages are part of the assessment in an online course. These can be as informal as a forum message such as "You analyzed that very well, have you thought about . . ." to much more formal evaluations. These messages may be posted as part of feedback in a private grade comment area or included as part of a post to refocus or redirect a student toward a deeper, more critically written posting.

Instructor messages can include email, text messages, chat, as well as discussion postings and mini-lectures. All these types of messages can build or hinder community or collaboration in the online environment. The facilitator concerned with best practices will work toward building community with every message.

BEST PRACTICES ON THE DISCUSSION BOARD

The discussion board is perhaps the area that requires the most facilitator skill sets to be in use at the same time. Clegg and Heap (2006) found that:

> The promotion of learning through online discussion groups requires skilled facilitation by educators who are able to recognize when and how to respond to expressions of student need and how to shape, promote, and respond to group interaction. Successful facilitators combine critical judgments about the content of contributions with clear decisions about the intervention process. The complexity of this process means that facilitators need to exercise skills of self-awareness in relation to how they make decisions with regard to student learning (p. 6).

GOOD DISCUSSION FACILITATION TECHNIQUES

To most good traditional classroom teachers, the following techniques to facilitate an online class discussion may be review. Running a good discussion online is somewhat similar to running one in the classroom. Still, it is important to review some basic discussion techniques and then look at how they might apply in the online environment.

- Ask thought-provoking questions to lead to deeper critical thinking.
- Summarize the discussion to validate the views of people who responded so far and encourage others to participate in the discussion.
- Review the points made to encourage additional points or opposing viewpoints to be posted.
- Provide group feedback to a small or large group.
- Ensure that no one is being ignored.

What does each of these techniques look like when used online? How can human connectedness occur in the discussions? The following examples showcase the techniques one by one. Some examples may actually showcase more than one technique. Look for ways that human connections are made through humor, sensitivity, and warmth.

Ask Thought-Provoking Questions Leading to Deeper Critical Thinking

The following is an instructor posting a response to a group of teachers discussing student records for mobile students:

> Could student records be put on a "smart card," which looks like a credit card but holds information? Could they be put in a secure location on the Internet? Could they be transmitted electronically from one school to another? I would love to see this group expound on these ideas.

Summarize the Discussion so Far

The following is an original instructor posting to the same group of teachers discussing student records:

> Gary, Steve, and Maria noted that getting the records can be problematic. Sonya suggested that even if the records with IEP hadn't arrived yet that the classroom teacher at least be told the nature of the student's special needs. That seems like a very reasonable suggestion! Darlene suggested that students not be allowed to enroll until records are received. What about the rest of you? How could getting student records transferred be improved in your school? Is anyone in a school that has a great method they could share?

Review the Points Made

To many people, summarizing the discussion so far and reviewing the points made may seem to be the same thing. Perhaps. The main difference is to whom the message is directed. The technique called "summarizing the discussion" validates the people who have participated in the discussion. It is a subtle message to those who have not yet participated in the discussion to get with it and *Review the Points Made*. It encourages them to get with it and serves as a virtual pat on the back to those who bravely got things going. In this technique, the topics under discussion are validated, and this will hopefully encourage new topics to surface.

The following is an original instructor posting to a discussion that reviews some of the majority points and encourages new points to be made:

> So far several people have mentioned that our students will need these skills when they get to the real world. Others have said that technology improves motivation and interest in the topics. I haven't yet seen this in the thread. One of the best ways to work with a negative person is to invite them into the classroom to see students using computers to work on reading, writing, math, and more. If technology is truly integrated, then it is just one of many tools being used in the classroom. Has anyone tried a direct invitation? What were the results? Would this work with teachers who are computer phobic? Are there some other ideas to share that haven't yet surfaced besides my suggestion of a direct invitation?

Provide Group Feedback

Sometimes it is important to respond to the entire learning community in mass, rather than as individuals. What follows is an example of providing group feedback.

The following is an instructor response posting to a small group learning a new teaching technique:

> I am so impressed with this whole group! Your enthusiasm, ideas, and willingness to try new things amazes me. Speaking of trying new things. . . . In Lesson 2 we will be using a technique called Think-Pair-Share.

Ensure That Everyone Is Involved

Watch the threads to make sure that every person has had a response to their original posting either by you or fellow students. An original posting is the student answer to the instructor-posted discussion prompt. It can be hurtful to students to post a well-crafted message and have no one respond to it. The instructor should respond to any original postings that have gone unnoticed for more than two days. Another method of making sure students are not ignored by their peers is to direct students to a posting that has gone unnoticed or which has not yet been fleshed out through discussion.

The following is an original instructor posting that directs others to fellow students who are inadvertently being ignored or whose points need to be fleshed out:

> Cleo and Gary have both said they do not have an ESL population or ESL resource people. What advice could those of you who do work with ESL students give them that they can file away for that inevitable day when an ESL student does arrive in their schools?

BENEFITS OF ONLINE DISCUSSIONS

Online discussions can be the most powerful part of a course. The learner-learner and learner-facilitator interactions in a discussion forum or chat offer the online student the ability to learn from not only the materials, but also the instructor and every single other student taking the class. Online discussions have some features that face-to-face discussions cannot match.

The first advantage to online discussions is that the entire discussion remains available because it is done in text form. Anyone, at any time, can review points made in the discussion by reading back through the discussion forums or the chat archives.

Second, everyone can, and should, participate. Unlike a face-to-face discussion where quiet students are rarely ever heard, in the online environment everyone has an equal chance to voice their thoughts. If a student does begin to dominate the board through overposting, instructor feedback helps to limit the participation to a more appropriate level where the student can then learn how to learn from others rather than holding center court. A clearly defined expectation for participation is very helpful in encouraging appropriate participation by all.

Third, for many students, the online environment releases them from inhibitions keeping them from being full participants in face-to-face discussions. Shy people often are emboldened; physical speech difficulties are nonexistent, and nonnative English speakers can take as much time as necessary to compose and edit their postings. In the online world, there are no prejudices based on physical appearance since student images should only be shared voluntarily. In fact, preserving this anonymity may be very important to some learners, which is a fact online teachers should keep in mind. Any requests to post digital photos of participants should be optional and part of the student lounge discussion, not the introduction forum where an optional request may feel more like a requirement.

DIFFERENCES

Text-Based Communications versus Face-to-Face Communications

Where do you begin with developing good communication techniques and patterns? First of all, it is important to recognize how text-based communications differ from face-to-face communications. The majority of communications in online courses are text based: email, discussion forums, chat, instant messaging (IM), and comments on assignments are all text-based communications. The use of audio and video for instructive purposes continues to grow, but text-based communication still reigns supreme. Audio and video do allow the learner to hear the inflections and tone of voice; video even provides the learner with facial expressions and body language.

Compared to audio and video or face-to-face communications, text-based messages can seem cold and harsh, leading to the myth about online courses as impersonal. Without some effort and a few tricks on the part of the message sender, text-based messages can, at times, seem more like a slap in the face to the recipient than the intended warm embrace.

Let's look at text-based communication from another angle. Books or articles can make you laugh out loud or create a lump in your throat. Some of the earliest text symbol shortcuts created by the first electronic bulletin board users to denote those same emotions were :) (the happy) and :((sad smiley). LOL followed quickly. Therefore, it is obvious that not all text-based communications feel harsh or lack emotion. It is important to create messages that can hug, tickle the funny bone, or draw a tear from recipients in an online course to reinsert the human connectedness that may otherwise be missing.

Humor

One of the first things that most online instructors-in-training are told is, "Humor does not work. Do not even try to be humorous in your communications." At least this was the advice given in several training sessions in which we took part. That advice was difficult to reconcile with our personalities and the observation that emails from family and friends often required a reply of LOL! Humor does work; however, it must be handled with care. But it can and does work.

It Has to Be Natural

Those people who do not naturally use humor in daily verbal communications should not attempt it in written communications. Humor cannot be forced. It needs to be a part of the message writer's everyday personality in order to have it work well in text. A fine online instructor, Walter McKenzie, introduced one method of inserting naturally humorous messages. McKenzie used tag lines after his signature when posting to the discussion board. Here is an example modeled after McKenzie's method:

> I cannot find the email address of the ESL expert that I wanted to try to put you in touch with, darn it! I wish I could have found that old email.—Signed, Kay *who is covered in virtual dust from rummaging around in old email folders*

Poke Fun at Yourself

Almost every circumstance of tension or problem in a class can be erased by the facilitator's ability to poke fun at him- or herself. It would be highly unusual for someone to be offended by a message in which the instructor was the buffoon. Here is an example of an email message meant to be humorous but still get a point across to the class and where the facilitator pokes fun at herself:

> Good gravy, did you see the spelling and grammar errors in my last email? Yikes! I know that I should compose in Word, use spell check then copy/paste it into the courseware email system. That's what I get for composing emails before my first cup of coffee in the morning! Oyyy!!

No Sarcasm

While humor does work in text-based communications, sarcastic humor does not. Never try to use sarcasm as humor in written messages. Sarcasm relies heavily on voice inflection to indicate the message is supposed to be taken in jest and not as it appears. Many individuals, including second-language learners, have difficulty with sarcasm even when it is spoken. Often the emoticon text indicators or other clues that the sarcasm is intended to be funny are not even noticed because students are too upset by the message. Here are some examples of attempted humor using sarcasm. Note the way smiley faces or emoticons are utilized to indicate the messages are meant to be humorous.

This is an example of an instructor response to a student:

> Whichever project you choose, please make sure you LOOK at the rubric for the project in the Assignments/Week 3 information. What I have seen happen in the past is that people use a project they previously created or they have a great time making something new but do not compare it to the rubric and end up with a very low score. Strange as this may sound, I use the rubrics when grading the projects. Is not that crazy?! ;-)

This is an example of an instructor response as part of an email directing a student to a folder in a course site:

> There are tech plan links in the Week 5/External Links folder called (this is going to sound crazy) Technology Plans. ;-)

This is an example of an instructor announcement posting:

> Just think, you only have two discussions and 1 real paper left to write for 6661 . . . plus the website, plus the revised concept map. . . . OK, well, we are almost there. The end is in sight! Or is that site? Get it, website. . . . Yeah, I know that was a bad one. ;-)

Ultra-Positive Is Better than Humor

What works even better than nonsarcastic humor? Being positive! It is important—very important—to maintain a positive tone and outlook in all instructor communications.

We have taught many online courses involving technology integration into the classroom. Occasionally someone in a class is not terribly proficient with technology and begins to wish the instructor was physically present to help instead of reading the student's posted pleas or emails requesting help. In fact, he or she wants to give up and quit the class. One experienced classroom teacher, but a technology newbie, who lived halfway around the globe from the instructor, was a student for whom this ultra-positive technique worked well. She was showered with glowingly positive emails such as this one:

This is from an instructor response:

> Wow! This is great! I know you said it's only partially completed, but look at how much you accomplished on your own before you had to ask for help! I am so impressed with your progress!

This student replied later with a message stating she knew exactly what the instructor was doing with all the positive talk. She could see that the messages were designed to build up her self-confidence in her own abilities, and even though she knew exactly what was occurring, she still said it worked.

Even an experienced teacher who had used positive reinforcement many times in her own classroom and knew we were using the technique still found it effective. It does work. Here is an additional example.

The instructor sends out announcements identifying the members of small groups for cooperative work. Via email, one student asked how the cooperative groups had been formed. The tone of the short email was terse.

This is the instructor response:

Good question! I must have forgotten to put that in the message in which I introduced the groups. I used the survey that everyone filled out before the class began to try to get an idea of tech skill levels. Then I tried to put people together by the grade or subject they teach. . . . I hope this helps out! I work really hard to balance things but at the suggestion of previous groups I do it earlier in the class so I have less personalized knowledge of each individual and their working style.

   If there is a problem I would like to know about it. I have been known to do some rearranging but I hesitate to do it until the groups give working together a try. It is a rare occurrence that I move someone out of or into a group but I have done it.

   Thanks for asking a great question!

Take Responsibility for Everything

Along with always being positive, there is a related tactic that should be employed. Take responsibility for everything. You will not be excusing students from work, but you will be removing shame and embarrassment from their having made what they perceive as public mistakes. It removes the *excuse* from things that may or may not be under your control as far as your institution is concerned. As the instructor, you need to have thick enough skin to take responsibility and be positive about everything.

   This advice was sent to a new online teacher as part of the mentoring process. It was obvious from her first reply that she was not sure this was the right way to go. Before the first week of her course was over though, she employed the *Take Responsibility, Stay Positive* approach. She emailed quickly after receiving the student's reply to her "I take responsibility" message. The new teacher was overjoyed with the results of this technique.

Quickly Won Over

When the instructor takes responsibility for something that is really the student's fault, it will be appreciated. Often students will awkwardly admit afterward that whatever occurred was, in reality, his or her fault. Generally, that sheepish student will be so grateful at not having an accusatory finger pointed at them that he or she becomes a model student from there on out, if not an out-and-out cheerleader for the instructor and the course.

Sammy, great job completing this week's assignment and being the first one to post it. The assignment needs to be placed in the *Post Assign. Here* forum, I should have noted this in my weekly announcement. I have moved your assignment to the Post Assign. Here forum. I will do a better job being clear in my directions from here on out.

Face of the Institution

Ultimately, the instructor is responsible for everything about the course. Students do not want to hear excuses; they want someone to take responsibility. Even more so than in a face-to-face course, students hold the online teacher responsible for every part of a course: the course materials, all the links, assignment choices, and the like. Perhaps this is so because the only real point of contact most students have in an online course is the instructor. While clearly the instructor is not responsible for everything, a good instructor will not pass the buck.

Time to Answer

Except in a rare instance when using chat or IM, the online teacher can take time to think and edit as he or she formulates a response to student communications. The student generally has no idea when his or her message was read. The online facilitator can use this time advantageously. This is especially true if a comment strikes a nerve. In a face-to-face classroom, a particularly harsh comment must be dealt with immediately—even if the method is to ignore the comment (which is a message in itself). Online communications give the advantage of time to craft a response. This thinking period before responding should not be excessive, but an overnight delay may give an appropriate amount of time to take a deep breath, write, rewrite, and only then send a response the instructor would not later regret. Think of it as counting to ten, digital style. Here is an example.

This message was sent via email to the instructor from a student confessing his difficulties with writing. His original spellings have been left intact:

> I read your comments about my writing and I agree. I must contests to you that I have a profound disability when it comes to writing. You see, I'm a hillbilly from Kentucky! Also I have been teaching children to spell was "wuz." God help us all. Talk to you later.

This is the instructor response:

> Well, then, there is a lot of room for improvement, isn't there? How exciting for both of us! We will just work together to see how far we can get before the course ends. OK?!

Once in a while a message arrives which is just difficult to answer in a positive way. The following message took several drafts to answer in a positive, yet truthful, way.

This is an instructor email to a student who has posted an assignment before the week even began and for which the instructor has just posted some additional requirements:

> I saw this morning when downloading files that you had already completed the paper for next week. Wow! You are really on top of things. I must apologize to you because I may be causing you some additional work. Just what you needed, right?! I just now posted the APA formatting requirements for next week. I try to do this before the previous week ends, just in case anyone is trying to get a jumpstart on the next week like you did. I failed to get that done before the week began. You should look over the APA formatting posting I made in the Q&A forum and double-check that your paper meets those requirements. I apologize. I know how busy teachers are and how badly we all sometimes need to get a jump on things.

TWENTY-FOUR HOURS

Research supports a best practice of prompt response to student communications. Twenty-four hours for email response has become the industry standard for high-quality programs. This is not a universally held expectation for all instructors or institutions as evidenced by this comment from an online student.

This is a comment about another instructor sent via email:

> I took an online class. It did not require all that this class does; we simply wrote responses to questions and sent them as an attachment. I had numerous questions for clarification because the syllabus was poorly organized. I emailed him 5–6 times. The class assignments were due each week. Without clarification some of my assignments were graded low. He never did email. I had to call him on the phone.

Let's look at this from another angle. The teacher in a face-to-face classroom knows when a student has a question. This might be indicated by the student raising his or her hand, hanging back at the end of class, or visiting the teacher in his or her office during a nonteaching time or office hours. One way or another, the student gets a chance to ask a question, and he or she has a reasonable expectation that there will be an answer from the instructor who is right in front of him or her. The answer might be "I do not know," but if the teacher fails to answer the question and the student is totally ignored by the teacher, the student will be insulted and hurt by this patently rude behavior.

It is hard to picture an instructor in the face-to-face scenario completely ignoring the student, is it not? We all know it would be incredibly rude, and extraordinarily unprofessional not to answer the question or to state, "No questions will be taken." Yet many online students report this is a common occurrence in some online courses.

This is an email from a former student complaining about another course:

> I do not know if anyone from the group has already emailed you, but some of us are pretty upset. We have not heard one word about the papers submitted so far and it is the beginning of Week Three. No feedback on the writing. Is this normal? Signed, Upset and Confused

This is the response from the instructor:

> Hmmm, is it normal? I do not think so. Is it ideal? Definitely not. But have I heard similar things from previous students? Yes, I am afraid that I have. I hope that you have done your best to contact the faculty member and ask for feedback. . . .

This is the return response from Upset and Confused:

> [T]hank you for the "prompt" and honest reply. I haven't emailed and asked for a response from him; I was feeling timid and figured I would hear something. I will try that and let you know how it goes.

Students, as our customers—as people—deserve to have their questions answered in a reasonable amount of time. This is a major responsibility of educators. It is a major responsibility of anyone wishing to be seen as a professional educator.

ANSWERING QUESTIONS WHILE ON THE ROAD

The best practice for answering email is for every query to get a reply within twenty-four hours. Sometimes the answer may have to be, "I will have to get back to you on that." That response at least informs the student their email has arrived and been read. Once in a while there are periods of inaccessibility when instructors are traveling. Students should be told this in advance and encouraged to contact one another for help until the instructor is back online. It is not conscionable to be out of contact for longer than two days during a course.

Those of us who have made online teaching our full-time job usually invest in a laptop computer for access to courses and email while traveling.

Broadband access cards make the Internet accessible almost anywhere. Even without a laptop, there are public libraries and cyber cafes where email can be answered and course shells accessed. Instructors expect their students to be available to their courses this often; they should expect no less of themselves.

LEARNER-LEARNER INTERACTIONS

Learner-learner interactions can be some of the most valuable in an online course; they also can be some of the most problematic. Instructors wishing to create a collaborative environment tread a fine line when postings and messages between learners become tense. Good dialogue can, and according to Wenger (1999) should, involve some conflict—that is, conflict between viewpoints and ideas.

The difficulty is recognizing the difference between *conflicting ideas* and *personal conflicts*, which occur between online students and require instructor intervention.

Humor with Peers

Advice about the use of humor in written communications applies not only to the instructor but also to the students in their learner-learner communications. It will be important for the instructor to offer guidance. How and when to provide that guidance is the question.

Advice about how to appropriately use humor in course communications given too early may hinder students in developing a friendly rapport. Students may be so cautious their communications become stilted. Instead provide guidance about humor in communications if a teachable moment presents itself. For example, if a learner-learner posting or email message looks like it could be misconstrued, contains sarcasm, or if a particular student is developing a pattern that has not yet, but may, prove troublesome.

In the first case, where a message looks like it may be hurtful, private emails to both students should be sent. This lets the message writer hear the instructor's thoughts about his or her message without losing face in a public reprimand. It also reassures the recipient or victim that the instructor is looking out for everyone. Many times the victim of the hurtful message will later relate that this reassurance from the instructor kept him or her from shutting down. It does not take much negativity in an online course before some students will drop the course entirely.

At the same time the private messages are sent, a carefully worded, positive-sounding all-class message should be posted. If this is not done, an underground rumble may begin to occur. The following is an example that could have grown into a full-blown underground rumble if not quickly caught by the instructor. The responses sent to the individuals and the group posting are included.

Message from one student (Fred) who inadvertently thought another student (Ellis) may have plagiarized:

> Great article! I agree! It looks like you did a little hitchhiking on Betty's post, using her Pros and Cons. That's really coming to agreement quickly! Typically, you'd want to reply to her post if you were going to do this, so that everyone knows you are expanding on her pros and cons. . . . The other option would be to include a citation with her pros and cons, giving her credit for them. . . . Otherwise . . . a suspicious person might think you both plagiarized them, and just happened to pick them up from the same source. Ouch! I know this is not the case, but it's so easy to alleviate any suspicions, that I just thought I should bring it to your attention.

This is the facilitator post to the whole class—working to diffuse the accusatory tone of Fred's posting:

> Fred is doing a great job of reminding everyone to be sure to give credit where credit is due. I do believe Ellis referenced the article he was referring to and provided the link—but we can still use this as a quick reminder. We have had issues with plagiarism in the past, and in the "copy/paste" world of online learning, it can be easy to do.
>
> Here are a couple of quick tips:
>
> If you are referring to another student's words, an easy way to do this is to write something like: When Lisa said "yada yada yada," it made me think "bim bam bloom."
>
> Referencing a website by providing the link and mentioning the author or title is also fine—this would clarify that your words are either a direct quote or your synthesis of the material.
>
> Set off long quotes by using the indent tool—it saves time from having to change colors, etc., to make the quote stand apart.

This is Fred's response to the facilitator by email:

> In your reply to my post, you said, "I do believe Ellis referenced the article he was referring to and provided the link." I noticed that both sets of pros and cons were the same right after Ellis made his post. . . . I've been in a class with Betty before, and I would have been shocked if she had done it. Then I got an e-mail from Betty in which she asked me what I thought was going on . . . she was wondering why Ellis copied her pros and cons. She was a little upset by this. I called her on the phone and told her how I intended to handle it. She was cool with that.

This is the facilitator by email:

> Hi Fred, I would like to phone you today to discuss the situation. When might you be available and how would I reach you?

THE UNDERGROUND RUMBLE

What exactly is the underground rumble? This phenomenon occurs when students in a class start communicating privately via email, phone, or in person to gripe or grumble about the course or the instructor. In other words, the students are talking behind the instructor's back. This private airing of ill will is negative learner-learner communications.

The rumble can be quite damaging to the class morale, but the instructor is often unaware this flurry of communications is occurring. As the online teacher, the best thing to do is prevent the rumble from ever starting by encouraging students to communicate openly and early whenever there is a question or problem. As a facilitator, you need to develop the deep level of trust necessary for honest communications with your online students who can then express directly the occasional frustration. It is when students are intimidated about asking questions, or questions go unanswered, that the rumble generally begins. And since the rumble communications are done in secret, it is unlikely an instructor will find out about it unless a student contacts him or her directly to pass along concerns.

TOOLS FOR INTERACTION

Communication is what separates true online learning from web-based tutorials. It is through the use of communication tools that learners are able to connect with other learners and with their facilitator. These tools bring the human and humane aspects to the virtual classroom.

CRITERIA FOR QUALITY INTERACTIVITY TOOLS

Many times, online instructors have no choice as to what interactivity tools will be used for a course—they get what comes with the CMS. There are usually several possible tools from which to choose for any particular need.

How does an instructor know which tool to choose? There are three qualities or criteria that must be present for a tool to be used successfully in any interaction (Figure 9.1). The tool must be in the student's possession, reasonably accessible, and operable by the student.

Criteria for Interactive Tools

Figure 9.1. Three-legged stool whose legs represent possession, operable, and accessibility, the three criteria for choosing interactive tools.

What do these criteria really mean to the facilitator? First, if the facilitator is in charge of deciding which tools will be used in an online course, he or she must make some judgments about hardware and software requirements. Those judgments must then be communicated to students before they sign up for the course. For the instructor who has a range of available tools, which tool will be best in which particular situation? When it comes to communicating important messages to the whole group, use at least two communication tools each time (i.e., post a message to the announcements and send it out by email). For a variety of reasons, some students will get the message from one tool but not the other.

Applying the Criteria to Email

Applying the three criteria of possession, accessibility, and operability to a simple example—email—should help clarify the characteristics. Virtually every online course states that students taking the course have to have an email account. The following is an analysis of email as a tool.

- Possession—Students either must possess an email account at the time of registration or be assigned one from the institution in order to participate in an online course. Those who do not have an email account at all cannot participate. Most students registering for an online course will already have an email account. On the off chance someone does not have an email account, they should be guided to their Internet service provider (ISP) for an email account, or they should sign up for a free web-based email account such as Hotmail, Yahoo mail, Gmail, unless their institution provides students with a free email account.

- Accessibility—Students have to be able to check their email regularly during an online course. In most courses, near-daily access would be a reasonable request. If a student only has access to an email account via the computer at their place of part-time employment and they only work two days per week, then the tool is not reasonably accessible.
- Operability—Students must know how to receive and send email messages. If they do not know how to run their email program, then this tool fails the operability criteria for the course and for the student. Depending on the course, operability with email may also mean a student can attach documents to an email, as well as download and save documents sent to them as an email attachment. If attachments are a requirement for a course, this should be stated technical requirements list that a student sees before registering for the course.

Applying the Criteria to Video

Many courses now require students to view video segments as part of the course materials. Video often requires a player, a piece of software that will allow the computer to run the video. Players can usually be downloaded for free from the Internet if a video program is not already installed on the computer. Video can be very memory intensive and often requires a minimum connection speed. What does all that mean in regard to your ability to use video to interact with your students online? Let's examine it more carefully. Here are the criteria applied to video.

- Possession—Streaming video requires that information be downloaded quickly enough that the data can be reassembled as the video is playing without lag delays midviewing. Otherwise the video will stop and start like a bad videotape as the computer waits, or buffers, more data so it can play another bit of video. A student with a slow Internet connection or slow processor likely will not be able to download the stream fast enough to play the video continuously. The video may not assemble fast enough to work properly. It cannot then be defined as being in their possession.

- Accessibility—If the video segment is not a streaming video, that is, if it is a file the student must download into the memory of the computer before being played, it will take a lot of storage space. Someone whose computer is just about out of space may experience a computer crash trying to download a big file. If the student has a slow Internet connection, the video file may take a long time to download. This is time the Internet connection and possibly the whole computer cannot be used for anything else. Students who are paying long distance fees or who pay by the minute for their Internet connection will find this costly in terms of both time and money. While many U.S. students now have broadband availability making downloading of large files quicker and more reliable, international students may or may not. Either way, the video may be essentially inaccessible for them.
- Operability—Video requires current and consistently upgraded hardware and software such as **codecs**. A codec is technology (hardware or software) that both compresses and decompresses audio and video signals to be transmitted and received. Both sender and receiver must have the same protocol such as MPEG. If a student is on a computer without the correct codec and they cannot or will not download the update, the video is not operable by the student. This is not to say video should not be used in a course. Simply that careful consideration of any tool must happen before it is arbitrarily added to a course and affecting interactions between learners and the content—either positively or negatively.

HARDWARE AND SOFTWARE COURSE REQUIREMENTS

For every tool included in a course, the criteria of possession, accessibility, and operability should be considered and a determination made about whether the tool should be required. Students should be told in the course marketing materials and syllabus what tools are needed to successfully complete the course. For example, if it is decided that streaming video is essential to the course and will be included, the course description should state the minimum connection speed, memory requirements, and that students will need to possess a video player such as Windows Media Player or Real Player.

Every new hardware or software requirement added to the list limits the potential market of students. It also increases the number of things to troubleshoot, both through the operation of the tools inside the course site and students' ability to utilize them. The goal of considering the criteria is not to eliminate all tools from the course but to proactively plan for all exigencies before a course begins. Every tool comes with advantages and disadvantages.

It is up to the course designer and the instructor to determine whether the advantages outweigh the disadvantages in each situation. Since interactivity tools are key to a successful course, examine them closely using the criteria listed in this chapter.

WEB 2.0

Technology is ever-changing, and it is likely that tools for online education will continue evolving as well. Some of the emerging tools developed for the public at large may have a place in online education in the future as well. Internet tools that were created particularly with the idea of collaboration and interactivity in mind have come to be known by the term *Web 2.0*. The collaborative plus interactive nature of these tools is what differentiates Web 2.0 from Web 1.0

Web 1.0 is what most of us would call the Internet of the 1990s and early 2000s. Web 1.0 was passive. The user read web pages without interacting with other users of the page or the page author. It was a one-way tool or what Marshall McLuhan (1994) would call a *hot technology*—in other words, all the meaning was created for you and told to you. Web 2.0 tools are what McLuhan called a *cold technology*. The meaning is not created for the student—the student has to bring meaning to it by interacting with the content or with others and the content—students must interact with this cool content thereby by warming up the place.

Web 2.0 tools are being adopted into CMSs at an ever-increasing rate. Blogs, wikis, photo sharing, and other collaborative tools also are almost always free to the user—another persistent criteria to the rise of the Web 2.0 tool. This has added to their adoption rate by faculty members even faster than the technology can be incorporated into CMS development.

Let's look at how a Web 2.0 tool like a blog meets the three criteria mentioned previously. First the blog is free to anyone who registers for one—so a blog passes the possession test. Next, it is accessible 24/7 on the Internet and requires only a web browser to read or write within the software; therefore it certainly passes the availability test, and finally, to sign up for a blog a student simply enters their own email address and first and last name. To write blog articles, the message box uses *what you see is what you get* (**WYSIWYG** pronounced *whizzy-wig*) protocol, so students simply type, copy and paste, and even insert pictures like they would be using in a standard word processing program. As far as difficulty of use, blogs have one of the shortest learning curves of available tools, so they pass the test for operability and resoundingly meet the criteria for successful course implementation.

Voice over Internet Protocol

While much has been said in course design and throughout this book about the use of discussion and dialogue as a way to enhance online learning, much of that discussion has focused on asynchronous technologies, such as discussion boards, email, and feedback. Purposeful synchronous instruction also can be highly engaging and community building—especially between the facilitator-learner and learner-learner when done using live voices.

Voice over Internet Protocol (VoIP), or voice-over-IP, means using the existing Internet infrastructure to send and receive live audio using broadband or dial-up connections. There are many services like Skype and Elluminate to do this, and some are free and others are fee based, but the basic elements required are a good microphone, the software, and an Internet connection. Because a facilitator is using his or her Internet connection, there are no long distance charges—not even when calling students internationally.

VoIP has the ability to reach an audience of learners and a learning style that otherwise might not be as engaged with just a text-based, asynchronous interaction. In his research on the use of VoIP in distance learning J. M. Lehmann (2008) found "Student L talked about bonding in relation to VoIP. She stated 'VoIP' creates a bond and mutual respect between classmates that cannot be formed through text chat or discussion boards" (p. 80).

Furthermore, when students are engaged in a synchronous VoIP discussion, the spontaneity of the discussion allows for faster paced debate and conversations that can turn more quickly than those in an asynchronous discussion forum. "VoIP can take diverse detours. . . . These dialogue detours encourage risk taking and learning. By bringing up new areas of content and focus, other students can be encouraged to take a risk by commenting, providing feedback or debating" (J. M. Lehmann, 2008, p. 70).

The Criteria and VoIP

How does VoIP meet the criteria for a successful interactive tool in an online course? Again, let's apply the three criteria of possession, accessibility, and operability to find out.

- Possession—Students with newer computers may have the software for VoIP in their possession already. Newer laptops often come with webcam and microphones built in, as well as, the accompanying conferencing software. Even most entry-level desktop computers built within the last five years have the capability; however, they do not automatically come with built-in microphones. These must be purchased. Headsets, while not expensive, are a technical requirement and must be stated in the syllabus as is the software, therefore possession cannot be guaranteed from the outset of the class.

- Accessibility—assuming all students are able to have the needed software and hardware to run VoIP, accessibility comes down to the ability of the facilitator to schedule a VoIP session at a time when all students are able to attend. Remember, synchronous schedules mean different things to the online world where students living in Taiwan take the same class with students living in Washington State. Which time zone is accessible? Does the facilitator go with majority rule despite the fact that the Taiwanese student will have to get up at 3:00 a.m. to participate?

This is where the facilitator walks the fine line of blending both the art and science of teaching. The science suggests that breaking the class into smaller groups may diminish the impact of the discussion by dividing the number of learners present—especially if the class is already small. The art is to find a way to stop that from happening and yet still serve the needs of the learners where they live.

In the case of large, disparate time zones, facilitators should break the class into as few groups as possible while creating time zone discussion groups that become manageable for synchronous assignment and discussion purposes. While the diversity of voices may lessen, it will make for much less frustrated students when trying to align participation schedules. In addition, students should be encouraged to read the transcripts of the other VoIP chats to support a broadening of ideas beyond just their own particular time zone group. In this way, the accessibility criteria can more easily be met without sacrificing the pedagogical need for the tool in the first place.

One other consideration with accessibility is the issue of meeting Section 508/ADA compliance. Because the technology is still fairly new, visually impaired students using screen readers may be at a disadvantage. Instructors should check with the software manufacturers before making VoIP sessions mandatory.

- Operability—VoIP does require a bit of technical set up and practice. Once learned, however, it is no more difficult that placing or receiving a phone call. In addition, if the network has problems, so does VoIP. Facilitators must make sure all students have correctly installed, practiced using, and are comfortable with VoIP prior to making participation in discussions a graded activity. For this reason, operability by the student is not a given, but it is something that must be determined on a student-by-student basis. Many facilitators will use low-level, low-risk activities in their first week to verify student skill level in required technologies—the ability to use VoIP would be one such area that a facilitator might employ this technique.

Interactivity between the learner-facilitator, learner-learner, and the tools that help us create those connections are just part of the picture of communication and learning in the online classroom. Another key component is whether students feel as though they belong to a learning community and the care and thoughtfulness a facilitator places in building that community—that will be the topic explored in the next chapter.

10

Building and Sustaining Communities of Practice

Creating learning communities is one of the cornerstones of best practices in online learning. The implications of feeling connected to other learners in a cold, technological environment, the ability to share ideas, and grow from the inherent conflict of them is at the very heart of social constructivism. Furthermore, students in communities of practice are actively and authentically engaged in their learning.

Why have learning communities become such an integral part of education? Because they are the natural outgrowth of much of the learning theory discussed in previous chapters. Lev Vygotsky, Jerome Bruner, and Jean Piaget all contributed to the understanding of how learning occurs. The basic philosophy of social constructivism is that students must work and dialogue with others while immersed in finding their own meaning in the curricular concepts. Put simply, learners make meaning of complex material for themselves and each other by their interactions with each other. It is within a learning community or a community of practice this happens most easily.

According to Wenger (1998) communities of practice can occur in any venue—the workplace, the neighborhood women's group, or the classroom. They simply require a group of individuals with a shared interest and a willingness to participate in a dialogue about that interest for purposes of learning. What each level of participant (e.g., individual, group/community, or organization/institution) gets out of the use of community of practice differs.

THE INDIVIDUAL

For the individual student, being part of a community of learners helps to humanize learning done via a machine. Bringing contributions to share with others breaks down the myth that online learning is cold and impersonal. When social learning theory is applied, the learner is constantly aware of what he or she brings to the educational table to share with the community since it is through this sharing that his or her own learning will evolve and take shape.

According to Wenger (1998), "Placing the focus on participation has broad implications for what it takes to understand and support learning. For individuals, it means that learning is an issue of engaging in and contributing to the practices of the communities" (p. 7).

THE GROUP

When a community of practice has been formed and individuals are truly engaged, a synergy of learning begins to happen. While individual learners concentrate their responsibility of contributing to the discussion, the group also begins to reciprocate by providing the learner with multiple viewpoints, challenging questions, and taking left turns in the discussion that the individual learner might never have considered on his or her own.

In this way, the individual learner has served the learning community and the community, in turn, has brought out the best in the individual learner. The give and take becomes something larger than any one discussion prompt, and the intangible benefits of a vibrant learning community pay off big dividends long after the discussion thread ends. Wenger (1998) states, "For communities, it means that learning is an issue of refining their practice and ensuring new generations of members" (p. 7).

THE ORGANIZATIONS

Vibrant learning communities form real bonds. These bonds tend to spread outward in a ripple effect, which can grow the whole organization or institution. This is especially true in the corporate world. A community of practice, which is growing, has a strong sense of belonging among its members. They feel part of the team. "For organizations, it means that learning is an issue of sustaining the interconnected communities of practice through which an organization knows what it knows and thus becomes effective and valuable as an organization" (Wenger, 1998, p. 8).

As you will discover, the community effect, like the butterfly effect, can be positive or negative for any individual, course, or institution. With positive community, the flap of the butterfly's wings can grow a whole forest, but with negative aspects to a community, it can knock the same forest down with the force of a hurricane.

BUILDING A POSITIVE COMMUNITY—INTRODUCTIONS

The novice instructor might think community begins in the first week of the course—perhaps with introductions. In fact, community begins with the first outreach of the instructor to the student—during precourse contact. Precourse and the all important first week activities (and how they relate to student retention) will be discussed in much more detail in Chapter 11. To discuss building community, however, we do need to briefly discuss the use of introductions within this chapter as well.

The first step in building an online community once the course has begun is through the use of introductions in the discussion forums. The importance of the social connections created in this first threaded discussion cannot be understated.

Most online courses begin with some type of an *Introductions* or *Get to Know You* thread. This allows participants to begin learning how to use the discussion board tools while establishing the social connections needed for a safe environment for the sharing of ideas. Nothing builds a community faster than allowing a group of individuals, sometimes complete strangers, to share silly little tidbits about themselves and bond over flavors of lattes, shared computer mishaps, or ideal vacation spots. Ideally, if the introduction topic can be fun and in some way relates back to the content of the course, it will be seen by students as more purposeful and therefore be more successful.

> Online classes can be tension-filled places, especially for newcomers to the online format, and facilitators should take the opportunity to lower the anxiety often in the first few weeks of a course. Ice breakers work in the online classroom the same way they work in a face-to-face course, or your neighborhood Tupperware party—they allow each person the chance to share a little bit of themselves in a non-threatening environment, to get over the hurdle of the initial posting without fear of "the grade" or "judgment" of their classmates, and to connect with others they may never meet in person on a more personal level. (Chamberlin, 2006b, p. 1)

NETIQUETTE FOR INSTRUCTORS

Netiquette is a set of norms that leads to less confusion and misunderstanding in a faceless, asynchronous environment. It is about courtesy and best practices for communication. It does not always make for the quickest posting, but it most certainly models clarity within the post. Instructors should strive to post with netiquette in mind each time they construct a message. By modeling netiquette for students (and even requiring its use), good facilitators will eliminate many misunderstandings in discussion forums—either from students misconstruing what has been posted by the instructor or from misreading each others' postings.

Be Consistent in Format

One of the quickest ways to develop a recognizable *voice* in a discussion board online is to use a consistent format. For instance, Bob always posts in Times, 10 pt. font, in italics; while Ramona prefers Comic Sans, 12 pt. font, and the navy blue color. Students who open a post by either of these instructors quickly recognize it as Bob or Ramona's posts (or their voice) before the students ever get to the signature or the *posted by* link.

Change the Subject Line to Reflect the Content of Your Post

Think of the subject line like the title of a good book, one which will draw other readers in. Subject lines that resemble addresses (e.g., Lisa to Kay) tend to close down discussions to just the two names listed. Subject lines that just repeat the original poster's subject line with the Re: added (Re: Re: Re: Unoriginal subject line) give no indication to the reader if the new or added content will benefit him or her as a learner, whether the conversation has evolved in topic or perhaps if it is veering off into a personal side conversation (which should then be directed to the student lounge or email). Each time an instructor posts or replies to a post, he or she should update the subject line to match the content of his or her posting.

Delete the Extra

When writing a **reply posting**, delete all extraneous information except the specific phrase, sentence, or comment to which you are replying. This not only helps the student reader know what you are replying to, but also helps him or her save time by not wading through a long post, or worse, the entire included thread. It also makes it quicker for students to download or print a particular posting.

Summarize, Quote, or Refer

Another way to help student readers engage in your responses is to give a frame of reference in your post by quoting or summarizing the content to which you are responding. For example, "When Nick wrote he always formatted his posts the same way I began to think . . ." is much easier for the reader to follow and understand than "Yep, me too, that's why I . . ."

To look at it a different way, some students choose to arrange their discussion board by *unread* posts only—the quote gives them their frame of reference for the topic of the thread.

To Personalize or Not to Personalize

If the goal of a post is to be inclusive of many students—or perhaps all the students in the course—avoid starting the post by addressing it to an individual student. "Dear John, I believe . . ." sends the unintended signal that this post is just for John's benefit. Other students may skip reading the post altogether or, at the very least, skip replying because they didn't want to intrude on the conversation between John and the instructor. If the goal is to only reply to John and not for the benefit of the entire class who may also read it, consider whether posting to the academic thread is the appropriate place? Or should the correspondence move to a *student lounge* or off board through email?

Add a Question

If you want to encourage deeper thinking and help encourage students replying, try adding an open-ended question at the end of your post. Beginning questions with *what*, *who*, *which*, *why*, and *how* will open more discussion and tend to avoid simple yes or no answers.

Color

Red and yellow are difficult colors for those with poor eye sight to see online; and those who are color blind may not delineate red at all. Furthermore, red can have negative connotations in some cultures. Try to use colors other than these for text.

Off-Topic Posting

Save nonacademic posts (except icebreakers) for a *student lounge* forum—this will cut down on the number of posts students feel like they must read. Redirect students to post to the lounge when threads get too far off topic. The lounge should never be required reading.

> This is a great topic but a little too far off of our current discussion about the causes of global warming. Kaitlin, could you restart this thread in the lounge?

Politeness versus Too Many Posts to Read

Resist the urge to post *thank yous* in the academic forums. While we all appreciate good manners, a post that merely says "thank you" adds to the number of posts to read and does not contribute to high level discussion building. Again, this type of social posts should always be placed in the student lounge area. Good instructor modeling of this netiquette rule will encourage student follow-through.

Overposting and the "Drive-by" Posts

This is a caution normally saved for students only. Upon occasion, however, online instructor certification programs do have to warn away the occasional trainee from **overposting** (dominating the discussion board), or from being a **drive-by poster** (breeze in with one-liner, comical postings in the academic forums).

As an instructor, your posts should be somewhere in the 10–15 percent range of the total volume of postings in any given forum. While this is not an absolute mathematical forum, it is a reminder that the facilitator's job is to guide and prompt the student's own discovery of insight from the material and each other. It is not to pontificate and dominate the discussion.

When a student tends to overpost, facilitators can provide feedback by asking questions like the following:

> Will your post contribute, deepen, and help draw more discussion out of others? If so—post it. If it is simply a comment added to every thread just to make a participation requirement—this may not improve your grade (in fact, volume posting—also called "overposting" without depth may actually lower your score).

If a student is doing the opposite and being a drive-by poster, your feedback might include statements like this:

> One gentle caution . . . I would like to make you aware of a habit I've noticing where you are posting "one-liner" posts, as these can be viewed as clutter by some, and they do not meet the rubric guidelines for proficient. Remember my mantra, if its worth the time to post, make it a content-worthy post.

Me, Too, I Agree!

The *me-too* post certainly is a frustration in the online environment and does not add any depth to the discussion or learning. In a study by Stodel, Thompson, and MacDonald (2006), "Learners got frustrated with the constant agreements and comments such as 'Good point' and 'I agree'; feeling it made the conversation overly positive and fake" (p. 12). Therefore be sure to post substantive ideas and avoid the *I agree* posts which just clutter up a discussion board.

Use Nongender Specific Language

Quick—do Jordan, Pat, Loren, and Callon use the men's or women's dressing rooms? Not sure? Then how can we blithely use *him* or *her* or *she* or *he* in a post to them? Unless these individuals or others with like androgynous names have clearly identified his or her gender, assume nothing and avoid the use of gender-specific language in your posting to them. This way neither you nor the recipient will end up embarrassed and having to post something like, *"Ah . . . I hate to mention it, but I'm a guy. . . ."*

Reorder Forums by Importance

For ease of locating the most important items and to limit the amount of scrolling needed, facilitators should keep the frequently asked questions (FAQs) or question-and-answer (Q&A) forum at the very top of the discussion board. This should consistently be followed by the most current weekly module, which the facilitator will have to rotate as the next module becomes the most current.

HURDLES TO BUILDING COMMUNITY

It takes time to build a solid community. The problem with that is many online courses only run six to eight weeks long—so situations that can cause a block or hurdle to community building need to be dealt with swiftly and decisively. The following scenarios are true and have been culled from our own experiences or those of our colleagues in the online teaching field.

Negative Nellies

Students who communicate negatively in some way earn the negative Nelly label. Their unconstructive communication can take several forms:

- Starting off grouchy and stirring up trouble (i.e., "I shouldn't have to take this class," "I hope this class is not as bad as the last online course I took," or "Have you seen the syllabus? Did you see all the work we have to do?").

- Being rude and sarcastic to other students or the instructor.
- Using the board to constantly and repeatedly complain that they miss seeing the other students and miss the face-to-face interaction.

Negative messages are like a virus and they can become contagious in your class. A student who is flaming the board, or posting negative messages about the class, other students, other instructors or you, needs to be dealt with immediately. The first step is to immediately contact the student causing the problem. If the posts are negative enough, this contact should be made by telephone with an email follow-up for purposes of an administrative record.

An example of that email follows:

Zack, Thank you for taking the time to speak with me this afternoon. I would just like to recap our discussion so that we have a written record. While your frustration with having to take this required course is noted, your success in this class, and the success of your classmates is dependent upon our building a community of learners that is a respectful learning environment.

You are right, it is easy to sometimes let emotions take hold and sarcasm can easily be misinterpreted. As you and I talked about and agreed, all students need to refrain from posting messages that are off the content of the instructor's prompts, outside the context of course curriculum, or combative in nature. Further no messages should be directed at an individual in a way that diminishes the dignity of the learner. If we all follow these guidelines, we will build a community where learning thrives and with your background knowledge, you will be an integral part!

The next step is to post a message to the discussion board reminding students that, while the board is a place for the free flowing exchange of ideas including ideas that conflict, students need to remember to disagree with ideas and not individuals. Furthermore, students need to be encouraged to express alternative viewpoints with supporting research to bring the conversation back around to a more academic intent.

Hijackers

Hijackers are students who, in some way, take over the control of the class or an instructor's discussion. These students

- Feel they can lead a discussion on the discussion board on their own, so they pose an unrelated question to the group without the instructor's permission.
- Do not want to work at the same pace as the class and post work well in advance.

- Do not read directions for discussion board use closely enough to learn how to create a new topic and instead use the reply function when not appropriate.

Hijacking may be intentional or unintentional due to a lack of knowledge of the technology, assignment, or tool. Intentional or not, this situation can usually be handled the same way—by reteaching. A gentle group reminder on the discussion board posted where the problem occurred and a second reminder posted to the news or announcements section will reteach those who missed the directions the first time and gently redirect those who are more intentionally trying to take over.

Here is an example of a redirection when students were confused about posting personal conversations in the academic forums:

> [W]hile I have your attention, please remember that off-topic personal conversations belong in the Student Lounge. I encourage you to continue to be a community and post "real-life" comments to one another but to do so in a place that is not part of the "required reading" of the course. The Student Lounge is located at the very top of the forums page—have fun!

Just the Facilitator and Me

Sometimes students are attracted to online learning because they mistakenly believe coursework just will be between them, their computer, and the instructor. This is especially true of the first-time online learner. The *facilitator and me* mindset shows up in several possible ways. These students:

- Post two-sentence messages, are shy, and need lots of encouragement.
- Submit the assignments privately to the instructor but skip the discussion postings.
- Log in on Sunday evening and complete all of the postings with no collegial interaction throughout the week.

Without previous experience, students may envision computer-aided tutorials worked on independently in isolation. For some personality types this is the attraction. These are the same students instructors struggle to engage fully in the face-to-face class when students are required to discuss in small groups, work on projects together, or even just participate in Socratic-type discussions.

While we do want to allow for some flexibility and choice throughout the length of the course, we do not want to abandon what we know about social learning theory and the need for students to interact not only with content but also with other learners in order to construct full understanding about a given topic. The reluctant participant, whether from shyness, learning preference, or just procrastination, must be encouraged to be a vital part of the learning community both receiving and contributing to it.

Strong course design with multiple venues of participation and accountability is the first way to combat the reluctant participant. Students should be held accountable not only for posting assigned work, but also for contributing to the discussion by replying to their peers and taking the discussion to a deeper critical thinking level. Learners also can contribute to the community by providing peer feedback on assignments. Finally, instructors need to give their own feedback as to the quality and quantity of postings of these reluctant participants in such a way that the learners are encouraged to increase their postings, take risks, and share more of themselves in the course. This feedback should be specific and give suggestions. An example of such feedback follows:

> Jesse: I want to see you meeting the minimum requirements of participating on three days in the forum so that you can earn a "proficient" score next week. That being said, I really appreciate the content of your original post and replies to others—which is why I tapped you to be the next group moderator. As the moderator, you will need to log in more often next week and reply to your colleagues in a timely fashion (remember the rubric). Finally, one trick for helping to extend the discussion is to end your post with an open-question (a question that has more than one way it can be answered). You'll notice I do this as an instructor quite often. I am confident you will do great next week and look forward to seeing the improvement!

Technology Issues

Newbies and others often have problems related to the technology of online learning. These students:

- Barely know how to send an email and are scared to death of the discussion board and technology in general.
- Reside abroad in a country with restrictive filters (e.g., Saudi Arabia) and cannot get into some of the readings.
- Discard the log in information sent by the school and try to log in with home email address and Social Security number.

A student's level of persistence in the face of technological hurdles may impede community building and most certainly will affect the student's desire to stay in a course or take another online course later on. How the instructor helps the student overcome a technological gap in learning is the key to retaining the student.

There are varying degrees of technological problems that may occur, and you must make a decision as to how much the technology will impede the student's progress or ability to learn. If, for example, a student has never sent email, does not know how to save and attach a document, and had to have a spouse help him or her register through the online registration system because it was too confusing, then this student will certainly struggle throughout the course just with navigating the course shell, posting to a discussion board, and trying to communicate with the instructor about how to do the simplest of items in the course. Would this be a successful online learning venture for this student? Probably not. Instructors need to make the call very early if they feel a student is so far over his or her head with the technology as to make success in the class improbable.

When a student's skill level is appropriate for the course, there still may be some bumps in the road. A student may not have a minor skill, like creating a screen shot, necessary to complete a required project. Or a student may have technology filters getting in the way of accessing course material—this is often the case for high school students taking college course work and working through the K–12 school network. An instructor will need to find work-arounds for these varying situations on a case-by-case basis. This is further proof why instructors need to be technologists as well as subject matter experts.

Finally, instructors can use moments where many students seem to be asking the same question about a technology skill as a teachable moment. A quick post to the Q&A forum with some instructions and a screen shot might save hours of time answering individual emails about the same or similar question. An example of a teachable moment post follows:

> Hi Jeff, Sorry to hear about your struggles to create a screen shot for your "how to" newsletter. When you mentioned you were working on a laptop—I had a Eureka moment! The key strokes of CTRL+Alt+Print Screen do indeed create screen shots. However, most laptops require that you also press the Fn (function) key. Yep—that's right—four keys all at the same time: CTRL+Alt+Fn+PrtScrn. Whew, I'm glad we could solve that one easily enough!

Reducing moments where technology inhibits community is one of the easiest ways an instructor can build and maintain community.

BUILDING COMMUNITY THROUGH GROUPS

Anyone who has ever worked on a small group project knows sometimes this is a frustrating experience. A common complaint is that one person does most of the work, or there is one person who does almost nothing. Another lament often heard is that one person has taken over and is bossing the rest of the group. Knowing this, it begs the question: "If there are so many potential headaches inherent in small group work, why bother doing them?"

Creating Connections in the Online World

Small groups promote an increased level of communication and involvement that might not otherwise occur in an online course. While much has been discussed about the importance of creating connections between instructor and students, many of the truly lasting connections that will occur in an online course are inside the peer group. These are, after all, colleagues with similarities in age, work, or some other area of interest that brought them into the particular course or program. Some peers will connect with each other in an online course no matter what the instructor does, but with a bit of facilitation, many more connections can be made before the course is over—connections like the ones discussed here by a student named Stephanie who was grateful to Valerie, another student in the class, for posting a potential job opening.

> Hi, Valerie. It's posts like yours that remind me of how connected an online community of learners can be. Many times when I tell people that I'm enrolled in a Master's degree program taught entirely online, most of them immediately think that learners are isolated and alone. After one week of meeting new colleagues and renewing acquaintances with those from previous classes, I feel more connected in this environment than I ever did in all of my on-ground courses. (Stephanie Watts, personal communication, 2002)

Problems with Self-Selection

Many online instructors, especially in the beginning of their careers, allow students to self-select their groups. This is especially true in higher education where andragogy suggests giving students choices when possible. However, self-selection in an online course can be very awkward, time consuming, and have potential negative effects on the community-building efforts elsewhere. If a class is only six to eight weeks long, students rarely have had enough time to form relationships where they feel comfortable choosing any particular person out of a group of virtual strangers—the earlier the grouping is required, the more true this becomes. Furthermore, since students lack the visual stimuli and cues needed for quick bonding, these group choices may simply become guesswork, or more often than not, simply based on who responds first to an email request by another student (which is not really self-selection of peers in the ideal sense of building on commonality).

Online teachers who choose to let students self-select groups need to be very clear, up front, about group size. When the instructor forms the groups, the size is easy to control. When students begin contacting one another about forming a small group, there is often a tumbleweed effect. For example, Josey contacted Sue about working together in a group. Sue said she contacted June who will get back to Sue as soon as William answers the email June sent to him. Pretty soon what was supposed to be a group of two or three will be four or five strong because no one wants to hurt anyone else's feelings by saying, "I joined a different group after I emailed an invitation to you."

On the flip side, there needs to be a mechanism for people who are completely left out of the groupings to contact the instructor and be placed in a group. This scenario is also awkward and has the potential to be very painful for the student who is excluded, even if it was completely unintentional. Being left out is more likely to occur online because it is impossible to see the groups forming. In the face-to-face environment, the instructor can see who is on the periphery, in danger of being excluded, and can subtly correct this problem.

Instructor-Selected Groupings

A better option than self-selecting of group members is to use information and observations to create instructor-selected groups. The information source might be a preclass questionnaire or the introductory postings. The advantage to instructor-created groups is that no one will be left out. The disadvantage is that the instructor still has a limited amount of knowledge that can be used to create the groups, especially if groups need to be formed early in the course. As discussed in Chapter 8, students tend to be most satisfied in working in groups when they've been grouped with students of a similar attitude and drive. The key is finding the right tool to get to that information as quickly and as accurately as possible.

An online instructor who will be using cooperative peer groups needs to first determine the purpose and functions of the groups. This will help in the selection process. For example, in a highly technical class it would be helpful to put students with lower technical skills or knowledge with students of higher ability. The higher-ability students can assist those with less knowledge while working on the project. Very likely they will continue in an unofficial mentoring role after the project is completed. Once a relationship is formed, groups usually communicate and help one another throughout the course. This is one way the community can help broaden the learning within the course.

If the purpose of the groups is to learn to work in a diverse group—like a product development team—then the instructor needs to put people from different employment tracks or departments together. Preplanning the purpose and functions of the group process is critical.

When groups are formed with a community of practice in mind, great things begin to happen. But it all starts with the relationships the students form from their initial placements.

> I really enjoyed this week because it was the first time I got to work closely with a small group of people. I met my group for the first time and we found that our interests and experiences complemented each other (probably encouraged by you!). You did a great job matching us up. (Kelly Sommers, personal communication, 2003)

Communicating and Monitoring

It seems to help alleviate some of the anxiety that results from forming groups if the instructor is honest about the perils of group work. Encourage everyone from the beginning to keep the instructor informed. In fact, one way to stay informed is to be an unofficial member of every group. For example, if copies of group emails go to the facilitator as well as all the students, the facilitator can listen in, or lurk, on the group conversations. A good facilitator avoids the tendency to get involved or meddle in the group. There is a fine line between proactive monitoring and meddling in the group dynamics.

Even with marvelous efforts at carefully forming groups and monitoring them, every instructor will eventually hear from someone who does want to switch groups. Sometimes there is a strong, rational reason to say yes to a switch. However, this is awkward because the result will disrupt two groups, not one. The group the student is leaving and the group being joined will both be temporarily out of balance. Making the switch in a way that does not leave hurt feelings is a communication (and community) challenge for any instructor and should not be done lightly.

Take, for example, the situation where Eileen wrote privately to the instructor requesting to be moved into a different group as she found Larry's lack of academic integrity in her small group more than she could bear. Her frustration with Larry's emphasis on bells and whistles over substance was beginning to spill out publicly and so a move was necessary—but how to do it with the least disruption to the remaining group members? In this case, the facilitator thought it best to blame an imaginary technical glitch rather than put a human face on the move.

Here is an example of the post letting the group know that Eileen would be leaving—note the lighthearted humor used to ease the situation, yet the instructor took responsibility for the move. This helps to keep the value of the small group community intact, preserves the moving student's dignity, and allows everyone to accept the move as necessary for the learning:

> Hello Plum group members! I am very sorry to inform you that I am going to have to relieve you of a colleague. I had a technical glitch in my records and had Eileen assigned to two different groups. Yikes! Since Eileen cannot possibly be in two places at the same time, I am going to settle her in the Green group and relieve her of the stress of feeling like she needs post enough for two people. I am so sorry to do this, but I know that this is a strong group and you will be able to carry on without Eileen even though you will miss her. Please accept my apologies.

No one should be allowed to work solo on a project when others are required to complete it in groups. It is a rare group that does not struggle to complete a project and many people would much prefer to just do it alone. If the instructor allows one individual to do the project solo, discontent will result.

Connectedness

Many, many students have emailed or posted in classes we've taught to say that while the group process was difficult in some way, they knew that they were better for having participated. Here are some comments about group connectedness that state it more eloquently:

> I've never done a group project with people I've never met before. This is an interesting experience for me in that regard. I'm also rather frustrated with the process as well . . . it would be easier for me to do this project individually instead of with a group. With that said, I have enjoyed receiving my group's input and sharing ideas with them. We were very slow in starting to communicate with each other, and we definitely procrastinated getting started on the project. Once it got moving, though, progress was made quickly. I enjoyed making suggestions and seeing them implemented by others and implementing others' suggestions myself. (Jonathan Hoffman, personal communication, 2003)

> Thank you for sharing your sentiments about the connectedness of the group. I feel we've all been able to share our experiences and ideas, and that there is a level of trust reached. I am happy to be a part of this insightful and caring group as well. You make a good point about feeling responsible for material when you know other members of the group are counting on you. (Meghan Caylor, personal communication, 2008)

The most important time for creating a community is before the course starts and throughout the first week of the class. The next chapter will explore this most important time period in detail.

11

The All-Important Window of Time: Precourse Work through the First Week

There is a critical phase in any online course, bound by the period before the class begins through the first week, which will be known in this chapter as **the window**. Approximately 70 percent of an instructor's total effort for the entire course takes place during the precourse-through-first-week window, this is known as the **70/30 rule**. Preparation and communication are the keys to success in all types of education but most especially in online education. The window of time is critical because this is the time when students are most likely to give up or withdraw from the course.

Students who are unsure of themselves as online learners or who are squeamish about this new environment will most generally back out of a course during the window. This phenomenon occurs in face-to-face classes as well, but the unfamiliar nature of online learning compounds the anxiety level for students, particularly first time online learners. Any investment of money already made can usually be recouped, and their investment of time and energy is minimal. This makes it easy for students to cut and run when things get tough. Most of the time, unfortunately, people drop a class they would have enjoyed and benefited from when fear and anxiety get the better of them. Many would remain enrolled if given some encouragement, guidance, and assistance during the window.

Once the window has closed after the first week of the course, students are less likely to drop out. By this far into the course, students will have made connections with peers and the investment of both time and money will have grown. Those students who drop out of a class after the window has closed are, in general, declaring themselves as not fit for the online environment. They have come to realize they do not have the attributes of good online learners. One other thing to keep in mind is that there will always be life circumstances that cause students to drop out throughout a class. The online instructor cannot prevent all dropouts; however, they can prevent those who are dropping out because of fear and anxiety.

COMMUNICATION IS THE KEY

Maintaining enrollment is not even the most important consideration when thinking about the window. Getting everyone off to a great start is the most important task of the online instructor. So what can the online instructor do to help maintain full enrollment in a class and get everyone off to a great start? To rework an old real estate phrase—communication, communication, communication. Helping new online learners get settled in and off to a great start requires lots of instructor interaction. Later in the class, the instructor can begin to ease him- or herself out of discussions, letting the learners take the lead. Early on the facilitator carries the majority of the load.

Precourse Communications

How does a facilitator begin communicating with students before a class has even begun? Start with an email! Prior to the start of class, most institutions send the instructor a roster of students and their email addresses. The email addresses are important. If the institution does not send them, see if there is a way to get them through the class list in the course site. Contact needs to be made as early as possible.

The first step is to send all students an introductory email message including a brief instructor introduction and directions to respond to the email. Students should be encouraged to ask questions at any time. Not only does this reassure the students, but it allows the facilitator to check that students can receive emails and that they read directions. It is recommended this first message be kept short. Here is an example of an introductory message where the directions actually start with the email subject line. Notice the subject line states the name of the course and the start date. This helps ensure that the learner will open the message rather than deleting it because they think it is **spam** email.

Subject Line: Welcome to Collaborative Communities beginning 6/9 Print this Email

Wahoo!! Let us introduce ourselves, we are Dr. Kay Lehmann and Lisa Chamberlin, your facilitators for Collaborative Communities. Our course, which we cowrote and now coteach, will be starting soon. We both live in Walla Walla,

WA. Yes, it really exists! We have been friends for over 15 years and coworkers for most of that time. We each have many years of experience teaching online courses. Once you have access to the course site you can learn more about both of us. We would like to have you complete the following in preparation for the start of Module 1 on June 9.

Please go to this page [course page URL would be listed here for the students' ease of use] and complete all orientation and preparatory activities including checking your browser, completing the orientation, and much more.

In addition to these preparations please respond to this email so we know that you received it. When you reply, please format your subject line with your name and the course title, which you can abbreviate as CC or Collab. Also include the subject of your message. Therefore your subject line for the reply might look like this:

Su Wong, CC, Replying to welcome email

We ask that you use this subject line protocol for all course communications. And be sure to always copy both of us on your emails. We look forward to working with you! This is a fun class!

This contact will generate several emails from grateful students who will confess their anxiety level was high and how they appreciated this simple contact for it reassured them. Guaranteed!

Administrivia

This first email is just one way to be proactive when teaching online. Another way is to send quick, informative emails or post a frequently asked questions (FAQs) page with information about how things work in the online course. Joan Vandervelde of University of Wisconsin–Stout's Professional Development department refers to these as **administrivia**. These administrivia messages include all the little things that would be covered in an orientation or in the first few days of a face-to-face course. Making this information available just-in-time is another way to reduce student anxiety. A few days before the class begins, plan to send another welcome message with more details, including how to log into the course site and how to proceed once the student has logged in. If the institution or entity has an orientation program, this step may not be necessary.

There Are No Dumb Questions

For the first few weeks of a course, many students will continue to be highly anxious whenever they do not know how to proceed, yet they are reticent to contact the instructor with what they feel might be a *dumb question*. Anticipating some of these questions and providing the answers before the questions are even asked is highly reassuring. These can be posted in a FAQ section throughout the first week or two so as not to overwhelm the learners.

One sign that an administrivia message should be shared with everyone is if more than one person has asked the question via email. If two or more people have a question and are willing to email it to the instructor, it is very likely that many more people have the same question and are still not comfortable contacting the instructor with what they think is a dumb question. Encourage learners to use the question-and-answer (Q&A) forum in the course site rather than emailing the instructor. That way all students get the benefit of the instructor's answer. This also is more efficient for the instructor than responding to multiple emails asking the same thing. Here is a gentle way first-time learners can be redirected to use the course Q&A forum.

> Great question Josef and no, I do not mind answering questions at all! I would like to see you place this in the Q&A forum in the course site. That will allow others to see the answers to questions they, too, might have. If the matter is personal, then by all means email me. Would you please share your questions and my responses with the group in the Q&A? I would love to have you do that, if you do not mind, in case others are wondering about similar issues.

No question is a dumb question if it is causing anxiety to the student. Instructors will receive questions that make their eyebrows rise and their heads shake, but this disbelief should never be communicated to the student. Ever. If an instructor answers curtly or suggests in any way that the question was idiotic, it will shut down communication with the student. Then, when a more important question about the course comes up, the student will be unwilling to contact the instructor and his or her assignments or participation will suffer because he or she didn't know how to proceed.

Students willing to contact the instructor with questions should be praised. This is part of the process of making connections. Students who begin to feel comfortable asking questions will then encourage others to ask questions. Better yet, many will begin to feel comfortable enough to answer questions posed by others. That empowerment of the learners is a major goal of the online instructor. Though it takes time to be highly communicative and proactive early in the course, it pays dividends later in the course when students are empowered to conduct their learning without as much instructor attention. Here are a couple of ways to let students know that questions are welcomed and encouraged:

- Great question, I am so glad you asked this!
- I am so glad you brought this up. I am sure others are wondering the same thing.
- Thanks for asking a terrific question!

GETTING LEARNER-LEARNER CONTACTS STARTED

Not only do students need to be comfortable with instructor-student communications, but it is also important in most online courses to encourage peer interactions. At first, many students find this awkward since the visual aspect of the face-to-face connection is missing. For some reason, not being able to see the faces of others really impedes some online learners. Most get over this quickly when peer communications begin to blossom. How can the instructor encourage that blossoming?

Introductory Activity

Providing students with an introductory activity that encourages them to post something about themselves personally and professionally will help community blossom. The instructor should post his or her own response first as a model for others. The activity needs to be specific enough to encourage students to post more than name, rank, and serial number, as it were. The more substantive the information learners post about themselves, the more connections will be made with others. The introductions prompt needs to provide some opportunity for students to respond in a unique way. Some of our favorite introduction prompt ideas are shared next.

Introduction Prompt Ideas

The introduction prompt needs to remind students to share a little about themselves personally and professionally as well as respond to the specific idea in the prompt. Some students get so caught up in the prompt they forget to state their location and other pertinent data. Others post the minimum, what might be referred to as name, rank, and serial number, but they do not respond to the prompt. Later in the chapter, some ways that instructors can resolve these common issues will be shared. But first, the prompts:

Mis-comm-puter-unication [used in a training course for online instructors]
Share your most embarrassing computer mishap (keep it clean everyone!). Reply to several of your colleagues, but remember you do not need to (nor should you) reply to every single person. Look for colleagues who have had few, or no, replies.

Tech Tips and Tricks [used in an educational technology course]
Tell us your biggest tech integration challenge OR your best tech integration tip. If you have a great shortcut or "trick," share that here as well. Reply to at least two postings with an in-depth posting about how to solve the challenge, or with a tip or trick that adds to or extends the idea to which you are responding.

Vacation location [Used in any class]

Where is your favorite vacation spot? In other words, where do you "go" in your mind's eye when you begin to stress a bit (like when taking an online course for the first time)? What should a first-time visitor to that vacation spot know before they go? Reply to at least three colleagues with questions about, or memories of, the vacation locale.

Tell One Lie

Share three things about you, two of them true and one of them false. Colleagues should reply to at least two postings guessing which one is the lie and why it appears to be a lie.

No One Would Guess

Share one thing about yourself that no one would ever guess. Respond to at least three colleagues by sharing similar experiences or asking questions about the unique characteristic.

Color Personality [For an art or photography class. FYI: There are several color personality tests online. There are other types of personality surveys that might be used as well. Some favorites are shared in Chapter 15.]

Share the results of your online color personality test and explain why you think the results do or do not match your personality. Reply to at least two colleagues with questions or comments about your own results or the colleague's findings.

Multiple Intelligences or Learning Styles [for an education class]

Complete the multiple intelligences/learning style survey and share your results here. Explain what you discovered about yourself as a learner. Reply to at least three colleagues.

Whether or not specific introduction prompts like those listed are used, students should be told what to include in their introduction. The expectation for responding to colleagues and how many colleagues to respond to should be stated. Students should *not* be encouraged to respond to every colleague; the whole forum becomes unwieldy when this happens. Students *should* be encouraged though to look for colleague's whose introductions have had few, or no, replies.

While students should not respond to every introduction, it is important that the instructor responds to every one of the personal introductions. This reassures the individual student, validates his or her posting, and provides the instructor an opportunity to model some discussion techniques for everyone's benefit. In all other discussions in the course, the instructor should not respond to every posting. This will subdue peer interaction, as everyone will be looking to the instructor for *the answer*. The instructor needs to be visible in the discussions by posting some thoughts each day, but the majority of the discussion should occur peer to peer.

As the course continues and peers become more adept at responding well, the instructor can continue to reduce his or her **visibility** in the discussion. The facilitator's presence should always be felt, but it should fade somewhat as the course matures. The students' presence will grow over time, but the instructor has to know which student is making contact. Signing all communications is a must.

Signatures

Students should be asked to sign emails with their full name. Names should also accompany postings although the student may not need to type their name because the course management system (CMS) may provide their name automatically. Early in the course asking for name and location in postings may be helpful when the group is geographically diverse. The instructor can model this for students and then celebrate those who follow the pattern. The same holds true for signing email messages; the instructor should model good signature lines in all instructor-student email communications and should encourage students to do the same. In addition to signatures there is another place the instructor's name should appear in all emails.

Instructors should make sure their email programs are properly set up so that the instructor's name shows up in the *From:* field when email is sent. Having a separate email account for professional use is encouraged and part of setting up that account should be putting in the instructor's full name. Students and a few instructors have set up their *From:* field with just a first name. The email appears to be *from* Marian or the email is *From:* their email address hotchick61@hotplace. Others use two names like Joe and Marian Thomas, yet only Marian is in the class, or in rare instances, the *From:* field appears completely blank. Correctly setting up the email program will help make sure precourse and first week communications are not routed to a spam folder.

FIRST WEEK TIME COMMITMENT

Every instructor should allow extra time in his or her schedule for answering emails and student postings during the first week of a course. Encouraging student communication is an important goal and promptly answering the first flurry of anxious emails and postings will go a long way toward meeting that goal.

Students new to online learning should have an easy workload during the first week. Assignments and readings should be kept purposely light to encourage the learner-learner interactions in the introductions. The first assignments should be manageable, even easy, so that each student feels successful at the end of the first week. This also allows for a learning curve while mastering the CMS. Many new online learners are easily overwhelmed, especially if the introductory discussion becomes lengthy or if, for some reason, they log in late that first week. Late arrivals can happen for a variety of reasons including technical problems. These latecomers are almost always stressed because of their late start. Extra attention must be paid until they are well underway.

CONFIDENCE BUILDING

Much of the first week is spent building the confidence of the learners. Confidence building does not end after that first week. In Chapter 5, some ways to build student confidence through communication were explored. In Chapter 8, assessment of student's work was discussed. It may seem like assessment would not fall under the confidence-building banner, but it very much does. Good assessment techniques will help students develop skills while improving their self-esteem.

COMMUNICATION ISSUES IN THREADED DISCUSSIONS DURING THE WINDOW

Keep in mind during the first week in nearly all online courses there is generally some type of *Introduce yourself posting* activity. Many instructors are tempted to ask students to share digital photos as part of the introductions. While this addition of the *face* to go with the name is at first appealing, many students are not comfortable sharing photos of themselves. First of all, if a student does not have a digital camera or access to one, they may feel left out. These days, however, most people can find some way to get an image using a camera phone or other device. Just because they can get an image does not mean they want to share it though.

These feelings may stem from a desire to be physically anonymous (physical anonymity is one reason that some people prefer online courses). Students may be uncomfortable with photos of themselves in general, or they may have real issues about their appearance. Others may fear that sharing photos on a course site could lead to misuse of the photo. The latter possibility has to do with identity theft and privacy issues and is a very real concern. The final caution with digital photos is that many students do not know how to set their digital camera or compress the resulting images, and they end up sharing monstrous files. This leads to a whole new set of technological challenges the instructor must be prepared for in the first week. The bottom line is photos should always be optional. With or without a photo, the students should be expected to introduce themselves to the instructors and their colleagues.

Even with a well-written introduction prompt, some students respond in ways that are challenging for the online instructor to handle skillfully. All of the following scenarios occur with some frequency. Possible responses are shared after the scenarios to offer insight on how to handle such situations with best practices in mind.

INTRODUCTION POSTING SCENARIOS

Name and Not Much Else

Sue Ellen posts the absolute minimum, basically the message is the equivalent of name, rank and serial number, and she may or may not have responded to the introduction prompt.

Students sometimes need to be encouraged to say a little more about themselves. Here is an instructor posting that encourages the student to flesh out her introduction and offers some suggestions of what to include.

> Glad you joined us, Sue Ellen! Tell us what fun things you are doing this summer. Do you have any hobbies? Are you planning to read any good books? Do you share your life with friends, family, or pets? The more we know about each other, the more connections we can make to help us enjoy this course together. Thanks for introducing yourself!

If the instructor had just posted, "Tell us more about yourself," the student may have floundered or even been somewhat insulted that his or her posting wasn't good enough. Remember that text can come across as cold or terse, and it is possible that a short, declarative statement, like "Tell us more about yourself," could be more harmful than helpful in encouraging communication.

If the student didn't address the introduction prompt, the instructor might respond this way,

> Suzy I found what you had to say about XYZ intriguing. I am wondering what you think about [Restate part of the prompt here.]

Replying in this way validates the effort the student made without defeating them. At the same time the instructor has let the student know that more is expected and specifically what more is needed.

You Can't Make Me

Students may be taking a course for reasons other than their own. They may need to take the course for certification or to keep their job. Sometimes students must take a class they feel is below their abilities. A bad attitude may be exhibited in their early postings with statements such as:

"I should not have to take this class," "I hope this class is not as bad as the last online course I took," or "Have you seen the syllabus? Did you see all the work we have to do?"

If the instructor does not address these issues, the introductions forum may turn into a big gripe session, which would defeat much of the community building that should be occurring in the first week. A brief upbeat message in the forum from the instructor may resolve the issue, or an email or phone call may be needed to help this student keep a more even tone in their messages.

Juan, I am so glad you have joined us. Your past experience with this subject matter will make you a valuable asset to your classmates.

This response is appropriate if the student feels that they are being forced wrongly to take the course.

Gracie, I hope that you have a great experience in this class. Let me know what I can do to help you be successful and enjoy the course.

This reply is appropriate if the student has had a bad past experience or if they are worried about the workload. Offering to have the student contact the instructor with issues usually defuses most students. Those who have serious gripes will generally respond favorably to a personal email or phone call.

Only an Intro

Students sometimes post an introduction of themselves and never respond again in the introductions forum. This also occurs with curricular responses. Many students will write out their original response to a prompt and then never set foot in the discussion again. In either case, after the week has ended the instructor can let the student know in the gradebook comments that replying to colleagues was an expectation that was not met.

Chang, thanks for introducing yourself. Your comments about "xyz" were interesting. Responding to the prompt is only half of a discussion. Just as in a face-to-face conversation, our online discussions need give and take. You need to reply to the original messages posted by your colleagues, and respond back to them when they reply to your original message. This deepens the conversation and creates connections with others. The more you participate, the more you will learn, and the more fun you will have in the class.

Remember that our weeks run from Monday morning to Sunday night at midnight. Participation is required during that time. For more information on the participation expectations please see the Syllabus. The points for discussion participation in week one are now lost, discussions cannot be made up. However, this loss of a small number of points should not impact your final grade. I look forward to your full participation next week. I know you have a lot to add to our discussions and everyone will benefit when you share your thoughts.

In the first part of the message the instructor is letting the student know that their message was read. The instructor should refer to a specific comment in the posting so the student's work is validated. Explaining that an online discussion is the same as a face-to-face discussion helps the student understand why their participation is expected. Most newbies do not, at first, see a threaded discussion the same way they would a face-to-face conversation. After this is brought to their attention however, many of them have an *Aha!* moment.

Reminding them when the module or week begins and ends is helpful, especially if the course has an odd schedule such as Thursday through Wednesday night. Conveying this information as well as the lost points is also one way that an instructor can document that students were made aware of course policies should the student protest later on that "I didn't know that was the policy. I insist you change my grade." Documentation can be important in the isolated but vexing event that a student protests a grade or other instructor action. Therefore, clearly stating policies, when such statements are appropriate, is a good idea.

No Shows

Occasionally a student does not *show up* at all their first week. The student's name is on the roster, but they never introduce themselves or participate in the discussions. This can happen for a variety of reasons. Some students do not realize that the course has started. Remember that the instructor welcome email may go into a spam folder, so the student may not have seen the welcome message. Occasionally students provide an incorrect email address or they simply do not check their email. In other cases students think that because online learning is flexible, they can begin and complete the coursework whenever they want without any deadlines or timelines interrupting that flexibility. Just before the week ends, the instructor should send a brief email to all the no shows with the word URGENT in the subject line. The email message should encourage participation rather than scolding the student for not getting started.

> Hi Angelica, Our XYZ class began several days ago [state the exact date] and week one is about to end. We haven't gotten to meet you yet. Is there anything I can do to help you get started? Let me know what you need. I am here to help.

The word *urgent* typed in all caps, which according to netiquette is shouting, usually gets the student's attention, and they will open the email even if the instructor's name and email address are unfamiliar. Asking if the student needs help is a nonthreatening way to get a response back from them. If the institution or agency sponsoring the course has counselors or other people assigned to assist students, copying the message to the counselor as an FYI helps them stay in the loop in case the student turns to them for assistance. By all means, utilize these support people if they exist and turn to them to contact students who have attendance or other issues. Anything the instructor can do to legitimately lighten the workload is encouraged!

A variation of the no show is students who respond to the first curricular discussion, but they do not introduce themselves in the introduction forum. Students may simply have overlooked the introductions, or they may feel they only need to do the parts of the course that are *required* (or: graded). However, many instructors and a lot of students revisit the introductions throughout the course as a way of reminding themselves about personal details of the people in the course. A quick email to the student requesting they complete an introduction is all that is usually needed. This can also be placed in the gradebook comments at the end of Week One. Here is one such message where the instructor takes ownership, even when it is not the instructor's fault, to allow the student to save face.

> Hal, I cannot seem to find your introduction in the Introductions forum. Perhaps I am overlooking it. I wanted to remind myself what your job title was so that I could tailor my comments to you in response to your message in the XYZ discussion. Did you post an introduction of yourself? If not, please do so as soon as you can. Many people, including myself, use them throughout the class when we cannot remember personal details about another person in the course.

Unprofessional Writing Style

Occasionally a student will fail to use appropriate writing conventions. In most courses there is an expectation that punctuation, spelling, and grammar and syntax will be correct. Occasional typos and mistakes occur, but students, especially secondary and postsecondary students, should be expected to use electronic tools to edit their messages into a final form before posting. In some cases students are using the abbreviated spellings common in text messaging. Reminders must be made to the whole class about the importance of making the messages clear to everyone. Punctuation, capitalization, grammar, and correct spelling are all part of writing clear messages. The instructor should first begin with a whole class message.

> Quick reminder for everyone—In our class we need to make sure that all our communications are as clear to others as possible. Correct spelling, grammar, punctuation, and capitalization help to clarify the meaning of our messages. Use your word processor to spell and grammar check your work before posting messages. The added advantage of using a word processor and saving your drafts is that your message will not be lost if your Internet connection blinks or your computer freezes.

Usually an all-class message suffices to solve the problem, but once in a while a student needs a personal reminder to edit messages before posting. This should be done by phone if possible. The phone will allow the instructor to deliver the message in a tactful way and allows for a chance to assess verbal communication skills. On rare occasions, a student's writing is symptomatic of larger communication issues and a verbal conversation can help the instructor identify such problems without offending the student.

ISSUES IN POSTINGS IN THE QUESTION-AND-ANSWER AND OTHER MISCELLANEOUS FORUMS

Issues during the window do not occur just in the introductions forum. There is usually an ongoing Q&A forum where students can ask questions and find answers without sending an email to the instructor. Occasionally difficult first week scenarios occur in a posting to the Q&A forum, other threaded discussions, or via email to the instructor. Here are some of the most common issues occurring during the window with suggestions.

Flexibility to the Max

"Can I finish the whole course today or this week?"
"Can I complete all assignments in the shortest time possible and be done with the course?"
"Can I wait to do all assignments on the last day or week?"

"Why are there weekly deadlines?" "I thought I could work at my own
   pace."
"Isn't online education about flexibility for the student?"

Online learning *is* flexible and in a course that is not facilitated or that is
a type of computer-assisted training or tutorial, students do have a great deal
of flexibility. The courses advocated in *Making the Move to eLearning* are
courses with active communities of practice in order to employ social learning theory. Some students have heard that online courses are flexible, so
students are not prepared for weekly deadlines and other expectations that are
often part of a model based on communities of practice. A kind but matter-of-
fact explanation of the way the course is designed generally suffices.

> An underlying theme for this class is community, specifically becoming a com-
> munity of learners. According to social learning theory, students have to discuss
> the course concepts among themselves for true learning to occur. Therefore
> much of the "work" occurs in the module forums. The work in those forums can
> only be done during the dates the module is active. This creates an opportunity
> for the cohort of learners to discuss the topics from just one module deeply and
> thoroughly. If some learners were working on Module 4 while others were still
> adding to Module 1, the group would not be focused on one set of topics.

Too Brief or the Drive-by

Often, especially early in a course, a student will post a message that is only
two to three sentences in length and does not address the prompt or assignment. This is also frequently accompanied by postings to colleagues all
within a time span of a few minutes. This type of posting is called a *drive-by*.
The student entered the course site and did the absolute minimum as fast as
possible, sometimes without even reading the course materials. If the student
never enters the discussion forum for the remainder of the week, or if the
drive-by posting occurs at the 11th hour for that module, the student is not
really participating in the community of learners.

The student is missing out on valuable opportunities to converse about
the course topics with others, and the rest of the class is losing out on the
student's wisdom and expertise. This happens in the first week many times
because students have not yet familiarized themselves with the course policies on participation or because they have not managed their time well and
haven't set aside an appropriate amount of time in their life for the course.
If there is still time for a student to see an instructor comment in the forum
urging the student to flesh out their original posting, that is a good step. Unfortunately most students who do *drive-bys* never see the instructor's posting

asking for their response to be developed further. In that case, or if the postings occurred at the 11th hour, the communication with the student on this matter is done in the gradebook comments or via email.

> Doug, I see you posted your thoughts in our XYZ discussion and you did reply to a couple of colleagues. Unfortunately your original message didn't address the entire prompt. Your thoughts on (xyz) would have been valuable for everyone else to read. I posted a message to you asking for more information, but you didn't respond. I noticed all of your postings were made within a 17-minute period and that you never re-entered the discussion forum.
>
> Keep in mind, participation in the discussions is a key to your own learning, and the learning of your colleagues. In order for that learning to occur, you must participate throughout the week and reply to colleagues with a message that adds to or deepens the overall discussion. The grading policies and the discussion participation rubric will provide more guidance to you so you might earn a better grade the next time.

Late Arrivals, Vacationers, and Absentees

A particular vexing set of issues surround attendance issues. For one reason or another students fail to *attend* their online course. This lack of attendance can be at the beginning, middle, or end of the class. Communications with them may include the following messages.

- "Can I finish the whole course today or this week?" "Can I complete all assignments in the shortest time possible and be done with the course?"
- "I'm going to miss the first 10 days of the course because I'll be on vacation and there may not be Internet access on my cruise (in my hut in Tahiti, etc.), will this be a problem?"
- A student has surgery (or has a baby) and is missing from class for several weeks. He or she does not let the instructor know in advance and does not submit his or her work in advance of the absence.

Many online instructors shake their head and mutter, "Would they ask if they could miss 20 percent of a face-to-face class?" The answer is generally, *no*. Most students would not approach a face-to-face instructor and make such a request. The anonymity of the online environment and the cold nature of text does seem to empower students to ask things they wouldn't dream of saying in person to an instructor.

Students fail to participate appropriately for a variety of reasons, but ultimately it comes down to not recognizing the integrity of the online course in the same way they would for a face-to-face institution. While some students think nothing of missing 20 percent of an online course for a vacation, the awkwardness of approaching their face-to-face professor from a land-based institution to ask for permission to miss the first one-fifth of class to bask on a Hawaiian beach would inhibit most students. The anonymity in the on-line environment lowers the inhibition level for students to, at times, make requests that are otherwise academically inappropriate or detrimental to the student's education.

Engagement with the content and engagement with fellow learners is an important part of the process of the community of learners. When a learner fails to contribute to the community, either by not logging in, not posting, or rushing so far ahead as to not be present with the majority of the group, the community is diminished. Each learner has something to contribute from their own experiences and perspective on the content. Each learner needs to be encouraged to share those perspectives and to help deepen and expand the conversation. This is how critical thinking builds.

The following email message is one for students who want to miss the beginning of class for vacation:

> Hello Sumi, this is a highly interactive course. One of main focal points of the course is collaboration between members of the class. We believe a major part of the learning takes place in the discussion forums. One of the course requirements is participation on the discussion board X/7 days each week, and the participation grade counts for X percent of the course final grade. More importantly, the first week of any online course is critical, even more so in this course because of the collaborative nature of the social learning environment.
>
> If you are going to be absent the first week-plus of class, it would be better to wait until next session to take this class. From what you have indicated you will be absent 10/56 days which is nearly 20 percent of the course. We hope you will join us in the summer for this course.

This request to miss a substantial part of the course also comes up once a course is underway and puts it outside the window. The scenario is closely related to the preceding one. Assuming the course is past the point when the student could drop the course, solutions other than dropping have to be considered. The instructor can be hard core and give the student a zero for all work not submitted during the vacation, however, such an action usually angers students greatly and does not make for good public relations for the instructor's organization. Another possibility is that the student may, depending on the type of institution, be able to take an "Incomplete" and finish the work after the course ends. This is an option that should be a last resort because many students never finish their incomplete courses.

Neither of those solutions mentioned have proven successful in terms of instructor-learner relationships or student completion of the course. What works is to have the student complete what they can in advance of their trip and then suffer the late penalties for work submitted after their return. Discussion participation should not be allowed to be made up after a module ends, therefore those points are a zero. This must be made clear to students as in the email, which follows:

> How exciting for you Fran that you will be going on a well-earned vacation with your family! I suggest you do as I do. Try to find a way to be online every couple of days while traveling. Using a combination of laptops with wireless networking cards, Internet cafes, libraries, and other solutions, I have taught our courses during hurricanes, while suffering the wishing-for-death flu, and from the lanai while vacationing in Hawaii. If you absolutely cannot get Internet access and participate in the discussions during the week, you will lose those points. Sometimes, however, I have to make trade-offs and this may be one of them for you. Those few points will likely not impact your overall grade for the course and trading them for a little R&R might be a good bargain.
>
> I would encourage you to complete the assignments and submit them in advance. You will find that you will be tired and the piles of laundry will steal your attention from your coursework when you first return home. Completing assignments in advance will allow you to leave with a lot of peace of mind, instead of a lot of anxiety worrying if you can get them completed when you return home. Enjoy your vacation!

Every instructor will have students who face emergencies taking them away from a course for a substantial amount of time. Emergencies are completely different than vacations, and handling students who have extended course absences because of emergency situations will be discussed later. The definition of an emergency is something unexpected, something which could not be planned for. Anything that can be written on a calendar in advance is not an emergency.

I'm Lost

Students sometimes cannot see the forest for the trees in an online course. Remember the whole environment is foreign to most students, which skews their ability to *see* buttons and navigation links. What seems obvious to the course designer or the instructor is, in fact, not at all obvious when a new online learner is anxious and frantic.

"I cannot find the discussion forum (or the assignments)" is a message frequently received early in a course. Keep in mind that generally students have

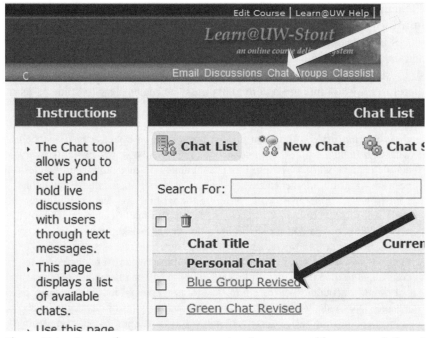

Figure 11.1. Image of a course management system screen with arrows pointing at links that the student should note.

completed an orientation of some type to familiarize them with the CMS, and in many cases, these items are clearly marked buttons in the course site or have been explained in emails or news and announcements. Nonetheless, for the student, they are all but invisible. A brief message with a screenshot attached is usually the answer. Seeing the visual with a bright green or yellow arrow or circle around the *missing* information or element is all that most students need. An example of this type of screenshot is shared in Figure 11.1.

ASSISTING STUDENTS WITH NAVIGATION

Many students who are first time online learners have a hard time figuring out the navigation of course sites. For the first few units of a course it is helpful to offer explicit directions to the materials. It is better to offer too much direction and instruction rather than not enough until students get comfortable with the course.

Another proactive step is to double-check all the links in the course site. The instructor should do this before every new module, but it is especially important in the first week or two. Again, running into a bad link for a required reading can make the new online learner highly anxious since he or she has no idea how to proceed from that point.

Some students do not understand that links to readings or resources may take them outside the course site and into the vast beyond of the Internet. One way to help students avoid that confusion is to set up all links so that they open in a new browser window. Students will at least still have the course page open behind the current window. For some tech novices, even that may be confusing because the Back button on the browser would not take them back to the course site. They do not realize it is still open behind the window they are viewing.

AFTER THE WINDOW IS CLOSED—THE OTHER 30 PERCENT

After the critical first week is over, the facilitator must maintain that level of enthusiasm in the students. Approximately 30 percent of the instructor's communication efforts go into maintaining student interest from the second week through the final week of class. These percentages are not scientifically derived, but the literature does note the importance of orientation and the period at the beginning of an online course. This 70/30 rule of effort and preparation by the instructor is key to course success. Instructors will be well served if they put a majority of effort into student communications that occur during the critical window of time prior to, and at the start of, the course.

Using 70 percent of the time and effort during the window will pay dividends in the long run. The instructor can be more efficient with the remaining 30 percent of their course efforts because of the good foundation laid at the beginning of the course. Tips on being as efficient as possible are always needed. Instructor efficiency is the topic of the next chapter

12

Time Demands and Efficiency Tips for Online Teachers

Time is different for online instructors. While it might seem teaching would be teaching whether it is done in a classroom or online, the fact is time is an entirely different commodity for online facilitators. There is no classroom schedule, and the instructor does not need to be in Room 201 from 3:30 to 5:30 on Tuesdays and Thursdays. This reality seems very appealing to those whose lives are overly scheduled, but there are some drawbacks. An online class is always in session, 24 hours per day, and 7 days per week. No matter the time of day or night, some student somewhere is probably inside the course site.

The online instructor has to be self-motivated as well as self-correcting. Supervisors rarely make an *appearance* in any online course. The instructor cannot rely on management to provide the incentive to get up and get to work—this drive must come from within when working online. Students may feel adrift in cyberspace when taking an online course, and they seek instructor help whenever the students are online, 24/7.

Students, if pushed for an answer, will say that they do not really expect an instructor to be online constantly. However, some student somewhere is always seeking help and his or her reality is the only one that counts. This means there might be 30 realities in a class if there are 30 students. Each one is *in class* whenever he or she is in the course site, and he or she wants service from the instructor when *in class*. Furthermore, students will be *in class* every day of the week. Realistically, high-quality online instructors must plan to be online virtually every day.

Sometimes only one hour will be needed to read email and postings, sometimes more time will be needed. Research clearly shows for students to be satisfied with their online learning experience, timely help from instructors must be available. While the rest of the world might work from 8 to 5, Monday through Friday, online learning is busiest over the weekend and on holidays. Online learners do their course work when they have time in their schedules, and most of them have that time available on weekends and on holidays. Midweek is *the weekend* for online instructors because this is when learners are less likely to be online.

Does this mean the instructor can never take weekends or holidays off? No, of course not. However, these should be rare occasions, and students should be apprised that the instructor will be completely offline during those times. That is the *take*, but the *give* is your availability to attend your daughter's school play at 10 a.m. on a Tuesday. Flexibility in scheduling is a give-and-take.

While instructors are expected to be online for at least a little while every day, their online time might be conducted from a cybercafé in Paris, while traveling by car, or from the comfy confines of their king-size bed. Online learning may be 24/7, but there is no specific schedule (unless a synchronous event such as a chat is planned), and it is not place bound. Being able to log on for an hour in the morning from a lanai on the island of Maui and spending the rest of the day on the beach, more than makes up for answering email every day. The online instructor can work from anywhere, at any time they choose. Yet there is work to be done, and how to do it efficiently, allowing for time on the beach, is the topic of this chapter.

ONLINE INSTRUCTION TAKES MORE TIME THAN TRADITIONAL

Everyone is busy these days, online instructors are no exception. In fact, research shows that an online instructor spends more hours than a face-to-face instructor preparing and teaching the exact same course. In contract language for faculty in distance education, the American Association of University Professors (AAUP, 2002) recommends:

> [W]orkload provisions should take into account the anecdotal evidence that distance education course development is taking two to three times as long as comparable courses taught in the traditional manner. The same evidence suggests that the investment of faculty time involved in teaching a distance education course is substantially greater than that required for a comparable traditional course. The time spent online answering student inquiries is reported as being more than double the amount of time required in interacting with students in comparable traditional classes.

O'Quinn and Corry (2002) in a study of traditional, distance, and combination instructors who taught both traditional and distance found, "The factor which posed the greatest concern to all faculty and division chairs regarding their participation in distance education was the workload that faculty incur as a result of participating in distance education" (p. 14). There are several studies that have been completed since AAUP developed the contract language on distance education confirming the anecdotal evidence that course preparation and teaching online are more labor intensive than the same courses taught in a traditional manner. The purpose of this chapter is not to scare potential online instructors with tales of the workload involved in online education, yet the reality is online education, done correctly, takes time.

The workload may deter some instructors; however, those who have studied this profession closely have also seen many motivating factors including flexibility of work space, teaching while traveling, student diversity, and creating real communities of practice. In any profession there are pluses and minuses. While workload could be an inhibiting factor, this chapter should help instructors be more efficient, thereby lessening what Bruner (2007) refers to as "the hassle factor" of teaching online. There are many **time management** techniques that lessen the total amount of time to teach a course online.

COURSE FAMILIARITY

Experience with a course will create efficiency . . . eventually. This is also true in traditional education. For example, during student teaching in a regular K–12 classroom, most preservice teachers find it takes them hours to accomplish what their master teacher gets done in minutes. This is because the student teacher lacks two things: practical experience and the specialized knowledge of the job. In any endeavor, things tend to go smoother and quicker with some practice or experience. In addition, some of the workload will be lessened when the student teacher picks up the little tips and tricks that allow the master teacher to be more efficient. These are the tricks of the trade, as they could be called.

The same could be said about learning to be an online teacher. At first the facilitator is inexperienced and slow. Some things just require practice. There is no substitute for these experiences and it certainly cannot be put into a book. However, the tricks of the trade, which improve instructor efficiency, can be put in a book and have been! But how much time does it take to teach an online course? This question has no simple answer.

The time commitment is dependent on many factors. The first of these is the familiarity of the instructor with the course materials. The first time through a course, everything always takes longer than in subsequent sessions of the same course. Pachnowski and Jurczyk (2003) confirm this in a study of online instructors who have taught the same course multiple times, "Faculty members who begin to engage in distance learning teaching, particularly web-based teaching, may require some additional accommodations during their first semester for the additional time it takes to transfer the course into the alternate teaching environment . . . after the first semester or two, most faculty do not spend a great deal of additional time for preparation" (p. 9). Pachnowski and Jurczyk took note that faculty were interested in, and would participate in, workshops that helped them better manage their time and workload.

BILLABLE HOURS IN ELEARNING

The term **billable hours** is an adaptation of an admonishment Lehmann received when signing the contract for a consulting job. *Do not make this a $2 an hour job!* The contract was estimated at more than 10 times the $2 per hour. The point being made, however, was that overworking the project would lower wages per hour. This statement comes to mind quite frequently when discussing the workload for online teaching. Many institutions and agencies pay a set amount for the course. An efficient instructor, who uses their time well, increases the dollars per hour when compared to an inefficient instructor.

For example, if an instructor is paid $1,200 to teach a six-week course, the income will be $200 per week. If he or she can complete all the work satisfactorily in 10 hours per week that makes the income about $20 per hour. If someone else teaches the same course for the same $200 per week but spends 20 hours per week, the income is down to $10 per hour. This is referred to as billable hours. The more efficient any instructor can be while still doing the job well, the more *billable* hours they will have to devote to additional jobs or personal endeavors. After all, the first instructor could have taught *two* $1,200 courses in the time it took the second instructor to teach just one. The first instructor therefore had the potential for twice as many billable hours. Over the course of many years teaching online, experienced instructors discover many ways to maximize billable hours.

Tips to Make Time Count

Instructor time is valuable. First, consider whether an action needs to be done at all. If it is something the student would not notice, do not do it. Examples might be searching for a cute piece of clipart or fixing nonvital formatting on a web page. If the artwork will draw student attention to an announcement, then it might be worth the time to seek it out. If the formatting will cause accessibility issues for students using screen reading software then, yes, take the time to fix it. Evaluate each action and determine if there is a need for it to be done.

If an action does need to be taken, complete it as efficiently as possible while still doing the job well. For example, do not spend more time leaving comments than a student spent doing the assignment. If it is something the students can do for each other or for themselves, have *them* do it. For example, establish a question-and-answer (Q&A) forum as the first topic area on the discussion board. Require students to post course technical questions in this area of the discussion board *before* sending an email to the instructor and encourage students to assist each other. This forum will need to be monitored to provide assistance as needed. In many cases students will help resolve each others' issues without instructor assistance.

Student Self-Reflection Made Easy

Use online tools with a really simple syndication, or **RSS**, feed or email notification for student self-reflection or self-grading. For instance have students complete their reflections on a blog and set up an RSS feed so that all new entries arrive without having to log into the student's blog. If the course management system (CMS) has a journal tool make sure that it can be accessed from the gradebook. This allows access to the journal entries from the grading page. The instructor can read the entries and score them on one screen. Self-grading can be done using surveys inside a CMS or using an online tool such as SurveyMonkey.com. Surveys can often be downloaded into an Excel document so that the instructor can see several students' scoring and comments in one spot.

Shortcuts

Use keyboard shortcuts to save time. This will also help prevent physical issues like wrist problems caused by overusing the mouse. Use the Help menu in any program and search for keyboard shortcuts. These will become second nature in no time. Ctrl+C for Copy, Ctrl+V for Paste, Ctrl+Z to Undo the last action, Alt+A to Save As a file when renaming the document after grading (more on this later), and Shift+Tab to move backwards in a form are just a few commonly used keyboard shortcuts.

Use desktop shortcuts, too. For example, if a major assignment is due and the folder has to be opened frequently, make a shortcut on the desktop to save time navigating to the file. On a PC right click on an empty area of the desktop, choose New/Shortcut from the menu. Navigate to the folder and save. This shortcut can be deleted when the need for it has passed.

Proactive Steps to Cut Down on Email Traffic

Instructors can cut back on the number of questions sent by email by proactively informing students about projected turnaround times, virtual office hours, and any expected instructor days off or vacation travel days. In addition, tell students how long they should expect to wait for a response to an email. This should be no more than 24 hours. By stating that students can expect a response within 24 hours, they are much less likely to send a second email six hours after their first communication asking if the instructor received the first email.

The same goes for the expected turnaround time when grading assignments. If students know an assignment will not be graded until the unit or week ends, they are less likely to send a "did you get it" message about their submission. Likewise if students are told in advance that assignments will be graded within three days of the end of the unit or week, they are less likely to ask the instructor about when they will get feedback. It is acceptable and sometimes necessary to tell students that instructors do not remain online 24/7. If students receive timely responses to emails and prompt feedback, most will relax and not contact the instructor unnecessarily.

Proactively arm the students with contact information for other professionals who can better assist them. If they do not have the information for course support, they will contact the instructor about technical issues. When they have the contact information for course support, they are more likely to contact the support people directly without involving the instructor. If there is no syllabus for a course, or the syllabus does not contain all the necessary contact information, the instructor can create a *cheat sheet* for students. The cheat sheet should have phone numbers and email addresses for the library support staff, university or course management technical help desk, and any other professionals to whom the student should turn for help. Place the cheat sheet in a prominent spot in the course site and direct students to this document if they are having difficulty.

Full or Part Time

One factor that relates to billable hours is whether online teaching is full-time work or if it is part-time employment sandwiched into an already busy life. Online teaching can be a terrific part-time job. The work can be done at any time of the day or night and at any location that has an Internet-capable computer. While time of day does not matter, it does matter that a little time be set aside every day during a course to answer questions from students or to respond to postings and assignments. The obligation to be available on a regular basis is an expectation students and employers very rightly hold.

HANDLE IT ONCE

Productivity expert David Allen (2001) suggests that you take one of three routes for any action,

> *Do it, Delegate it, or Defer it.* If an action will take less than two minutes, it should be done at the moment it is defined. If an action will take longer than two minutes, ask yourself, *Am I the right person to do this?* If the answer is no, delegate it. If the action will take longer than two minutes, and you are the right person to do it, defer acting on it until later and track it on a list. (p. 35)

The more things that are dealt with immediately, the fewer tasks there are on the to-do list. These management suggestions are true in all settings including online instruction. There are some specific tasks done by online students where the handle it once rule is particularly apt.

Email

If an email message requires a reply or an action, very likely it fits in the *under two minutes* rule, therefore do it right away. Put emails that need to be kept, but not acted on, in a specific folder before closing them. If the email is pure junk or not needed, delete it; do not keep it just in case. An exception to the *reply right away* rule for emails is when it raises an instructor's hackles. If a message is irritating or downright infuriating, set the message aside in the *to be handled later* folder. Replying immediately to such messages is dangerous. Wise instructors allow a little time for the emotions to subside before writing a reply. The lack of immediacy in replying is outweighed by the need to write a message with a professional tone, free of emotion. More about email in a moment.

Discussions

Reading discussion postings takes a certain amount of time no matter what an instructor does. There are, however, a few efficiencies that can occur in the forums to save time. If a discussion posting needs a reply, respond right away. Also, keep an Excel sheet open or a paper grade sheet handy and make note of important contributions while reading discussion postings. This will speed up grading and commentary when the unit ends. Learn to flag items and make use of sorting features of the CMS as well.

Assignments

As assignments arrive, make notes or fully grade them and save them to a hidden *instructor only* area. Posting grades in the middle of the unit is not recommended. When grades are posted before the unit ends, students often will request a chance to redo the assignment, thereby doubling the work of the instructor. Keep the notes about the assignment handy and transfer the comments to the gradebook after the week or unit ends. There are times when students do need to redo an assignment, but the Type A students will want to continue redoing everything until perfection is achieved even if the point deduction was one-tenth of a point.

If the assignments are documents, make sure students name them using a file-naming protocol. The easiest way is to have them use their last name, perhaps a first initial, and then the title of the assignment. This way the instructor knows exactly whose work has been received and which assignment has been submitted. The instructor needs both name and the assignment title, otherwise files might get overwritten by the computer.

If, for example, a student submits the Week One reflection as WongS .doc and then submits the Week Two reflection as WongS.doc, the computer will allow the new file to overwrite the old file. That means the instructor will have lost the Week One assignment. If the student is required to add the assignment information then WongSReflectionWk1 will not overwrite WongSReflectionWk2. The computer sees these as completely different documents. Further, saving work to folders labeled weekly or unit labeled on the instructor computer can help keep files from getting lost or overwritten.

With last names first the order of the submitted assignments will match the order students are listed in the gradebook. No-name papers are as common in the online realm as they are in traditional classrooms. If the student's last name is part of the file name, it is much easier to identify no-name papers. Of course it also helps to expect papers to be properly headed with name, date, and the like, but the instructor still has to open each document to see the name on the assignment.

Instructors should also add to the filename so that it is immediately clear which items have been graded. For example GarzaMPowerPoint.ppt would become GarzaMPowerPointGRADED.ppt. When the instructor glances at the folder of assignments, it is very obvious which documents have been graded and which still need to be graded. Using the Ctrl+A keyboard shortcut makes this a simple operation.

HANDLING EMAIL MORE EFFICIENTLY

Get a Separate Email Address for Online Teaching Work

Instructors need a separate email address for online teaching. If the institution or entity does not provide an email account, the instructor will have to arrange for their own separate account. Most Internet service providers (ISPs) offer their subscribers more than one email address with an account. Use one of these unused-but-free email addresses from the local ISP. The drawback to an ISP email account, especially if the provider is a small local company, is that it can often only be accessed from the main home computer on which it is set up. Those who have good technical abilities can use **POP3 forwarding** from a laptop used while traveling or access it from **Webmail** portals when away from home.

Instructors who regularly use more than one computer or who travel frequently would benefit from a free web-based email account. These email programs can be accessed from any Internet-capable computer. Some examples are GMail, Hotmail, and Yahoo Mail. One drawback is that these free accounts often receive a lot of spam or unsolicited commercial emails. However, one advantage is that the email domain is more universally recognized. A disadvantage of using these web-based accounts is the domains are often blocked by email filtering systems.

Why Get a Separate Account?

There are several reasons to get a separate email address for online teaching. First, it will be less likely to get overloaded. Many email accounts have storage limitations. If personal and teaching emails are combined into one account, it is easier to reach that overload limit. For example, if Aunt June sends pictures that have not been resized and compressed or if the online students begin sending their projects via email attachment, it is likely that the home email storage limit will be reached. This will cause all further emails to bounce back or be returned to the sender until email storage space is reopened by deleting stored emails. It can be disastrous to have emails bouncing back since the online instructor is not even aware that messages from students have been rejected.

A separate email account also eliminates the possibility other members of the household will open or even delete course emails. Once a message has been opened it usually changes from boldfaced type to regular type. If someone else in the house opened a course email by mistake, it would be very easy to overlook this now *read* message in the Inbox.

Most email programs allow the creation of new folders to hold received mail. Instructors are advised to create email storage folders to hold messages from each course, or even every course module. With separate folders and good email subject lines, it is easy to quickly sort mail and then store it so that it can be readily located for future reference.

Filters

Most email programs also allow for rules or filters that will send certain emails into a folder. Students should be directed to write their subject lines in a specific way. Adding the course number to the subject line, for example, could be a trigger that causes the filter to put the email into the folder for that course. An example for a course named Math 111 might be written, *Subject: 111 Question about text,* or *Subject: Math111 Question about text.* Since it is unlikely that a spam email will have this same information, spam is usually not sorted by the filter into the folder. When an email does have this subject line pattern, it is most likely from a student in the course. This is very handy if the instructor is teaching more than one course at a time. The instructor must remember then to check each folder since new emails will not be delivered to the Inbox.

In addition to the course number or other course-specific information, students should be taught to put their name in the subject line. Student email addresses are often not very informative (hotchick61@ or idiotsdelight@) and some students have not correctly set up their email program to put their name in the *To: field.* In addition many students do not sign their full name to emails. Students should be encouraged to sign emails; however, having them put their name in the subject line acts as a nice backup should they forget to sign their email.

This information can be sent as part of the welcome email prior to the course beginning. An example of what the subject line would look like should be included in that email. *Subject: LastName Math111 Reply to your welcome.* The word *Help* or *Urgent* can be added if the message needs to be answered quickly. Likewise, a student could put *Not Urgent* in a subject line for a message that does not require an immediate response. It helps to include this information on the course pages wherever appropriate.

Type of Course

Time commitment is also dependent on the type of course being taught. As explained previously in the book, the level of instructor interaction with the learner depends on the type of course. And within those models, there is still considerable leeway. For example, a course that is part of a degree program may have multiple papers needing grading during a term, while an isolated professional development course or a course of a shorter duration than the typical quarter or semester will generally have fewer items to grade. In addition, these items may be projects. Projects can be less time consuming to grade. The time saved during grading of the projects may be overshadowed by the time spent downloading them depending on the type of project being evaluated.

Instructors should establish peer feedback activities using rubrics or checklists to provide an opportunity for students to revise and improve assignments before final submission to the dropbox. Peer review and evaluation of all types of assignments may save the instructor some time grading and writing comments. The additional benefit is that peer review can help develop community.

GET ORGANIZED

When working as an online instructor, especially when working from home or while traveling, organization can be an issue. The instructor should have an organized workspace to avoid hunting for things. This workspace should not be shared with coworkers or family members if possible. An alternative to a physical space is to have a briefcase or computer bag that contains all the documents and tools needed to work online. The workspace therefore is mobile and can accompany the instructor to whatever physical space is used for work that day. A mobile workspace is less likely to be disorganized by family members or coworkers.

All documents for a class should be in one folder on the computer—each section should have its own folder—each week or assignment its own folder. This folder should be backed up regularly by copying it to other media like a flash drive. Placing all documents in one spot in an organized system of folders creates efficiency for the instructor.

Also using a folder named *Late Work to be Corrected* can be helpful. This folder is used to hold any late assignments until they are corrected. If late assignments are placed into the regular weekly folder, it is easy to forget to grade them since other assignments in that folder have presumably been graded previously. No matter what late policy an instructor has, there will always be instances of late assignments due to illness, emergency, or other understandable and unforeseen circumstances. Filing these late assignments in a special folder serves as a reminder to get them graded. After grading, the late assignment is moved into the appropriate weekly folder and deleted from the *Late Work to be Corrected* folder.

After a course ends it is a good idea to copy all the files to CD-ROM or other storage media for archival storage. It is rare that files from a previous course need to be retrieved, but it is possible to have a past student challenge his or her final grade. Some institutions require that records be kept for a certain length of time. Either way, it is just a good idea to archive files. Then the files can be deleted from the hard drive or network drive to free up storage space.

The instructor should use a calendar to keep track of course and module or unit start dates, assignment due dates, and so on. Most online instructors are scheduled well in advance, and course start and end dates are easy to forget when the contractual communication about teaching the course occurred months ago. Figure 12.1 shows an Excel sheet with each course color coded and all dates assignments are due.

Create an online course calendar or checklist with due dates and deadlines for the students' benefit. Post it in a central location in the CMS where it's

A	B	C	D	E	F	G	H	I	J
	1	2	3	4	5	6	7	8	9
February 2008	1	2	3	4	5	6	7	8	9
CSUEB	M4	M4	M4	Annc	M5	M5	M5	M5	M5
UW-Cc	M0	M0	M0	M1	M1	M1	M1	M1	M1
UW-729	M2	M2	M2	M2	M3	M3	M3	M3	M3
USD								W1	W1
March		1	2	3	4	5	6	7	8	9
CSUEB	M8	M8	Draft	M9	M9	M9	M9	M9	M9
UW-Cc	M4	M4	M5	M5	M5	M5	M5	M5	M5
UW-729	M5/6	M5/6	M5/6						
USD	W4	W4	W4	W4	W4	W4	W5	W5	W5
UW-729									

Figure 12.1. Screenshot of an Excel spreadsheet used to keep track of dates for multiple courses.

easy for students to check each day. Do not post any dates within the content or modules. This will reduce course maintenance time each semester, as there will be only one place to update due dates. This reduces the chance of having information in two places which do not match.

Record notes each week in a teaching journal identifying thoughts about revisions for the next semester. Some fixes, like broken links, can be done on the fly during the current run, but others, like the rewriting of a section, need to wait until the students are no longer present. At the end of the semester reflect on the notes. Having a current, reflective list will help make the revisions easier, more relevant, and save time. Cross off the revision from the list after it has been completed.

COMMUNICATION TIMES

Efficiency can also be gained by setting up regular communication times. This includes setting at least one time per day for answering email and reading discussion postings. Another type of regular communication is to hold online office hours at certain times each week. This can be done via chat or instant-messaging (IM) software. If students know that the instructor can be contacted in real time one or two times per week, this may cut down on the email load. The advantage of online office hours is that the instructor can be accomplishing other tasks until a student logs into the chat or IM system. Usually the entrance of someone into chat or IM is accompanied by a sound announcing an arrival.

The disadvantage of online office hours is that the instructor needs to be faithful about being online at those times. Remember that any synchronous communications like chat can be a challenge to schedule if participants in the course are geographically diverse.

STAY FOCUSED

When working from home as an independent contractor without a fixed location or fixed set of working hours, it can be very easy to get distracted. Learning to stay focused will help the instructor be more efficient. The first step is to find a quiet place with no distractions. While this sounds simple, it is a key to staying focused on the task at hand. Defining *quiet, nondistracting place* varies from person to person. Some people can tolerate some background noise and movement, others need silence.

Part of staying focused is making sure others can tell the facilitator is working. When working from home this means family members, whether in the home or not, need to understand online facilitation is *work* requiring focus and concentration. Phone calls and conversations need to be dealt with firmly if the facilitator is to remain professional and efficient. When working from an office, this may mean closing a door or putting a sign at the cubicle entrance letting others know that the instructor is not to be disturbed.

Use email efficiently and keep the email program closed when working on other tasks requiring concentration. Email efficiency might mean flagging emails for follow-up that cannot be dealt with immediately. In addition, prioritizing emails improves efficiency. Replying to a future student who wants advice about taking a course may not need to be taken care of as quickly as a current student's question about an assignment. Responding to email regularly is important, but that does not mean reading email while grading assignments. Handle email at specific times each day and do not be tempted to check it at other times. Whatever it is, it can wait, and it is just a distraction from other *less interesting* tasks such as grading or revising course materials.

An important aspect of staying focused is counterintuitive, take quick breaks. Productivity will increase if short breaks are taken regularly. Not only is this good for improving efficiency in thinking, it will help prevent physical issues from developing.

EXPLAIN CLASS POLICIES

Students will more likely follow course policies if they've read them. A precourse agreement or syllabus quiz is ways to make sure that students read important policies. Those course policies need to be stated very clearly to eliminate loopholes students might try to exploit. Having to deal with students who are looking for loopholes is time consuming. Establishing clear policies and ways of being certain that students have read these policies before the course begins, will save time answering emails from the **Loophole Generation**. According to Summerville and Fischetti (2007), these are the students who spend more time trying to find ways around doing assignments than they spend completing the actual assignment. Student access to the Internet is one course policy that needs to be loophole free. Here is suggested language for proactively eliminating the *My-connection-is-down-I-can't-do-my-course-work* loophole:

> Since this course is online and email never closes for bad weather, illness, etc., there is always a way to get the assignment in. Computers are available on campuses as well as public libraries, internet cafes, etc., therefore problems

with home technology will not be accepted as an excuse for late work. Seek out alternate locations you can use to access the course just in case.

Providing the syllabus in a printer-friendly format will eliminate yet another loophole. Students should be told to print the syllabus for offline use. After all, if they cannot access the course site, they cannot access the syllabus stored in the course site. Students may need phone numbers or email addresses for the instructor or information technology to report their access issues. Having a printed copy of the syllabus will ensure they have the contact information they need when technical issues arise.

ORGANIZE THE DISCUSSION FORUMS

Like email, avoid checking for postings to the discussions or submissions to the dropbox several times a day. This is not necessary. Set a schedule such as checking for new discussion postings only once a day. The instructor's presence should be felt on the discussion boards at least every other day, though daily is best. Postings should be read every day, even if the instructor does not post a message. Once the postings are read for the day, complete any grading or course organization tasks and then close the course site.

Train students to write good subject lines for their discussion postings. If students create a subject that conveys the main point of the comment, it will garner more interest from colleagues. Good subject lines require the author to summarize their message, which improves learning. Tell students that writing a good subject line is like writing a book title or an advertising teaser, it needs to convey the main point but be compelling so others want to participate. This practice of good subject lines allows the instructor to quickly see how the discussion is going by scanning all the subject lines even before opening the new postings. In addition it provides students with an advance organizer, which helps in organizing and prioritizing response postings.

If the class size is 16 or more students, consider creating groups of eight students where students can discuss, debate, and interact. This will create less reading for everyone. Some instructors limit students to responding to three other students' original postings per forum topic. This may vary based on the class size. Structure the discussion to a routine such as *post your original no later than Wednesday, and then make your responses no later than Sunday night.*

At the end of each unit or week, reorder the discussion forums so that the current unit or week's forums are at the top of the page. The time it takes to change the order of the forums will be saved by not having to scroll down to locate the correct forum.

ONLINE TOOLS THAT INCREASE EFFICIENCY

Use the Right Tools

Using the right tools and using them efficiently is a key to maximizing bill-able hours. Some of these ideas have been shared previously in the book. They are listed here to maximize efficiency when returning to this book to look for tips after the first reading. When grading use comment features in word processing programs to leave notes throughout complex or lengthy pa-pers. Use Del.icio.us or other social bookmarking sites to keep track of book-marks no matter what computer is being used. When working from multiple computers this eliminates transferring bookmark files.

Use a flash drive or other portable storage to backup the hard drive and remember to back up the flash drive as well too. Lost files equal time spent looking for files, or worse, re-creating documents that cannot be found or were lost to a technology failure. Use a split computer screen, or two browser windows, to see the assignment and a spreadsheet or gradebook at the same time. And by all means, if a graduate assistant or intern is available to help with the mundane tasks of online teaching, use them!

Proactive Course Set-Up

Set up all aspects of the course in advance to open automatically at the appro-priate times. Open the new unit, in a read-only format (no posting allowed) two to three days before it is due to begin. This allows students some flexibil-ity of preparing ahead while keeping them focused on the current materials. If the entire course is open right from the start, students will be working far ahead and posting assignments and discussions before the instructor or col-leagues are ready.

Most CMSs allow a start date to be set so that an announcement, discussion forum, or course materials will be invisible to students until the start date is reached. Setting these start dates is time consuming, yet it will ultimately add to instructor efficiency. All materials will open on time without the instructor having to remember to unhide the next unit. In addition, when students see something new appear they think the instructor has been in the course site to do something. Students should see the instructor in the course site several times per week. Setting start dates helps the instructor's visibility quotient.

This is not an invitation to instructors to be absent from the course at all. If however, the instructor has no need to post anything in the discussion forums and all work is graded, there is no way to appear visible. Automatically open-ing the materials helps with visibility, even if it is illusory. Again, this is not a way for the instructor to avoid being in the course site regularly.

If an instructor has multiple course sections including future course sections on their instructor home page, changes should be made to all course sections at the same time. We both teach for one institution that often has two or more future course shells set up and ready to go well in advance of the course start dates. Once those courses are copied by the institution any changes that must be made have to be made to each section individually by the instructor.

By using multiple windows or browser tabs, the changes are made to every current and future course section at the same time, one after the other, to ensure the change is made everywhere. This is much more efficient than trying to remember to update a link in the November class when it begins if it is currently September. By November, the instructor will likely not remember to fix the link, creating confusion for students who will email the instructor about the bad link. This is one of those tasks that seems counterintuitive. Fixing a link in four different course shells at the same time is tedious work, but doing it to all available course shells will save time and headaches in the future. This also means future course shells copied over by information technology will have the corrected link.

Surveys

One handy tool for gathering background information and facilitating the formation of small groups or troubleshooting group dynamics or technical skills is to gather data through a precourse survey. Some CMSs have a quiz or survey feature the instructor can utilize for this. There are also online survey sites. An alternative to an electronic survey would be to formulate a survey as a word-processed document to be sent and returned via email attachment.

Some good items to include on the survey, besides the basic demographics, would be technical data. Knowing whether a student regularly uses a Macintosh computer or a windows-based PC, for example, can speed up troubleshooting dramatically. Also, having on hand some information about the general processor speed of the student's computer most regularly used for the course and his or her Internet connection speed can be helpful. Sometimes slow computer or connection speeds can cause the student's computer to *time out* or stop downloading if the process is taking too long.

Keep in mind that many people do not know their exact computer processor or connection speed. The survey can be formatted in more general terms depending on the instructor's suppositions about the technical knowledge level of the group. A group of people taking an online C++ programming course would generally be much more knowledgeable about their computer equipment than those taking a course on the basics of word-processing software.

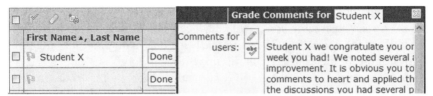

Figure: 12.2. Screenshot of a gradebook item just for weekly comments with a Done message.

Online Gradebook

The instructor should streamline grading as much as possible. Touch-It-Once grading is most efficient. Whenever possible the comments and score should be entered into the gradebook when the project or assignment is first opened. If there are multiple elements in one week to be graded, one way to streamline the commentary is to put all the comments for all of the elements in one comment box. For example, create a separate gradebook item that has no point value for each week or unit. Place all comments in that weekly item. Signal to students that feedback is ready by using a *done* or + score, whatever the grading system allows. Figure 12.2 shows an example of a weekly comment box and the Done grade recorded to get the student's attention.

This eliminates email questions about whether grading is complete or not. The score must still be put in the proper spot in the gradebook, however, not having to enter a comment to go with each score saves one click for every score in the gradebook and waiting for a pop-up window to open for every click. The time and effort to make the click and wait for the pop-up window adds up in the long run.

The Good and the Bad of Always Being in Touch

Online instructors may find that a Blackberry or other **smart phone** allows them to complete many of their online teaching duties on the fly. Checking email on such a device allows the instructor to handle problems quickly while in the waiting room at the doctor's office. What would have been wasted time has been made productive by using an electronic device.

There are some downsides to such tools however. The keypads on smart phones and Blackberries are quite small. It can be aggravating to compose long replies on such a limited keypad. In addition it can be tempting to answer email whenever it arrives, even during social gatherings and family time. Finally having email always arriving can be distracting. One of the tips already shared was not to read email while working on other instructor tasks. When the smart phone is ringing constantly, it can be terribly tempting to look to see who the email is from and read it, thereby distracting the facilitator from the task they were doing. Staying focused is much harder when the smart phone is a distraction. Knowing when to put it on silent helps.

WORK SMARTER, NOT HARDER

Keep comments and news announcements from previous semesters. Organize announcements and news items, welcome letters, regularly used commentary, and such in Word documents or make it a permanent part of the *course-within-a-course* content, and set release dates at the beginning of each semester. Use rubrics to make grading easier and to clarify expectations for the student.

Customize feedback comments for each student or course section; students hate (as well they should) canned comments. However, there is no reason to type out everything again if some comments remain the same from student to student or section to section. Adapt or reuse them the following semester. Spread out the grading. Schedule self-graded or shorter assignments after a long, complex assignment to allow time and energy for grading the longer assignment properly. Carefully set due dates so that a two-day turnaround time for grading assignments is possible. Link the dropbox folders to the gradebook to facilitate faster grading and feedback.

KNOW THYSELF

Each instructor has a time of day when they are most alert. If possible schedule online work for that time of day. Hopefully this coincides with the best time of day to check and respond to email and postings. For example, the household computer should be available to the instructor while they are at their most alert. The instructor should try to complete as much work as possible when they are mentally alert and able to concentrate.

Another factor that determines how long tasks take is the speed at which the instructor reads. The majority of information in an online course is text based. The faster the instructor reads, the more efficiently the work can be completed. The same goes for typing speed. Unless the facilitator is using a voice-activated system for word-processing, such as Dragon Naturally Speaking, the ability to type quickly speeds up the rate at which work can be accomplished.

What may be considered an overload for some instructors is not for others. Before accepting teaching assignments look at the other courses already accepted for that calendar month and consider whether the workload is too heavy. Factor in family obligations and planned vacations when considering personal work capacity. An instructor can work online when vacationing, but no one wants to spend six hours a day on vacation answering postings and emails.

One final area where the instructor must *know thyself* is in the area of temperament. As noted previously, any email that irritates or aggravates the facilitator should not be answered immediately. This is true of all communications including responding to discussion postings, assignments, or reflections. Even if the student phones and wants to vent, it is acceptable to schedule another time to finish the conversation. Being caught off guard by an angry student can lead an instructor to answer back angrily. Ask to return the call later or set aside the email, then wait for a cooler head to ensure a professional response. Likewise when working with frustrating technology problems on the instructor's own equipment.

Obviously, working through technology glitches rationally is the best choice but at times even the calmest person is inflamed by balky equipment, lost Internet connections, or documents that have seemingly disappeared into the ether. Each person must know when to walk away from the computer and cool off before trying to continue with computer-based tasks. Technology problems will occur; this is inevitable. Online instructors should be skilled with technology and armed with strategies for troubleshooting. Troubleshooting is the topic of the next chapter.

13

Troubleshooting

In your courses, despite having the help of information technology professionals in the form of course concierges or a Help Desk, it will be up to you, the instructor, to troubleshoot some of the more common technical problems found in the world of online teaching. Some of these problems may be specific to the course management system (CMS), and others will be software specific, like difficulties with operating system compatibilities. Lastly, you will have user-related problems based upon the technical proficiency level of some of your students. It will be up to you to first determine from where the problem stems, and then offer the quickest solution set.

ISSUES WITH LEARNERS: NEWBIES

Orientation Is a Must

Students who are taking their first online course and who have little-to-no technology skill or confidence are often referred to as newbies. Newbies require a lot of time and patience on the part of the instructor as they often are quite afraid of their computers or the Internet. They are sure they can break one or the other or both.

Orientations were created with newbies in mind. If your institution does not have or require an orientation separate from your course, create a **module zero** and require students to complete it prior to beginning your actual course work. Include basic course survival skills in it such as sending and receiving email, discussion board posting, dropbox usage, and any other quickly teachable and desperately needed skills to help the true newbie make it through the first few weeks of your course.

Encourage Community

Create a frequently asked questions (FAQs) thread and a question-and-answer (Q&A) thread in your *Support* forum. Provide answers to commonly asked questions and encourage newbies to read through the FAQ before posting questions. When they do have a question, encourage them to post to the Q&A rather than email you—that way other class members can jump in to help new students through the learning curve.

Positive and Encouraging

Newbies are the population most likely to quit or drop a course. Their frustration level is high—not only with the technology, but in the case of adult learners, with the fear of looking foolish. Instructors need to constantly be positive and reassuring to this group in particular. While statistics vary widely and questions abound about the validity of the research when trying to assess an overall dropout rate of online learners in comparison to their face-to-face counterparts, it is generally accepted that those students who are first time online learners struggle the most, and thereby are at the most risk (Tyler-Smith, 2006).

Low Technological Skills

Sometimes students enroll in courses with the necessary academic prerequisites but lacking the technological skills to complete certain project requirements because the assignments are completed in a virtual environment. While the student may have basic word processing skills, they may never have been exposed to web conferencing software or made a screenshot before.

For these students, and for all technologically based assignments, instructors should provide alternate step-by-step instructions on how to use the technology. These instructions need to be independent of the instructions for the assignment itself. If the technology is very complicated, a practice session should also be provided. Providing visuals for students including screenshots with bright arrows and labels pointing to areas they should focus upon is extremely helpful. This was shown in Figure 11.1.

Finally, as an instructor, take advantage of all resources available to you to help your students. One of the most simple and often overlooked resources is the telephone. Oftentimes instructors can walk a student through a problem resolution in a real time conversation that might otherwise take hours of frustration by sending emails back and forth. You should also not be afraid to refer students to the Help Desk or course concierge for issues beyond your technical ability or when you've exhausted your own explanations and examples.

Assisting Students with Navigation

Many students who are first time online learners have a hard time figuring out the navigation of course sites. For the first few units of a course, it is helpful to offer explicit navigation directions to the learner (i.e., *click here* to go to the readings) along with the traditional links in the navigation bars. It is better to offer too much direction and instruction rather than not enough until students get comfortable with the course. The scaffolding can be slowly taken away as the comfort level increases.

STUDENTS WITH SPECIAL NEEDS

When a student with a disability makes his or her disability known to the instructor, Section 508 of the Americans with Disabilities Act (ADA) comes into play. Institutions and instructors are legally bound to make the course and its materials accessible to the student. ADA compliance officers and disability support services personnel can help you provide the student with software or hardware capable of handling the CMS. Good course design principles like alternate text for images, transcripts for audio or video files, and the use of headings will also make ADA compliance easier and more effective.

It is important to remember that not all compliance issues come in the form of meeting the needs of the visual or hearing impaired. Students with physical limitations of the arms or hands may also need accommodations to help with the level of typing required in online courses. These students often require voice recognition software such as Dragon Naturally Speaking. Again, support services will be the best department to turn to for help for the student.

UNDERQUALIFIED STUDENTS

Just as in a campus-based course, occasionally students who are underqualified for an online course do register and get in. However, due to the public participatory nature of online learning, this student's lack of knowledge will become glaringly apparent not only to you as the instructor, but also to all of the other students in the course who read all of this underperforming student's posts and shared assignments. If the course does not have a prerequisite, the student does have a legal right to attempt to take the course, but his or her performance can inhibit community and certainly his or her own frustration level will surely rise if the class is too far beyond his or her academic ability. So what should the instructor do?

This is where the advising hat from Chapter 4 needs to comes out—very quickly—while students still have an opportunity to make changes to their schedules, if need be. An instructor should also reach out to a department chair or program coordinator by private email to make sure the student wasn't accidentally placed in the wrong level of course work. Encourage the student to speak with his or her own academic advisor. Discuss the issues you see—suggest the student first take a skill building course that may be a precursor to your own course, so they might have a better chance at real success. Ultimately, in higher education, it is the student's decision whether to stay in the course or not, but they need to have all the information prior to making the choice.

Poorly Advised

As online instructors we are at times surprised when we hear students say things like, "My advisor told me to take the class online even though I said I didn't have a computer at home. He said I could just work from the campus each day," or "I said I hate computers and my advisor said this was the only class that fits my schedule." Since one of the biggest predictors of success in an online class is the right mindset and comfort level with the technology, advising students who are *antitechnology* or lacking in basic computer technology skills to take courses online is setting them up for frustration and failure.

Again, the instructor may have to don the advisor hat and, if they sense a real hate-hate relationship with the technology or a student with extraordinarily low skills, the instructor needs to make the decision whether they have the space within the curriculum and time within the quarter or semester to remediate the skills and attitude surrounding the technology. If not, they should encourage the student to find a campus-based alternative that might better serve the student's needs. It is fair to say that while online learning does suit many individuals and many courses, it does not suit *every individual* and every course.

ROUND PEGS IN SQUARE HOLES

There are some students for whom online learning and social constructivist theories are just not a good fit. These students may be more successful learners and find more satisfaction in their learning if they take campus-based classes that align with their own particular learning style or work ethic rather than pursuing their education virtually.

INDEPENDENTS

Best practices have moved toward collaboration, discussion, and Web 2.0. For the independent student who just wants to read assignments, turn in homework by email, and take online quizzes—the choices have become limited. Social learning theory and the drive for better quality instruction as well as more assessment and accountability for both instructors and students and are beginning to overwrite the tutorial, low-to-no interaction electronic version of correspondence courses of the early days of online distance learning. The student yearning for this type of class will surely be frustrated by the types of interaction and collaboration with the instructor and fellow learners required in modern, well-written courses.

UNMOTIVATED STUDENTS

Unmotivated students are attracted to online learning like the proverbial moth to the flame. But like the moth, this is generally a onetime action that is self-curing. Unmotivated students want an easy class and they make an assumption that because a class is on the Internet, it must be easy—after all, the Internet is where MySpace and YouTube live. These same students are often shocked when they discover another interesting phenomena—online classes are often more difficult than their campus-based counterparts and often require more, not less work. This is one of the explanations for student drop out rates in the first weeks of online classes. It has more to do with unrealistic expectations rather than student or instructor ability.

OVERLOADED STUDENTS

On the opposite end of the spectrum of the unmotivated student is the student who will attempt to take on too much. This is the student who perhaps is already registered for a full load of campus-based classes and figures he or she can fit an online course in as well because it does not require seat time. This student often does not realize this the same thing the unmotivated student didn't realize—the workload for a well-designed online course is at least equal to if not slightly more than the average face-to-face class. Furthermore, even though the student may not be spending time sitting in a desk on campus, the student will need to spend time sitting at a computer. This Type A student is often very grade oriented and gets very upset when his or her grades reflect his or her inability to participate to the level the course demands.

The instructor, as pseudo-advisor, must detect very early on in the course if this overloaded student will be able to meet the challenges of a heavy schedule and the online learning environment. They must honestly present the potential pitfalls of such a schedule to the student so the student is making an informed choice of remaining in the course. This will also limit or eliminate student requests for incompletes at the end of the term. These students made an informed choice to continue at their own peril. Here is an example of this type of message:

> Tony, I'll be honest with you. This is a very intense class and you are now 10 days behind. You have missed the chance for a lot of brainstorming on a possible research topic with me and your colleagues and now need to dive right into finding literature on the topic. This is one course that requires a full commitment from the student if they are to be successful. You have to hit the ground running right now and remain running at full speed for the rest of the course if you are to be successful.
>
> I know I am being blunt with you here, but I feel I have to be if you are going to complete this class with any chance at a passing grade. My experience is this is one class where students cannot afford to get behind because they just never catch up. I will hope this is not the case, and that you will be the exception to the rule.

In higher education, continuing on in a class where a student is overloaded remains the student's choice. For younger students, it would be highly advisable to suggest to both the student and his or her parents that the student not take an online course as an overload. Statistically, success is not their favor.

ISSUES WITH THE COURSE MANAGEMENT SYSTEM OR CONTENT: ACCESS ISSUES

Temporary Access Issues

Upon occasion students will be temporarily unable to access the course site. Sometimes this will be the fault of the institution—a server going down, for instance—and sometimes it will be the fault of the student with a home network crash or virus problem. These glitches happen and usually last no more than a 24-hour period. It can, however, be frustrating for either side when it does happen. The instructor may be waiting for students to turn in assignments or the students may be trying to submit assignments on a deadline—either way, the drawbridge is open and no traffic can move.

The key here for instructors is to remain calm and flexible. Certainly, if the problem is on the institution's end, the instructor needs to extend any due dates by the amount of time the course was inaccessible—especially if the problem happened right at the deadline when an assignment or project was due.

Students should be advised to consider alternate ways to log into the course *before* they have an access issue. An example of a loophole-free syllabus statement about course access was shared previously. The wonderful thing about online learning is that it is accessible any place there is Internet access, so if a student loses a home computer to a virus, he or she is still able to log on to the CMS from a public library, Internet café, local community college, or even a friend's house.

If the problem was with a particular student's home system—the instructor should remind students to consider their alternate Internet plans so the student can still meet course requirements and not fall behind. By storing their work in the CMSs student locker, learners should always have access to all their work—regardless from which computer they access the course.

Major Issues with Access

Major issues with access do not occur very often, but when they do, they can be highly impacting to a course that only lasts six to eight weeks to begin with. Major access issues might include weather situations like winter storm power outages lasting up to a week, damage from hurricanes or tornadoes leading to several weeks of inaccessibility, student soldiers going on extended week-long missions where they are not able to access the Internet, or unexpected illness or injuries, like heart attacks and car accidents. Like temporary access issues, major issues can affect either the student or the institution or both.

Health

For students experiencing life-threatening health issues, the answer is easy— these students need to prioritize their health and seek a medical withdrawal from the course just as they would in a campus-based course. Once they are back in good health, they can pursue their educational goals again.

Military

Student soldiers, especially deployed student soldiers are in a unique situation. They specifically take online courses to continue with their education while serving their country under extreme circumstances. Instructors need to find a way to educate these men and women while working around the issues of short-term absences. One suggestion is to encourage the soldiers to work ahead in the module when they know about an impending mission. Another suggestion would be to allow the soldier to complete the discussion portions ahead of time and turn in the remaining work when he or she once again returns to an area with Internet access. Either way, it is important to be flexible in meeting the needs of our military students and not to penalize their military-related course absences.

Weather

When major weather is the culprit, only some students (or the instructor) may be affected. As a global classroom, it is important to remember others in the course may be completely unaffected and wondering why the instructor or half the class simply disappeared. Communication before the event is very important in this instance:

> Hurricane Alert: As some of you may be aware, Hurricane Isabel is heading my way. I've looked through our class roster and it looks like I am the only one who may be affected—lucky me! I've put some contingency plans in place for alternate access to the course site in case my home and the surrounding area loses Internet access and electricity, but if you do not hear from your intrepid instructor for a couple of days, do not panic! It may take a couple of days for us to clear all the downed trees to get out of our neighborhood—at least that's what happened last time!
>
> Anyway, I've released Module 3 early, and our course concierge is aware of the situation. Should you have any questions or problems, you can contact the concierge if you cannot get a hold of me. I will post a news announcement to let you all know I am well and online as soon as I possibly can!

In the event of a lengthy power outage or Internet disruption affecting quite a few of your students or perhaps the institution, again you should certainly be flexible with due dates or consider eliminating an assignment or two to take the pressure off students when they return to the course site. This needs to be handled on a case-by-case basis.

Course Pages Not Showing as Intended

Instructors who design their own courses have the extra responsibility of making sure their course pages appear to students in the same way they do to the instructor. Depending on the CMS, instructors may be adding information using a what you see is what you get (WYSIWYG) type interface, or they may be required to design more advanced html-based pages using web page development software. No matter the way the pages get written, instructors should always take the time to view the pages from the student view. This may require impersonating a student or simply leaving the course author mode of the CMS.

When viewing your course site from the student view, you should look for some of the following potential problem areas:

- Does the layout of the page still work regardless of the browser text size settings? If students are visually impaired, they often set their text size to the largest setting available. Instructors should adjust their own browser settings both up and down to see the effect on the course web pages and edit accordingly.
- Are red Xs holding the place of missing images? Browser options may be set to not load images (which makes for faster browsing). A second reason for the red X place holder is when images are not stored locally but just referenced by a link in html. If the link becomes broken, the image will no longer show and will instead be replaced by a red X placeholder.
- Are student views missing information you know is available on the page? When browser histories are set to remember what has been viewed on web pages for many days, the page information is stored in a memory cache. The next time the student returns to the page, the browser loads what had been there, not the current configuration. To remedy this, students should set their browser to check for changes every time. This does make for slightly slower browsing, but if the instructor makes a change or updates a page, it is vital the students' browsers show them the changes and not old data.

Login Procedures

Students who are new to online learning often have trouble logging into the course site and course email systems. One proactive way to deal with this issue is to suggest in the precourse email that students printout or write down their login and password in case they forget it. In addition, students should store course support information like the Help Desk phone number and URL offline in case they cannot get logged into the course site to retrieve the needed contact information for help.

Broken Links

Broken or dead links, also called **link rot**, are a frustration for both students and online instructors alike. Broken links occur when the link is created, but the URL is typed in incorrectly. Dead links occur when the host of the page moves or removes the page to which the link is referring. In either case, students who click on the link will find themselves sent to the generic *Page Not Available* or *Page Not Found* message. This can lead to a flurry of emails to the instructor requesting the link be repaired, requesting the information from the missing page, or just venting over the broken or dead link.

As is the case in troubleshooting, for most problems in an online course, instructors can eliminate many of these emails by proactively scanning their course sites for inaccurate links. There are software programs, both free and for purchase, which are written specifically for this task. The instructor simply enters the URL for the overall course site and the software goes to work verifying the integrity of the links including referenced images, audio files, and even links embedded in attached documents. A quick Internet search for link checkers will bring up the most current titles available.

Once the broken or dead links are discovered, it is up to the instructor to quickly edit the course pages so that students can access the material. If the web page has moved, the instructor needs to search for the new location and replace the dead link with the new accurate hyperlink. If the URL was entered incorrectly, the instructor needs to make the correction. Some common mistakes when typing URLs include:

- Putting the period that ends the sentence in with the URL address so that http://www.Internet.com becomes http://www.Internet.com. with a period following it.
- Forgetting to put the .htm or .html extension at the end of the URL.
- Having a blank space somewhere within the URL.
- Forgetting to add the / mark at the end of the URL.

NO TEXTBOOK THE FIRST WEEK-PLUS

Students, especially those new to online learning, are often confused as to where they get their books. For some institutions, students still buy them through the school's bookstore. For others, it is up to the student to locate the required book information and purchase through a third-party bookseller like Barnes and Noble or Amazon.com. For the new student, even finding out whether they are responsible for finding out about the book procedure can be a daunting experience. There are several things the course designer and facilitator can do to help alleviate this stressful problem for the student and lower the number of students showing up in online courses the first week without a textbook.

First, place the required textbook information outside the CMS. Put the title and the ISBN number on the same web page as the technical requirements for taking the course. This way, any student registering for the course will know the book they need before the course ever begins.

Second, send the book title, ISBN number, and directions for obtaining the book in the precourse email. The institution may notify students of this, but students who are new to online learning often miss the first telling of pertinent information, so the redundancy certainly would not hurt. If a student is responsible for ordering the book from an online bookseller, be sure to send this email out with enough time for the student to get the book back from the company. Also, remember students may live far from a campus bookstore, so even if students are to order directly from the institution's bookstore, allow time for delivery to faraway places.

Finally, as you design your course, do not put textbook-dependent, high-point-value assignments in the first week of the course. Instead, create activities that rely on web resources, discussions, or PDF files included in the CMS. That way, if students are still waiting on books to arrive (or if there is a delay in shipment from the publisher), they will not fall behind.

TECHNICAL ISSUES: COMPATIBILITY

Operating Systems

Operating systems are the software programs that make everything on the computer run smoothly. They also help the computer interface with all the peripherals like printers, modems, and disk drives. More commonly known operating system platforms are Windows XP and Vista and Mac OSX.

Online instructors often provide screenshots and directions based on these common platforms to help students through assignment directions. When one of the computer software manufacturers does a major upgrade to its operating system, chaos may often be the result for online educators. Suddenly and literally overnight, directions may become obsolete for any students with the upgraded version. Furthermore, new releases of systems are known for their bugginess, so early adopters may experience other minor tweaks and glitches until new service packs are released.

When Microsoft Windows released its Vista platform, a major upgrade over its XP version, online instructors struggled to overcome a myriad of problems resulting from how different the two versions operated. This was further exacerbated by the roll out of Office 2007—a substantial version upgrade over the previous versions of Office. Directions had to be updated, glitches around some issues resolved or work-arounds figured out, and in some cases, the upgrade was so extensive students found their peripherals wouldn't work with their new system. It was certainly chaos for several months in the online world and continues today as the slower moving K–12 system works to *afford* the cost to catch up to the new upgrades.

Instructors need to prepare for these kinds of problems by making their course sites as universally compatible as possible and by requiring students to submit work in compatible formats as well. Furthermore, when a new roll out does happen, instructors should get access to the new version as soon as possible to begin learning and troubleshooting potential problems. Even though your institution may not yet support a particular software platform in its courses, you will still have students working on new laptops who need your help to be successful. Often the software manufacturer's website is a great source of information.

Browsers

The web browser is the software window to the Internet. All browsers will let a student see the web pages on the Internet, but not all web pages work the same way with all browsers. Instructors often have a preferred browser, but unfortunately, its newest version is not always compatible with all the institutions' CMS platforms. Instructors need to be conversant in more than one web browser.

It is a good idea for instructors to be familiar with most major web browsers and to look at their CMS through each one. This way, you will know if certain functions are problematic with certain browsers and can give a warning to students using that particular browser software.

Here is an example of one such warning:

Windows Vista Discussion Board Problems
    If you have a new computer running Windows Vista and are having discussion board problems, read on.
    There are some compatibility issues with this version of Blackboard for students using Windows Vista operating system and Internet Explorer 7 as their web browser. If that is the case, you may not see the toolbar for text formatting (e.g., highlighter, color changing, centering, bold, italics, underline, etc.) or the tools may not behave appropriately.
    The first thing to do is to turn off the tool box editor. Click on "Course Tools." Then "Personal Information," then "Set Visual Textbox Editor Options." Click the "Unavailable" button and "submit." Now you will be able to enter information on the discussion board, but you will not have the fancy editing tools. Please send me an email if you are one of these few individuals, so I will know not to expect text formatting in your posts or replies.

Document Format

Sharing documents may also have its share of compatibility issues. This may happen due to students sharing documents across platforms (such as Mac to PC), or it may happen when a software company does a major upgrade to a version of its software—new versions will sometimes be incompatible with machines running the older version software and the document may not open, or the formatting may be distorted or changed in some way.

Requiring students to save documents in universally compatible formats solves this problem. No matter the operating system or, in general, the application, most programs have an option to save the document in formats that can be read by other software and platforms. Some of the more common compatible formats today are rtf, PDF, and html.

Simple Solutions: Mac and PC

Currently the two most common operating system platforms are Windows-based PCs (PCs) and Apple's Macintosh computers (Macs). The most common problem occurring between the two operating systems is the way the computer indicates the software used to create a document. Macs do not add a file extension (a period plus a three or four letter indicator) to the file name to alert the computer to the software program used to create the file. Macintosh computers automatically encode this information into the file. On the other hand, Windows-based PCs need the three-letter file extension in order to know which program to use when opening the file. The extension is being added, whether the user sees it in the filename or not. Due to a file options setting, the extensions are often hidden.

Here is an example of how the same file name would appear to a computer user, depending on the type of computer on which the file was saved:

- Civil War lesson plan file created in MS Word on a Macintosh: Civil-WarLP
- Civil War lesson plan file created in MS Word on a Windows-based PC: CivilWarLP.doc

If a PC user shares a file with a Mac user, there are usually no problems as long as both computers have the same software program in their own operating system. Problems generally occur when a Mac user shares a file with a PC user. The Mac user must remember to add the file extension to the file name when saving the file in order for the PC user to be able to open it. As previously stated, a way to avoid this incompatibility is to require students to use file formats that are cross-platform compatible such as html, rtf, or PDF.

File-sharing problems can also occur even when all students are using the same computer platform. It is important to remember that all parties who want to view a file need to have the same software program, and sometimes the same *version* of the software program, to be able to open a file. It is helpful to state the software requirements, just like stating hardware requirements, before the course begins. The alternative is to make sure that all files are saved in a cross-platform, cross-application format. For example, files created in MS Publisher on a PC, will not be able to be opened by other PC users—unless they have MS Publisher. However, if the file is saved as an html file, anyone on any computer with a web browser could view the document.

Computer Lacks an Update

Multimedia programs and presentation programs are often the culprits when it comes to difficulties with updates and online courses. When video or audio technology makes a major advance, for example, it can take months for the updates to trickle down through all the users. Until then students get frustrated when they cannot play a file being streamed in your course. One solution is to provide a link to download recent updates alongside the media file. Another solution is to provide a link to the newest media player itself—so students can install and run the file, even if they lack the resident application. Anticipating the problem and being proactive with a solution will save a busy instructor much time in online teaching!

COMPRESSION ISSUES WITH IMAGES

RTF and Images

Whenever students are sharing word-processed documents across platforms, they need to be encouraged to share in formats that are universally compatible. Rtf, or rich text format, is one such format as it can be read by Mac, Linux, UNIX, and PC machines while keeping document formatting intact. The problem comes when students use rtf for documents with images in them. The resulting encoding makes for extraordinarily large files that might otherwise be quite small if other formats were chosen. To resolve this problem, require assignments with multiple images to be formatted as a PDF file. Students without the software to create PDFs can use some of the Web 2.0 tools available like Open Office to convert their files for free before uploading them to your class.

SCREENSHOTS

One of the quickest ways to resolve technical issues is through the use of screenshots. We use them to both illustrate examples for students and also have students use them to show us what they are having difficulties with when they lack the technical vocabulary to explain it. The simple key stroke combination saves hours of frustrated email or telephone phone call exchanges trying to describe the problems. The old cliché is true—a picture is worth a thousand words.

Desktop PC Screenshot—How To

Reduce the active window until it displays only the items you want included in the screenshot—this will save time cropping later. Press the CTRL+Alt+PrtSc (Print Screen) keys all at the same time. This captures the image in the active window. Open a new document and choose the paste option from the menu. The image should now be on your document. You can now draw arrows, label with text boxes, and otherwise indicate what a student needs to know about the image.

Laptop PC Screenshot—How To

Follow the same directions as you would for the desktop above except you will need to press four keys at the same time instead of three. Laptops usually require the user to press the Fn (function) key to active the Print Screen feature, so the screenshot key strokes are: CTRL+Alt+Fn+PrtSc (Print Screen). Remember to reduce the window to display just what you want in the image first, and then press all four keys at the same time.

Mac Screenshot—How To

The Mac has a useful utility called Grab that can be found in the Applications>Utilities folder. In this program, the version of the keystroke to capture a window is Shift+Command+W. Once you save the image, it will be in the tiff format that creates very large files. Instructors should convert this image using an image editor to a more universally accepted format of jpg or gif and compress to a web acceptable dots per inch (dpi) before sharing the image with others or inserting it onto web pages.

COMMUNICATION ISSUES

Email

The primary source of instructor—learner communication outside of the discussion board is email. Whether you are writing to one student or the whole class, this communication tool is often the best way to get information out to students quickly and efficiently. When there is a breakdown with the delivery system, it can be a frustrating tool to troubleshoot. Given here are some of the more common problems and their solutions.

Cannot See or Find Instructor Emails

When a student writes to an instructor stating he or she isn't receiving instructor emails, the first instinct is for the instructor to hit reply and explain the problem. This would not work, however, since the student would not receive that reply either! In this case the instructor will need to post a general news announcement and one to the Q&A forum stating that some students are having difficulties receiving instructor emails and then layout the troubleshooting solutions.

Potential problems and their solutions include:

- The instructor emails are being filtered to the student's spam or junk mail folder—students need to open their junk mail folders and approve the instructor or approve emails sent from the xyz.edu or xyz.biz domain.
- The student's email may be entered into the institution's email system incorrectly—students should check their profile and verify spelling of their name and email account information.
- The instructor's emails are not reaching the student due to a full "inbox" as some business or public school accounts have small storage limits. When the account limit is reached, all further incoming mail is bounced back to the sender. Students should be instructed to regularly delete messages from their *sent messages*, *trash*, and *inbox* to avoid reaching their account limits.

Student Not Reading Email

Sometimes it becomes quite evident a student is not reading their email. They fail to respond to feedback, follow directions, or reply to important questions from you or their fellow students. When this happens it can be quite frustrating.

The first trick in troubleshooting this problem is to be proactive about student email and teach students they will need to check and respond to their email frequently. As stated in Chapter 11, send out a precourse email asking students to reply to you. This is an efficient way to verify you have the correct email address, students can send and receive emails to and from you, and you can include in the message the need to check email frequently.

Some students who are not regular users of email may still forget to check their email. One way to get their attention is to post your request in their gradebook feedback. Here is an example:

> Sarah, Your web page design is missing an important element. I sent the directions for how to add this screenshot to you by email two weeks ago. Please check your email and reply to me by email. Remember, students in this class must check email at least four times per week as it is one of the primary ways we communicate information and feedback. If you need help in checking your email, please contact me or the IT Help Desk by telephone ASAP and we will walk you through it step by step.

Instructor Not Receiving Student Emails

Another frequent problem is students forget the institution assigns them an institution-based email account. These accounts are assigned partly for convenience and partly for security's sake. Instructors sending private messages to email accounts assigned to students at the time of registration are using good privacy practices. When instructors send emails out to haveagoodtime@ hotmail.com, they could be sending private information to anybody and this could potentially break student privacy laws. The business or institution has no guarantee that *haveagoodtime@hotmail.com* is the registered student. (See **Family Educational Right to Privacy Act** [FERPA].)

Students who use their free web-based email accounts sometimes are reluctant to use the school-based accounts. They do not see the point, so they do not login. The solution is to frequently remind students that all course communications will only take place through the school-based accounts and to only accept communications from students through those accounts as well. Furthermore, you can explain to your students that instructor spam or junk filters will often filter out web-based email accounts whereas school-based emails will always get through. An example of an announcement of what students might see when they first login to a CMS before Module One has begun follows:

> Click the Assignments button (on the left side of the screen) to find the first set of directions for how to put your profile in the system, including your com-

munity college email address. The Consortium of Community Colleges and this school requires you use this email address for online courses to protect your privacy and to assure that any messages sent to your email address actually get to you. Also, due to our excellent spam filter, we will no longer accept private email addresses as they are often blocked by the filter. School email addresses always get through!

Do not panic if you do not know your school address. The college assigns everyone an email address when they first register. You can find the directions for locating your email address here. Write the address down, then return to this page, and use it to complete your profile. (To get back here, click the "back" button on your web browser—very top, upper left hand side of the screen.)

THE TELEPHONE: PROS AND CONS

Pros

In the independent world of online learning, a student knowing that he or she can pick up the telephone and actually speak to a real live instructor on the other end is often the difference between that student dropping a course and sticking it out. The importance of the human connection can never be overstated.

With new webconferencing tools such as Elluminate, instructors cannot only talk with their students, they can also share files, draw out complicated math concepts, view each other on web cameras, and connect almost as much as if they were physically in the same room. This can be particularly helpful when a student is struggling with a concept and needing a one-to-one instructional session.

Furthermore, certain populations or age groups may be much more inclined to open up and share issues over the telephone than they might otherwise share in email. Those who are not early adopters of technology, for instance, may be much more comfortable discussing a problem by telephone.

With that being said, there are parameters for dealing with students by telephone an online instructor needs to consider, much in the same way an instructor would have to consider the same issues when dealing with students in a face-to-face setting.

Cons

When an instructor and student talk on the telephone, unlike with email, there is no written record of the conversation. While this may not cause a problem if the student simply needed some extra help with course content, it could cause a problem if the issue was regarding an academic dishonesty issue like plagiarism or a personality conflict with another student or even the instructor. In these cases, documentation is invaluable—so an instructor must, at the very least, follow up with a clearly written email restating the topics discussed, positions taken by both the instructor and the student, and any decisions made during the phone call. The email should be devoid of emotion and read like a summary transcript. The student should receive a copy as should the program supervisor.

Sometimes students will call you angry or upset over a grade or a posting in the class. If the student calls during your virtual office hours, and you are prepared to handle it, your job is to let them get it out of their system first. (This does not mean you have to accept abusive language.) Angry or upset students usually just need to vent a little and feel they've been heard—so listen to them without interruption. Take notes. Then, when the student is finished, verify you understand the problem by using a "Just so I'm clear, what I hear you saying is . . ." kind of statement. Allow any clarifications to take place. At this point the student is almost always calm and talking. Now you can work toward resolving the issue together.

If you are not prepared to deal with an unsolicited student phone call—perhaps it is not during your virtual office hours, you're lacking the information you need to answer the questions they have, or you may have company at your house—it is certainly appropriate to reschedule the telephone call to an appointment time when you are more prepared to deal appropriately and professionally with the student. Moreover, if the student is belligerent, giving him or her a little time to cool down (and giving you time to notify your supervisor of a potential problem) certainly would not hurt. However, be sure to make the appointment in the near future—a long delay will only exacerbate a problem.

There are students for whom the telephone is just an extension of their personality. These students will call for almost any reason at any time day or night. This may be truer for students in the millennial generation, who have grown up having a cell phone within arm's reach, than any other. These students may become problematic to an instructor who has given out a private home or cell number as their work phone. The student may need to be admonished to only call during office hours and use email for contact at all other times. Certainly it is within the instructor's rights to screen calls if a student abuses the use of telephone contact.

Technical Considerations

As you work with students, there may be times you do wish to contact them by telephone on more controversial issues. These are times where conference calls can come in handy because you can invite your supervisor in as a third party to help mediate the situation. It also provides you with an added layer of protection as the third party can act as a witness to what was said during the conversation. Conference calls can be done through three-way call or simply by using a speaker phone if two of the three parties are located in the same city.

One note of caution when using a speaker phone: many individuals in all walks of employment, not just online education, have been embarrassed or worse by statements made at the end of a call placed over a speaker phone. Users thought the phone was hung up, but instead it was merely taken off speaker mode and the party on the other end of the line heard the postcall analysis. When using a speaker phone, callers should hang up twice and wait until they can hear a dial tone. They should then ask "Are you still there?" or some other phrase just to be doubly sure the caller on the other end of the line has also hung up prior to launching into any discussion.

INSTITUTION-ASSIGNED VOICE MAIL

Some institutions who regularly employ many distance educators will assign a virtual office phone number to the instructor. This is certainly a question to ask about at the time of employment. New hires need to make sure they know how to access, program, and retrieve their voice mails. Even more vital is to find out how you will be notified that you even have a voice mail message waiting for you in the system. Some systems will send an email notification, others an instant message or cell phone message.

KEEP RESOURCES HANDY

At the end of the day, one of the best ways the online instructor can help him- or herself is to have a toolbox of reliable tricks, tools, and people at the ready to help with a problem at a moment's notice.

One such tool is social bookmarking websites like the Web 2.0 site Del .icio.us. The reason social bookmarking is such a handy tool is that an instructor can collect all his or her favorite troubleshooting websites together and have them available no matter what computer he or she logs in from. The instructor simply has to login to the Del.icio.us website to retrieve the needed websites.

Another way of keeping resources handy if an instructor works from several different worksites is to make good use of **remote access**. With remote access an instructor can, again, access files, email accounts, and other servers from home or other nonwork locations. Remote access is built into most operating platforms or can be added through third-party vendors.

Some instructors have chosen to untether from computers altogether and yet still keep an eye on their courses while going about their day. These instructors have taken to smart-phone technology like Blackberry to send and receive institutional email and check mobile websites. These instructors are able to respond to urgent student emails without students having to wait until the instructor has logged into a computer to know that the student has even written for help. Nonurgent emails can wait until virtual office hours for replies.

Perhaps the first rule of troubleshooting (and the last word on it) is to remind online instructors to remember they are not islands unto themselves. You have supervisors and program directors whose jobs are to help you with problematic students, program issues, and even with technical difficulties. When the going gets particularly rough, instructors need to be on the phone or email to their supervisor, even if it just means cc'ing them to keep them aware of a situation brewing. In the same way an instructor likes to be notified when a student is struggling—early enough to intervene and problem solve—so do program directors appreciate the heads up and chance to squelch potential firestorms before they ever start.

If troubleshooting the various issues listed does not frighten you away, you are more than likely one of the personality types this industry is crying out for. The next chapter looks at how the online instructor with your kind of potential goes about securing employment and keeping it.

14

Employment in Online Teaching

You've read the whole book, including all the troubleshooting you may need to do when teaching online, and you still want to be an online instructor? OK. How do you show you are qualified for such a job, and where do you find one? Once the job has been obtained, what are the issues that could cause the loss of an online teaching position? Obviously the answers vary depending on the field, the type of institution, and the qualifications necessary for the job. That said, there are some things you should know.

The growth in the distance education field makes it hard to predict what employers will expect in new employees in the years to come. Currently there is a need for the following characteristics: online communication and technology skills, subject matter expertise, training or experience in online teaching and learning. These qualities plus a combination of luck and good networking skills will help new online instructors get the job they are seeking. Once online instructors are on the job, they need to know how to keep their position in good standing.

The early part of this chapter is meant for those people who are actively seeking employment by an institution or company. This will also be helpful for those who are employed in traditional education and are being asked to move their courses online. There are the skills and tools that should be in the online instructor's employment arsenal.

FINDING AN ONLINE TEACHING JOB

What to Do Prior to Searching for a Teaching Position

According to Joan Vandervelde (personal communication, 2008) online professional development coordinator at University of Wisconsin–Stout, one of the first qualifications for getting hired is having an ePortfolio containing artifacts which showcase technical skills. Online education is becoming more and more technical and the technologically savvy candidate will have the edge. Having a website portfolio is just the first step. The site should have audio commentary recorded by the prospective employee as well as other types of media such as podcasts, Flash animations, and such. The assumption for the future is that instructors will be providing feedback and communicating with students using multimedia. Therefore having media that can be used to show prospective employers these skill sets will be important.

Preparing a good cover letter and resume is key, just as it is in face-to-face hiring situations. Sending an informal email saying "Hey, your program looks great, I would be interested in working with you. Signed, Just Checking" is not advised. While this may work in flagging someone's attention, there is a high probability of being seen as less than professional. However, sending a *feeler* message without there being a job opening is acceptable if it is a more formal letter spelling out your qualifications that would benefit the program.

Online programs are often developing new classes far in advance of needing instructors. Many institutions keep a list of possible future hires who can be interviewed when the need arises. Therefore a formal email message sent to the specific person in charge of the program may be a great idea. This message should include a link to your website but no attachments. Unsolicited attachments are the clear sign of being an amateur.

Wait until attachments, such as a resume, have been requested. Many firewalls will prevent emails with attachments from being delivered, especially if the sender is unknown. And even if the message makes it through the firewall, savvy online professionals hesitate to open emails with attachments from unknown senders. In fact, even with known senders, savvy computer users will hesitate to open a message with an attachment unless they are expecting a document because of the virus potential. Wait until the resume has been requested before sending it. Better yet, make sure your resume is a part of the ePortfolio then there is no need to send a document at all.

Online Instructor Interest Forms

Some institutions have online application or interest forms that can be filled out to show interest in future employment. Do *not* depend on these forms as your only method of contact. Unless the school is very active online, the results of these forms may never see the light of day and are more decorative than functional at present.

Online Learning Experience as a Student

Having experience as an online student will make anyone a better instructor advises Sheila Bartle of Kendall College. "Be in the online student's position and learn what it is like to wait for an answer" (Sheila Bartle, personal communication, October 5, 2008). Having been at the other side of the keyboard offers insights instructors will never have if they have never been in the online student role. It is a great idea, and should really be a requirement, to take a couple of online courses before applying to be an online instructor. Being an online student, and the epiphanies gained from the experience, should be noted in the ePortfolio or during the interview.

Training in Online Teaching and Learning

Most institutions have some form of training required of all online instructors. This is almost always related to how to run the particular course management system (CMS) and has very little to do with online teaching best practices. Future online instructors would be well served to have completed a certificate program in online teaching and learning prior to applying for such jobs. Such training currently is not a requirement, but it certainly is a selling point during an interview. Creating an ePortfolio should be part of an online teaching certificate program. If it is not, use the opportunity to create one anyway. Bear in mind though, even with a certificate or a full degree in online teaching and learning, employers will almost always still require a new employee to be trained on the CMS.

Teaching Qualifications for Educational Institutions

If your area of interest is teaching K–12 online courses, an extremely fast growing field, a current teaching certificate is usually necessary. The tricky part is that the certificate has to be from the state where the program is housed or the state housing the program must offer reciprocity for certificates from the other state. In other words, if a teacher in the state of Washington wants to teach with the Florida Virtual School the Washington teacher would have to have a Florida teaching certificate. Or Florida would have to recognize (offer reciprocity) for certificates from the state of Washington.

Not all states recognize teaching certificates from all other states. For those seeking employment in higher education, usually a master's degree in the field is the absolute minimum to be considered for an online teaching position. Often the standard is higher. A doctorate or another appropriate terminal degree such as a Juris Doctorate (JD) in the legal field may be the minimum requirement for an online adjunct position in higher education.

Job Search

Where to start with an online job search is the hardest element to define. The first step is to network with anyone who is already working in online education. This might be within your current institution or through other networking opportunities. If you have taken courses in online teaching and learning, use all your contacts from that program, including colleagues in the classes. Visit the websites of any programs that might be of interest to you and look for job postings or interest forms. Remember to look in the distance learning site as these faculty positions are often posted separately from traditional faculty jobs. There are some online sites that are also worthwhile to check.

Dr. Peggy Gaskill of Michigan Virtual Universities suggests joining organizations devoted to online learning such as the North American Council for Online Learning (NACOL). If you have a university or community college with whom you have a connection you will want to explore that first. Be on the lookout for programs that offer online courses in your area of expertise, and try to meet some of their instructors through online forums or sites such as LinkedIn. Some of getting hired is still *who you know*. Online learning remains a small world in many ways.

Internship

One of the biggest difficulties for people new to online teaching is that many programs are looking for experienced online teachers. This is similar to the old dilemma faced when young adults try to obtain their first job just out of high school. Everyone wants experience but how do you get experience if no one will hire you? There are a couple of ways to start but they are low or no pay positions. Try to work as an intern with an online instructor. In particular, if you participated in an online teaching and learning training program, ask for help from those teachers and administrators in getting some experience as an intern.

If your institution has some online education underway, ask to work with a current instructor, even if it is in a completely different department to get some experience. In the eLearning certificate program at University of Wisconsin–Stout, students participate in an internship at the end of the program.

INTERVIEWING FOR A POSITION

Prior to Being Hired

Once an interview has been set up, there are some specific things to keep in mind. According to Vandervelde (personal communication, 2008) a major key when interviewing is for the prospective employee not to overstate his or her qualifications. Whether the qualifications are technical skills or experience in the subject matter area, be completely honest with the potential employer. Vandervelde explains many people overstate their technical abilities and expect the institution to remediate these limitations after being hired. Be honest with yourself and the prospective employer about all job skills. Bartle (personal communication, 2008) suggests making sure personal respect for online students comes through in the interview. Occasionally interviewees would joke about students. This disrespect was noted resulting in the interviewee not being hired.

In addition to what the employer might ask, there are some questions you need to ask about any online position, especially if you will be working at a distance from the institution hiring you. Some of the following applies even if you may be onsite, but there are some special challenges when working at a distance for a new employer. The following items are not in any particular order.

Questions to Ask about Course Design and Instruction

Will you be designing the course and will you own the copyright to the materials or will the institution own those rights? If you will not be designing the course, is there someone from the instructional design department with whom you will be working? Who can answer questions about the materials and the assignments? Can you as the course instructor, make changes to a course if you find a problem? If not, who would you contact about broken links or other problems with course materials? Will you have a mentor? Be sure to find out what the maximum class load is, as well as the average number of students in a class.

Ask what the expectations are for amount of time you should be online, and how that online time is to be organized. Will you be expected to be online seven days a week? Five days a week? How much troubleshooting will be expected to be done by you and what is the availability of technical support for you and for students?

Questions about Pay and Administrative Issues

What is the pay structure for the course or teaching assignment? Is it per head or per course? Will the instructor be paid all at once when the course ends or in timely installments throughout the course? Are there benefits of any kind? (Hint: Do not count on it!) What training is required and what training will be available later on for professional development? If this is a higher education institution are tuition waivers available to take courses for free? Are there any faculty members working full-time online for this institution? Do they receive benefits and a salary equivalent to full-time traditional faculty? This will give you a picture of future advancement and tenure possibilities.

AFTER BEING HIRED

Assume, after you asked all those questions listed, that you managed to get hired to teach online. What questions now need to be asked? Some of these apply only to those working at a distance, others apply to all new hires. There are a host of questions to be asked about paperwork and how employees are paid.

If you are working at a distance, you need to find out if there is a state or local income tax in the institution's home state and how you can avoid having these taxes taken out of your paychecks if they do not apply to your location. This is much easier to do in advance of the first paycheck than it is after taxes have already been taken out. Distance educators have lost tax monies to states before they ever realized the states *had* a state income tax. It pays to ask!

Ask about direct deposit immediately as well. It is a hassle, not to mention risky, to have paychecks delivered by snail mail. This is especially true for distance educators who may travel while working online. Ask how and when you will be paid. Some institutions pay online instructors as independent contractors, others treat the instructors as employees. If you are paid as an independent contractor, you will be responsible for paying the federal income taxes on the monies from that institution.

This means you will very likely need to make quarterly payments to the Internal Revenue Service (IRS). Check with an accounting professional. You do not want to find out you owe $5,000 in income and self-employment taxes next April 15 when you get ready to file your forms! Some institutions pay in a lump sum after a course ends, others issue checks every pay cycle. Knowing how often to expect paychecks allows for some financial planning.

Establishing all the financial details is important but even more important than this, especially when working at a distance, is having contact information for everyone! Everyone equals your supervisor to whom you will directly report as well as to whom you can address questions, any and all other online instructors in your department so that you can network and ask questions, and you also need to know who to contact in technical support.

Once you know who to contact, ask those folks about any paperwork that will be expected. How will grades be submitted? What forms are needed by payroll so you can actually get paid for your work? What evaluation forms are required from the instructor or the students? When working at a distance you can be at a real disadvantage when it comes to submitting paperwork. In one case, one of us (Lehmann) was not told about a new form required for submission to the payroll office. When a paycheck failed to arrive in a timely manner, she asked about the delay and was told the new form was not submitted. By that time the deadline for the next month's payroll had passed and she ended up waiting more than three months for the paycheck to arrive.

At hiring is the time to ask whether you will be teaching the course on a continuing basis and how often the course runs. Will you have to be *asked* back each time the course is offered or will it be assumed that you are teaching the course until you are told differently? Does the course run regularly or intermittently? Does a contract have to be signed each time the course is offered or will you be on a continuing contract?

What is the evaluation process and how will you know what your supervisor and your students think about your instruction? What are the institution's policies and where can they be found? Is there an employee handbook? Are there policies concerning student conduct? If so, what are they and are the students aware of these policies? The new hire should not assume that *someone* will think to mention all these things. No one will remember to fill you in. You are just a name and an email address. You will likely have to ask about every one of these items to avoid being in the dark!

Sigh and Get Over It—The Annoyances of Telecommuting

Most institutions, whether educational or business, are not used to employees who telecommute, and this leads to a lot of annoying and just plain stupid communications to the online instructor. For those who work thousands of miles from their employing institution, the best advice is to *sigh and get over it* when . . .

- You are sent parking pass information.
- You are asked to stop by and pick up paper forms from someone's desk or office.
- You receive phone calls on their time zone, and they do not understand why you are not yet up in the morning or why you have already quit for the day.

- You have state and local taxes taken out of your paycheck despite filing tax exemption form.
- You are sent information about weather closures or other local emergency information (although some of this is helpful in being proactive with students who live in that locale).
- You receive invitations to attend events.

But, you should definitely not sigh and get over it if the institution fails to pay you and states they will *catch up* next month. Would you accept that treatment in a face-to-face job?

Working at a distance means you are the equivalent of a ghost at times. Rarely would an institution say to a face-to-face employee "we forgot to process your payroll, but we'll get to it next month." Unfortunately it happens much too frequently when instructors are ghost employees who work from home. You also should not sigh and get missing course evaluations from students or management, but you may need to fix this on your own. On more than one occasion it took institutions months to provide feedback to instructors. This is unacceptable. Just as students need prompt and informative feedback to improve their learning, instructors need prompt feedback so they can improve the course and their own instructional practices. In instances when feedback is not delivered in a timely manner, create your own survey to get information from students in a timely manner.

Keeping the Job

Once a teaching position has been obtained, how does the new hire stay employed? The following applies to those with adjunct or temporary contract status. Most new employees will benefit from connections with others in the department or institution. Making those connections when working at a distance can be much more difficult than when working face to face.

Mentor

Ask if an experienced facilitator from your institution can serve as an official mentor. Having a mentor allows an experienced online instructor to audit the class being taught by a new online facilitator. Students should be made aware a mentor is auditing the course for the sole purpose of helping the instructor. The mentor would lurk in the discussions but not participate. **Lurking** means the person is invisible to those in the class because they are not posting anything. The mentor would read the discussion messages and emails in order to offer ideas behind the scenes to the new teacher. Not only does the new teacher benefit, but mentors benefit through their observation of another teacher and their conversations with their mentee about online teaching.

In addition to seeking a mentor, find out if there is a **listserv** or discussion board that can be used to connect with other instructors. Ask for assistance in wording communications which may prove troublesome. Other instructors have likely encountered difficult situations similar to yours and can help you avoid *saying something stupid* or otherwise getting into trouble.

COMMUNICATION

According to Vandervelde (personal communication, 2008) the number one major source of student complaints is faculty who do not respond to student questions, especially emails, promptly. The next issue is instructors who are not professional in their communications. This may be because the messages are too harsh or curt, which then offends students. The flip side of this issue is instructors who are too informal in their communications. Students expect professionalism. Clearly communication is the number one issue for students and the top reason for instructors to be reprimanded in Vandervelde's experience.

Unless a communication was extreme in some way, it is unlikely that communication style would lead to firing or a failure to be continued, at least not at first. Problems that can lead to a probationary status or outright dismissal involve legal or policy issues such as plagiarism or harassment by the instructor. Hopefully those reading this book will not be involved in such serious problems. Being aware of institutional policies and all laws governing the particular area of education in which the instructor is employed are the keys to staying out of serious trouble.

STAYING CURRENT

Staying current with various CMS versions is almost impossible. You have to be ready to think on your feet and roll with it when a university upgrades to a new version or a different CMS. There is no point in knowing all the bells and whistles of various CMSs because most universities do not invest in every possible feature available. Other institutions do not bother with the upgrades so you will be working with multiple versions of a CMS packaged in multiple ways.

WELCOME TO ONLINE EDUCATION

The world of distance education is growing rapidly. Every instructor needs to give each online student the best experience possible. No book can discuss all the possible scenarios, eventualities, and duties of a profession. This is especially true when the profession is both new and evolving, as this profession is.

> The challenge calls. Clearly I must learn to stay out of my own way and realize that the future will not wait for teachers who are stuck in the past. In fact, the future has already begun and it belongs to our students. Only by embracing the challenge of making learning happen while integrating computer-based technology into the classroom will we prepare our students for the business relationships and friendships they will establish, the environmental troubles they will solve, the cures for diseases they will develop, and the peace among nations for which they must strive. I am grateful for the knowledge and skills I have learned in this course that have prepared me so specifically for this challenge. (Judith Arnold, personal communication, September 19, 2008).

This book hopefully has offered you some insights and ideas of value as you work to be the best online teacher you can be! Your online students deserve no less than your best! Welcome to teaching online!

15

Resources

In this chapter we have compiled documents and other items that may prove useful to other online instructors. You can find in this chapter:

- Table 15.1: Types of Online Courses.
- Precourse Survey.
- Course Support Checklist.
- Personality Type Survey #1 and #2.
- Checklist for Students of Weekly Assignments and Due Dates.
- Example of Grade Weighting and a Table 15.2 Grading Scale.
- Late Assignment Policy.
- Discussion Participation Explanation.
- Self-Reflection Survey for End-of-Module.
- Table 15.3: Reflective Writing Rubric.
- Table 15.4: Small Group Project Rubric.
- Collaboration Survey.
- Portion of a Mini-Module on APA Formatting.
- Figure 15.1: Email Filters.
- Internet Resources Used in *Making the Move to eLearning*.
- Suggested Internet Resources.

Table 15.1. Types of Online Courses

Course Type	Start/End Dates	Description	Instructor Interaction Level	Learner-Learner Interaction Level	Expected Outcomes	Institution Involvement
Online tutorial	Student choice of starting and stopping dates—self-paced time frame	Self-paced, learner-operated instructive web pages Assessment may be built in	No instructor Material is self-taught Help and support are for technical issues	No learner interactions	Low level recall	Free to gain traffic to website No credit/ no certificate granted
Self-paced course	Student choice of starting and stopping dates—self-paced time frame	Student progresses at own rate Assessment built in or with instructor	Either independent or with instructor interaction at certain checkpoints	Unlikely to have substantive learner interactions as students are at different points in the course at any given time	Mastery is determined by checkpoint assignments or assessments	May be used to gain traffic to a website May be charged credit or certificate could be granted
Asynchronous cohort course	Course start/end and unit due dates are primarily controlled by the instructor Times of attendance and interaction within the module remain student choice	A group of students working through the same course together Peer, instructor, and built-in assessment may be a part of the course Discussion boards are used to keep interaction on the learner's own schedule	Instructor-learner interaction is substantial from public and private communication to course assessment and feedback	The cohort model is designed for learner interaction and support As such this area is substantial Despite being asynchronous, some courses may require real-time interaction at times to aid the	The student learns through interaction with the content and processing it through interaction with peers and the instructor Assessments may be built-in, peer, or instructor with frequent feedback	Very like a moneymaking endeavor for the sponsoring agency or Credit/certificate generally granted for learners who complete the course

	within course parameters		cohort and push the learning to a higher level		
Synchronous course	Course start/end and unit due dates are primarily controlled by the instructor Times of attendance and interaction are also controlled by the instructor	Same as asynchronous course with the addition of synchronous activities, discussion, and so on	Same as asynchronous course with the addition of synchronous discussion	Same as asynchronous course with the addition of synchronous activities	Same as asynchronous course	Same as asynchronous course
Hybrid course	Online course times may be fixed or scheduled at the discretion of the course instructor	A course with both online and face-to-face components Learners are expected to participate in both This model is increasingly common in the K–12 setting. It includes attributes of the other models listed	Instructor-learner interactions are substantial They include face-to-face meetings as well as online communications	Learner interaction is highly dependent upon the design of the hybrid model If used for online tutorial, then very little interaction If designed as extension, then it could be highly interactive	This model includes characteristics of both asynchronous and synchronous models as well as standard learning from face-to-face environment Built-in, peer and instructor assessment all are typically used	Moneymaking venture for sponsoring agency or institution May be credit/certificate issued May also be used for remediation or training purposes

(continued)

Table 15.1. (continued)

Course Type	Start/End Dates	Description	Instructor Interaction Level	Learner-Learner Interaction Level	Expected Outcomes	Institution Involvement
Extended classroom online	Follows schedule of face-to-face class	The course instructor provides classroom extension activities such as webquests, extra links, extra readings, and student resources on a class webpage available to students and kept frequently updated	Instructor-learner interaction is by way of "announcements" on the webpage and perhaps a "comments" board build into the site	Learner-learner interaction in minimal, if any	Students have resources available to them 24/7 and feel an instructor availability without the instructor really being available	Provides resources for students who view these instructors as "current" and technically Server space is minimal investment

PRECOURSE SURVEY

This survey was completed online using the site SurveyMonkey.com.

Information about Who You Are and Where and What You Teach

1. First and last name. _____
2. In what school do you currently teach (please indicate city/state.) If you are not currently with a school indicate that.

   _____

3. What grade/subject do you teach? If you are not currently teaching please indicate what grade/subject you would like to teach.

   _____

   If you are an administrator please indicate your position and the grade level of the school. _____

   Information about your computer and your Internet connection.

4. Please indicate the type of computer you will be using most often for this course.

   - Older windows-based PC
   - Newer windows-based PC
   - Older Macintosh
   - Newer Macintosh

5. How will you usually connect to the Internet for this course?

   - Modem (phone line) 56K or 28K
   - Broadband or cable
   - T1 line
   - Wireless internet connection
   - Have no idea but it's fast
   - Have no idea but it's slow

SUPPORT CHECKLIST

(Print this, and keep it by the computer.)

Feel free to ask questions in the question-and-answer (Q&A) forum section of the discussion area. In an emergency you may contact the instructor at: onlinet@notadomain.com or home phone (555) 555-5555 (Pacific Time zone, keep this in mind when making early morning calls).

Course Support

Students can contact the Learn@UW Help Desk (6 a.m.–1 a.m.) at 1-888-435-7589 or 1-608-264-4357, option #3. Please indicate that you are a UW-Stout student.

For students who need help with the Learn@UW system, click on http://www3.uwstout.edu/lit/lts/learn/student_resources.cfm.

PERSONALITY TYPE SURVEY #1—
USED TO CREATE COOPERATIVE GROUPS

(This survey was completed online using the site SurveyMonkey.com.)

1. Enter your first and last name here _____
2. When referring to your own personal general tendencies for completing group tasks would you say you are:

- More of a Type A person—someone who likes to be in control, prefers to get started on a project as quickly as possible and can be impatient when waiting for others to complete their part of a joint task.
- More of a Type B person—someone who is willing to let others take the lead, prefers to wait until near the deadline to get started on a project and is laidback while others complete their part of a joint task.

PERSONALITY TYPE SURVEY #2—
USED TO CREATE COOPERATIVE GROUPS

This survey was completed online using the survey tool inside the course management system (CMS).

1. Enter your first and last name here _____
2. When referring to your own personal general tendencies for saving the world with group members, would you say your personality tends to be:

- More of a Jason Bourne type person—someone who likes to be in control, prefers to get started on "saving the world" as quickly as possible and can be impatient when waiting for the rest of the secret spy world to complete their part of the mission.
- More of a James Bond type person—someone who is willing to let others sit round the roulette table with him or her, prefers to wait until

near the deadline to disarm the bombs, and is patient while waiting for the rest of MI-5 to complete their part of the mission.

CHECKLIST FOR STUDENTS OF
WEEKLY ASSIGNMENTS AND DUE DATES

Module #1 ~9/03–9/07

- Topic: Introduction to Research/Researchable problems.
- Read: Gall, Gall, and Borg, Ch. 1, all, and Ch. 2, pp. 36–44 (to the heading Working on a Team Project); also read the APA manual pp. 3–9.
- Participate in weekly discussions.

Module #2 ~9/08-9/14

- Topic: UWStout's Library Learning Center/APA formatting/Literature Searches.
- Read: Gall, Gall, and Borg, Ch. 4, pp. 89–113 (to Synthesizing the Findings of Your Literature Review); Download APierson APA_Intro document from course site.
- Assignment: Locate a research article, complete the paraphrasing activity, submit it to the dropbox.

Module #3 ~9/15–9/21

- Topic: Research Objectives and Ethical/Legal Issues.
- Read: Gall, Gall, and Borg, Ch. 3, all; Ch. 2, p. 45 to the end.
- Participate in weekly discussion.
- Assignment: Complete Protection of Human Subjects certification training.

EXAMPLE OF GRADE WEIGHTING AND A GRADING SCALE

The grade weighting for this course is as follows:

40 percent	Large group discussions
25 percent	Small group discussions and scenario discussions
10 percent	Portfolio drafts
25 percent	Final fully revised portfolio

The grading scale for this course is as follows in Table 15.2:

Table 15.2.   **Example of Grade Weighting and a Grading Scale**

Grade	Percent
A	90–100
B	80–89
C	70–79
D	60–69
F	<60

LATE ASSIGNMENT POLICY

It is expected that you will find time to participate in the threaded discussions during the dates listed for the unit. It is also expected that you will complete and turn in assignments by the due date. Work is late after midnight Pacific Time on the due date. Work submitted within three days of the due date will earn 80 percent. Work submitted between four and seven days late will earn 50 percent. Work more than seven days late will not be accepted and a zero will be recorded.

It is likely that some participants will be traveling at various times during the course for conferences or family events or emergencies. In addition to notifying the instructor that you will be traveling and may be out of contact, you should plan to work ahead on unit assignments. The instructor will open units two days before they are to begin to allow this flexibility. The threaded discussions will be open one day in advance.

Emergencies arise in everyone's lives and the late policy can be waived, at the discretion of the instructor, for emergencies. You must notify the instructor as soon as reasonably possible (reasonable means don't call from the emergency room, wait until you return home!) about the emergency. An emergency is defined as anything that could not be written on the calendar in advance of the occurrence. Heart attacks and car accidents cannot be written on the calendar in advance, those are emergencies. Parent-teacher conferences, camping trips, and a child's wedding can be written on a calendar in advance. These are not emergencies. Plan ahead for the upcoming events in your life so that your work can be completed on time.

Since this course is online and email never closes for bad weather, illness, etc., problems with home technology will not be accepted as an excuse for late work. Seek out alternate locations you can use to access the course just in case. Do this *before* you have a problem! Computers are available on campuses as well as public libraries, Internet cafes, and so on. There is always a way to get an assignment in.

DISCUSSION PARTICIPATION EXPLANATION

(Posted as part of the syllabus in all classes now.)

Discussions are made of two elements that could be labeled (1) *You* and (2) *Colleagues*. Keep in mind that online discussions in this course are meant to be equivalent with the level of discourse in a face-to-face graduate-level class.

The *You* portion is (a) your own original response to the discussion prompt and (b) your replies to people who respond to your original message. Note that you must return to the discussion after allowing time for your colleagues to reply to your original message if you are to reply to them. This means you cannot fulfill the expectations for the You part of the discussion if you log in at the last hour on the last day of the week. Your colleagues would not have time to reply to your message, nor would you have time to then reply back to them. You must log in more than once during the week to fulfill the expectations. Participating at the last minute in a discussion is the equivalent of showing up in a face-to-face class with five minutes left in the class period and expecting to get full credit for participation. Below is an example to help you understand the You parts of a discussion. The You parts are in italics.

> *Original response: My thoughts on this question are supported by our readings . . .*
>
> Colleague replies: I disagree, I wonder if you have thought about . . .
>
> *Your reply to the colleague: Great question, I based my answer on my experiences and on the textbook which states . . .*

The *Colleague* portion of the discussion is when you reply to the original responses to the discussion prompt *made by your fellow students*. For this to be a true graduate-level discussion, your replies need to take the discussion deeper, further, or in a new direction and your reply should be meaningful to many people in the class, not just the original author. You **CAN** fulfill this expectation by asking questions, playing Devil's advocate, offering suggestions, providing new resources, etc. You *cannot* fulfill this expectation by answering "Great job!" or "Thank you!" or "I agree." These "rah rah" types of answers will not take the discussion deeper and they are meant only for the original author. Below is an example of the Colleague portion of the discussion. The Colleague portion that you would write is in italics.

> Colleague's original response to the prompt: My thinking on this topic changed as I read the textbook and considered how . . .

Your reply: As your thinking evolves on this you might want to read this article published recently . . .

You can earn up to two points for discussion participation. Your messages must exhibit graduate level thinking and analysis of the materials in order to earn the two points and meet the expectations stated. You *must log in more than once* to participate in the discussion in order to fulfill the expectations as stated.

SELF-REFLECTION SURVEY FOR END OF MODULE

(This survey was completed online using the survey tool inside the CMS.)

1. Enter your first and last name here _____
2. I read the Required Module X readings. True ____ False ____
3. My participation in the Scenarios discussion will be rated based on these criteria.

   - Original response to Scenarios forum posted by Wednesday night.
   - Answer supported with the readings or other relevant material and all readings/materials are properly cited.
   - Responded to the original messages posted by some colleagues on at least three separate days throughout the week.
   - Took the Discussion Rubric criteria into consideration

   I award myself a score from 5 (highest) to 1 (lowest). (Use N/A to indicate no participation.)
   Score _____

4. In the box below I will explain the score I awarded myself for the Scenarios discussion by reflecting on my own performance and learning in this forum. (*Please use a couple of specific examples.*)
   _____
   _____

5. Below I will score myself on the completion of the Portfolio assignment using these criteria.

   - Action Plan document submitted by the Sunday night deadline.
   - My methods of interacting with students are listed.
   - The materials and tools I will need are included.
   - A timeline for implementation is outlined.
   - The resources that can be used in times of trouble, or when I wish to have or will need are listed.
   - Document submitted in a universal format such as Word 2003 or earlier, PDF, or web page.

I award myself a score from 5 (highest) to 1 (lowest). (Use N/A to indicate not completed.)

Score _____

6. In the box below I will explain the score I awarded myself on the Portfolio assignment by reflecting on my own performance and learning portfolio assignment. (*Please use a couple of specific examples.*)

---

7. The class is half over. The most important things I have learned so far are . . .

---

what I would still like to learn . . .

Table 15.3. Reflective Writing Rubric

Criterion	Exemplary: Above and Beyond Acceptable Performance	Acceptable: Meets Expectations	Developing: Doesn't Quite Meet Expectations	Unacceptable: Needs Considerable Improvement
Thoughtfulness and clarity	Reflective, thoughtful ideas relevant to the assignment are clearly identified	Presents relevant ideas and connections to the assignment with some clarity	Presents some relevant ideas and connections to the assignment, writing lacks clarity	Few relevant ideas connected to the assignment but most ideas unclear
Organization	Exceptionally well organized	Is generally well organized	Needs more organization	Writing is poorly organized
Details	Reflective piece covers numerous facts and specific details of the learning experience	Some details are used but more detail would make this a better reflection	A few details are used but they don't relate to the examples or they are too few to show the connections to learning	Few to no details are used to show connections to learning
Transitions	Thoughtful transitions which clearly shows how ideas connect	Transitions are not strong or are lacking between some ideas	Transitions between ideas are not strong or are lacking in most places	No transitions between ideas

Table 15.4.   Small Group Project Rubric

Criteria	Pts.	Criteria for Full Credit	Criteria for Partial Credit
Small group process	6	Small group worked effectively to complete the lesson plan as evidenced by their correspondence with the instructor and the notation of their contributions in the introduction of the lesson plan	Sliding scale based on instructor's judgment after reading self-evaluations and peer evaluations in the reflective journals
Individual effort in the group process	6	Each person did a fair share of the work in completing the project as evidenced by their self-evaluation in their reflective journal and the assessment of their peers in their respective journals	Sliding scale based on instructor's judgment after reading self-evaluations and peer evaluations in the reflective journals
LP: Optimizes tech resources	2	Lesson plan clearly states the minimum technology requirements to carry out the plan and offers suggestions for extensions if other resources are available	For 1 point, lesson plan fails to state either the minimum tech requirements or extension possibilities
LP: Develops info literacy and problem-solving skills	2	Lesson plan includes scaffolding and rubrics that assist students in research and carrying out the lesson but allows for open-ended or varying types of results	For 1 point, lesson plan fails to include either scaffolding or rubric(s) or the planned outcome of the lesson is so tightly controlled that student problem solving is limited
LP: Promotes meaningful and effective uses of technology	2	Lesson plan involves technology to carry out operations, create results or products, or extends student learning in ways that would not be possible without the technology	For 1 point, technology is included without meaning or need in some aspect of the project
LP: Aligns with curricular benchmarks or standards	2	Lesson plan states the local, state, or national benchmarks and standards met. These may include curricular area standards, process standards such as reading, writing, or speaking and technology standards such as ISTEs NETS standards. Some of the standards should be national so that the lesson plan is applicable to teachers across the nation	For 1 point, lesson plan fails to address some possible standards or does not include some standards applicable to a teacher outside the state or local area
TOTAL	20		

COLLABORATION SURVEY

(This survey was completed online using the site SurveyMonkey.com.)

Identify yourself and your group mates and evaluate the collaboration in the small group project. This is an anonymous survey, only you and the instructor will see your responses. If someone did not contribute or collaborate, please be honest.

1. What is your full name?
2. Use the drop-down menu to indicate, which small group you were in for the collaborative project? Example, Group A, Group B . . .
3. Award yourself a grade from 4 pts. to 1 pt. how well you communicated with the group. _____
4. Award yourself a grade from 4 pts. to 1 pt. for how well you shared in completing the work. _____
5. Explain anything you would like to here about your own contributions to the group project.

   _____

   _____

6. Enter the full names of your group members here (DO NOT LIST YOURSELF).

   Group mate 1 _____

   Group mate 2 _____

   Group mate 3 _____

   Group mate 4 _____

7. Award a grade from 4 pts. to 1 pt. for each group member for how well they communicated with the group.

   Group mate 1 _____

   Group mate 2 _____

   Group mate 3 _____

   Group mate 4 _____

8. Award a grade from 4 pts. to 1 pt. for each group member for how well they shared in the workload.

   Group mate 1 _____

   Group mate 2 _____

   Group mate 3 _____

   Group mate 4 _____

9. Add any comments here that you would like to make about the contributions of any of your group mates

   _____

   _____

PORTION OF A MINI-MODULE ON AMERICAN
PSYCHOLOGICAL ASSOCIATION FORMATTING

References

There are a lot of picky nuances to note about American Psychological Association (APA) references but here are some of the main problems I see. *Study* the entries in the manual. Look at spacing, punctuation, italics and then emulate those entries.

Format the list with a hanging indent. Type all your entries without worrying about the indent, do not hit Enter at the end of lines, do not hit Tab. When you are all done, highlight all the entries then go to (MS Word directions—see the Help section of your word processing program for directions for other programs) Format/Paragraph, under Special, choose Hanging. Viola, hanging indents.

Learn to use formatting features to help you out. Put in a page break after the last line on your title page, or after the last line of text in your essay, rather than hitting Enter, Enter, Enter to get to the next page. Using a page break makes this much cleaner, especially if you edit something later. Insert/Break/Page Break.

EMAIL FILTERS

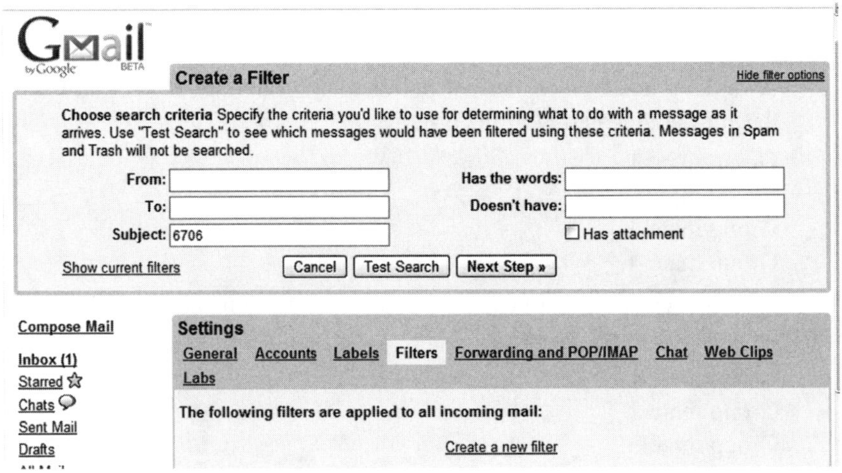

Figure 15.1. Creating a filter in an email program. The filter is the course number, 6706.

INTERNET RESOURCES USED IN
MAKING THE MOVE TO εLEARNING

AngelLearning, http://www.angellearning.com, Course management system, p. 14

Blackboard, http://www.blackboard.com/us/index.bbb, Course management system, p. 14

Desire2Learn, http://www.desire2learn.com, Course management system, p. 14

eCollege, http://www.ecollege.com/index.learn, Course management system, p. 14

PandemicFlu.gov, http://pandemicflu.gov, U.S. Department of Health and Human Services site about pandemic illness readiness, p. 16

VARK, http://www.vark-learn.com, Learning styles visual-aural-read/write-kinesthetic assessment tools, p. 29

Section 508, http://www.section508.gov, Explanation of Section 508 laws and policies concerning accessibility, p. 68

Flashlight Project/TLT, http://www.tltgroup.org, Teaching Learning and Technology group site includes explanation of Dr. Stephen Ehrmann's Flashlight Project, p. 71

Foundation for Critical Thinking, http://criticalthinking.org, Explanations and tools for incorporating critical thinking skills, p. 77

MyReadingLab, http://myreadinglab.com, Supplemental drill and skill site, which accompanies several reading textbooks, p. 86

Revised Bloom's Taxonomy of Cognitive Levels, http://social.chass.ncsu.edu/slatta/hi216/learning/bloom.htm, Taxonomy for incorporation of thinking skills in lessons, p. 88

GLOBE, http://www.globe-info.org, Global Learning Objects Brokered Exchange—Repository of learning objects for use in online courses, p. 104

Americans with Disabilities Act (ADA), http://www.ada.gov, Home page for all information about ADA, p. 107

TurnItIn, http://turnitin.com/static/index.html, Tool for verifying authenticity of student writing, p. 116

Rubistar, http://rubistar.4teachers.org/index.php, Repository of rubrics for all levels as well as tools for creation of original rubrics, p. 132

Skype, http://www.skype.com, Voice over Internet protocol tool, p. 172

Elluminate, http://www.elluminate.com, eLearning and collaboration tools, p. 172

Survey Monkey, http://www.surveymonkey.com, Free online survey tool, p. 229

Del.icio.us, http://delicious.com, Social bookmarking site, store and share bookmarks, p. 243

Family Educational Right to Privacy Act, http://www.ed.gov/policy/gen/guid/fpco/ferpa/index.html, Government site explaining this privacy act known as FERPA, p. 271

LinkedIn, http://www.linkedin.com, Tool for connecting with other professionals, p. 281

SUGGESTED INTERNET RESOURCES

AdjunctNation, http://www.adjunctnation.com, Site for adjuncts for support, advocacy, and job listings.

Higheredjobs.com, http://www.higheredjobs.com/default.cfm, Networking site for finding jobs in higher education. Hint, use the keyword online when searching to find online teaching positions.

MultiMedia Educational Resources for Learning and Teaching Online, http://www.merlot.org/merlot/index.htm, Known as MERLOT Learning object and publication repository.

North American Council for Online Learning, http://www.nacol.org, Known as NACOL organization for K–12 online education.

Readiness to teach online tool, http://depts.cc.edu/its/bb7docs/misc/USED-BB7_misc_faculty_self_eval.pdf, Unsure if online teaching is for you, this self-assessment may be helpful.

Sloan-C, http://www.sloan-c.org, Consortium of institutions interested in online learning. Great source of highly reputed publications about online education.

Glossary

70/30 rule: Seventy percent of an instructor's time is spent during the window of time from before the course begins through the first week of the course. The remaining 30 percent is expended during the entire remainder of the course. (*See also* the window.)

acceptable evidence: The result of a learning activity, which shows the learner mastered the content skills and knowledge in the lesson. This is tangible proof, which can be gathered and then evaluated.

accessibility: Provision of software, hardware, or adaptations to electronic tools such as web pages to allow all users, including those with disabilities to participate. Software includes screen-reading programs such as JAWS, which reads text aloud. Hardware includes alternate keyboards or touch screens. To be compliant with the Americans with Disabilities Act, courses need to be accessible for students requesting accommodations with disabilities. Web page accessibility means people with any disability can use the web page. (*See also* assistive technologies.)

administrivia: Short for administrative trivia. Administrivia are the little tidbits, facts, procedures, and policies that must be related to the students during the window. Instructors also deal with administrivia from supervisors and other personnel at the institution. (*See also* the window.)

adult learning theory: *See* andragogy.

advisor: One of the many hats worn by online facilitators. Students working at a distance often turn to the instructor for assistance and advice. While you may not actually physically register students for classes, you more than likely will be responsible for passing on information about where students can get their transcripts at the end of the course, who they contact regarding technical problems, degree programs, degree audits, add/drops, and so on.

Americans with Disabilities Act (ADA): 1990 act, which mandates access to private and governmental institutions for those with disabilities. To be in compliance with the letter and the spirit of the ADA, online courses need to be accessible for students with disabilities. (*See also* Section 508.)

andragogy: *See* adult learning theory; andragogy is a learning theory, which states that adults learn differently than children and the instructional practices for adults need to be adjusted to their needs as learners. Knowles and colleagues (1998) suggested there are six characteristics of adult learners, which should be considered when planning adult learning. These are the need to know, the learners' self-concept, the role of the learners' experiences, the readiness to learn, the orientation to learning, and the learners' motivation.

anonymity: Students in online courses are largely anonymous. In a text-based environment, it is nearly impossible to know the gender, race, age, or other physical characteristics of students or instructors. There may, in fact, be a desire to remain physically anonymous. Physical anonymity may be one reason some students prefer online courses.

argumentative dialogue: Conversation between participants in which there is constructive disagreement over the course concepts. Such discussion is healthy in building student understanding of the material, but the disagreement must be confined to the issues and not allowed to become personal. Students can disagree with the ideas but not the people.

assessment: Evaluation of student learning. Evaluation may occur during the lesson as the student is completing a task, or at the end of a lesson or unit to determine the extent of student mastery of the content. Assessment should not be confused with the term assignment. (*See also* formative assessment and summative assessment.)

assistive technologies: Devices of all types that help those with disabilities do the same tasks as those without disabilities. In online learning assistive, technologies may include software such as screen-reading programs or hardware. (*See also* accessibility.)

asynchronous: Activities that do not happen at the same time or simultaneously. Students and the instructor do not need to be logged in to the course site at the same time to post or read asynchronous messages. The message postings are stored for others to read in the future. (*See also* synchronous.)

authentic assessment: Authentic means to use in a realistic way. Authentic assessments are used to determine whether students truly learned the intended concepts and skills from a lesson by showing their knowledge. For example, in a carpentry class, an authentic assessment would require students to build something out of wood rather than taking a paper/pencil test. Authentic assessments require students to use the knowledge and skills in some way to show their comprehension.

backward diffusion: The movement of best practices in online learning from the distance classroom into traditional learning environments. Considered backward because it has been commonly believed that traditional educational practices infuse pedagogical skills forward into online courses. Best practices in online courses, however, are often superior to traditional courses. Those teaching in both environments have begun backward diffusion into their traditional programs with best practices from their online courses.

billable hours: Many institutions and agencies pay a set amount for the course. An efficient instructor who uses fewer hours to do the job, increases the dollars per hour when compared to an inefficient instructor who uses the same number of hours to do the same job.

blended learning: *See* hybrid courses.

blog: Short for web log. An online tool for self-publishing content, in particular text-based content. Blogs can be personal diaries, newsletters, editorials, portfolios, or journalistic in nature and are open for the entire world to view. Viewers can leave comments about the blog entries, but unlike wikis, cannot change the entries.

Bloom's taxonomy: An organized schema for describing levels of thinking skills in learning activities. This hierarchy was developed by Benjamin Bloom in 1956 and has been revised by Anderson and Krathwohl (2001). According to the taxonomy, learning activities start with low-level thinking at the base of Bloom's Pyramid of Cognitive Learning, and increase in cognitive skills at the higher levels of the pyramid where students are achieving and thinking at the highest levels.

branching quizzes: A computer-based test that uses intelligent technology to adapt the instrument based on students' previous answers.

chat: A synchronous communication tool that requires all learners to be logged in at the same time and in the same *room* in order to have a conversation. Chat is different than instant messaging in that the chat room is web based whereas instant messaging is specific to the computer on which the instant messaging program resides. (*See also* instant messaging.)

codecs: Technology, either hardware or software for compressing and decompressing audio or video signals to be transmitted and received. Both the person sending the file and the receiver must have the same technology on their machines. Codec stands for *co*mpress/*dec*ompress.

collaboration: Students working together informally at any point in the course. This is not the same as cooperative learning or cooperative groups. (*See also* cooperative learning.)

community: A group of individuals who care about and support one another. (*See also* communities of practice.)

communities of practice: A group of individuals who care about and support one another while working toward mutual goals. This goes to the heart of social constructivism. Furthermore, students in communities of practice are actively and authentically engaged in their learning.

computer-assisted instruction (CAI): Also known as computer-based training (CBT). Computer-assisted trainings are self-paced tutorials devoid of interaction with others in which the program assesses whether the student has successfully completed each learning unit.

constructivism: Learning theory which states learners need to experience and work with the concepts to learn them deeply. Learning is situated in real-life experiences and scenarios, activities are hands on, dialogue between learners and the facilitator is emphasized, learning is not prescribed, it is guided but allowed to be evolutionary, and assessment is authentic. (*See also* social learning theory.)

content-related messages: Messages explaining the curriculum. These postings may clarify the content, explain it more deeply, or add additional details.

cooperative learning: Formal activities in which small groups of students are expected to work together on a defined task. Both the process and the product are important components of cooperative learning. The process is the student-student interaction taking place to complete the task. The product is the final tangible result of the cooperation between the students. Cooperative learning, unlike informal collaboration, is often graded. Instructors need to grade both the process and the product.

correspondence course: Developed by Sir Isaac Pitman, the English inventor of shorthand, who came up with the ingenious idea for delivering instruction to a potentially limitless audience through the mail.

counselor: One of the many hats worn by online instructors. Students working at a distance from an institution often turn to the only contact they have, their facilitator, for help and advice on more personal issues dealing with personality conflicts, future employment, etc.

course conversion: Taking materials from a face-to-face course and turning them into an online course.

course design: May include writing, copy editing, or proofreading. Preparation of the online course materials from setting objectives, gathering materials, and determining the elements of the lesson to deciding how students will be assessed.

course designer: A person who writes or prepares online course materials.

course management system (CMS): A collection of software tools for management of curriculum and students in one website. The system has a log-in portal used to enter each course. Examples are Blackboard, Angel-Learning, eCollege, and Desire2Learn.

critical thinking: Engagement with the learning materials at high cognitive levels. Requires evaluation of information in order to utilize the information in new and inventive ways. (*See also* EASy, engagement.)

dialogue: The whole set of communications about a topic. A dialogue is more than just one or two individual messages; it is the whole conversation. Dialogues can be social, argumentative, and pragmatic. (*See also* social dialogue, argumentative dialogue, and pragmatic dialogue.)

differentiation: Designing the learning experience so that a variety of approaches and products are used to reach multiple preferred learning styles for optimal achievement.

differently abled: Students with disabilities of any type. Some online students are visually impaired and use screen reading software such as JAWS, or adjust the text size to its largest viewing capacity, while deaf or hard-of-hearing students need less visual accommodation but require scripts of any recorded messages, videos, and so on. To be compliant with the Americans with Disabilities Act, courses need to be accessible for students with these kinds of disabilities. (*See also* Americans with Disabilities Act, disability.)

digital immigrants: Term created by Marc Prensky (2001) to describe the divide between the current generation, dubbed millenials by some, and the older generation. Digital immigrants are those of an older generation for whom technology is not second nature. (*See also* millennials.)

digital natives: Term created by Marc Prensky (2001) to describe the divide between the current generation, dubbed millennials by some, and the older generation. The digital natives of this generation, in general, have very good technology skills because they have grown up with technology. (*See also* millennials.)

disability: Students who need assistance in some way because they are differently abled. Students may have difficulty with a sense such as vision or hearing, or they may have cognitive or neurological conditions that impact the ability to learn.

distance education: *See* eLearning.

diversity: Students in an online class may come from anywhere in the world to take the class together (geographical and temporal diversity); they may be of any race although race is often completely invisible in an online class (ethnic or racial diversity); students physical appearance and abilities or disabilities may be diverse although rarely do others in an online class see physical appearance or become aware of disabilities (physical and gender diversity); and students of any age may be in class together and again, unless students state their age, this is an invisible characteristic (diversity of age).

drive-by poster: Student, and very occasionally an instructor, who posts messages, which are brief, breezy, often off-topic, and posted within a short time span. Drive-by posters come into the course site, post a bare minimum as quickly as possible. Frequently these funny quips add little to the overall discussion. The student often is never seen on the discussion board again in that forum that week and therefore misses a chance for true discussion to take place.

dropbox: Tool in many course management systems into which students can upload an assignment for the instructor to download and grade.

EASy: Acronym for evaluate, analyze, and synthesize indicating increasingly more complex thinking skills. This is a change in the order of terms used in the original Bloom's taxonomy. (*See also* Bloom's taxonomy.)

eCertification: Programs taught online that lead to any professional certification.

eLearning: Fully online courses and programs without any traditional classroom seat time.

engagement: Learners active involvement and contributions to the learning community.

English as a second language (ESL): Students whose first language is something other than English, but whose studies are conducted in English. Such students often require some accommodations since they are both translating the material into the new less-familiar language and learning the content. Also may be referred to as English language learner (ELL) or English for speakers of other languages (ESOL).

ePortfolio: The compilation of assignments and reflections in an electronic format. Portfolios can be as simple as a web page with links to documents, and as elaborate as using a site specifically designed for ePortfolios, such as Chalk and Wire.

evaluative messages: Messages, which provide assessment information from facilitator to student or between students. These may be informal evaluations or formal comments on assignments or projects.

face-to-face (f2f): Traditional education conducted in a classroom with a live instructor.

facilitation/facilitator: Skills needed to guide learning without relying on direct instruction. In a constructivist classroom, the instructor assists learners as they come to comprehend the concepts in their own way. The term *guide on the side* is used to describe facilitation.

Family Educational Right to Privacy Act (FERPA): Federal law governing the privacy of student records including, but not limited to, grades. This law applies to the records of adult learners as well as the school records of children.

formative assessment: Evaluation of student learning while the learning activity is still taking place. Formative assessment lets the student know if they are headed in the right direction and what they need to change in order to master the skills and knowledge in the learning activity.

hybrid courses: Reduced traditional seat time in the classroom by placing a portion of instruction on the Internet.

icebreaker: A discussion topic or prompt helping students get to know one another at the beginning of a course.

instant messaging (IM): A synchronous communication tool requiring two or more parties to be online at the same time, and using compatible software programs (such as Yahoo Messenger, MSN Messenger, or AIM) to have a conversation. IM is specific to the machine, computer, or smart phone, on which the IM program resides. Frequently confused with chat that is similar; however chat is web based. (*See also* chat.)

instructional design: Design that includes setting objectives, gathering materials, determining the elements of the lesson, and deciding how students will be assessed.

instructional designer: May also be referred to as course designer, or course writer. Prepares the online course materials, which may include setting objectives, gathering materials, determining the elements of the lesson, and deciding how students will be assessed.

instructional technologist: Technology specialist who may handle programming, course infrastructure, as well as provide assistance to students and instructors.

instructivism: Guided instruction involving traditional teaching techniques familiar to most learners. In an instructivist environment, the teacher is the *sage on the stage*, the source of information, and the center of the learning activities.

JAWS: A screen-reading software program often used by students who are blind or visually impaired.

learner-content interaction: Interaction between students and the course materials and concepts.

learner-facilitator interaction: Interaction between students and the instructor of the course.

learner-learner interaction: Interaction between students in a course.

learning activity: The tasks students are expected to complete in an online course. These may be assessments or assignments. (*See also* assessment.)

learning disabilities: Diagnosed difficulty with some sense or ability that impacts learning. These include cognitive and neurological disorders.

learning styles: Preferred methods by which learners best comprehend course concepts. For example, those with a visual learning style benefit from photos, video, and other visual stimuli when learning a concept. There are a variety of defined learning styles.

link rot: Web page links which cease to work correctly. This occurs when websites are reorganized or taken offline. Maintaining links to web-based content is a continual problem for online instructors and those responsible for the course pages.

listserv: Group email program, which allows the user to send a message to the entire group by using one email address.

loophole generation: Term coined by authors Summerville and Fischetti (2007) for students who spend more time trying to find ways around doing assignments than they spend completing the actual assignment.

lurking: Spending time in a course site reading materials and postings without participating. A person who is lurking is invisible to those in the class because they are not posting or sharing anything.

messages: Individual postings. Messages may or may not be part of a dialogue. (*See also* content-related messages, technical messages, procedural messages, and evaluative messages.)

millennials: Slang term for current generation of students who came of age after the millennium in 2000. (*See also* digital natives.)

module zero: An orientation to be completed before a course begins.

multiple intelligences: Theory developed by Howard Gardner (1983) stating every learner has not one intelligence, but multiple intelligences. The first version of the theory described seven intelligences, currently the theory has eight intelligences with another one being considered. Everyone has a variety of intelligences in varying strengths. Some are more dominant intelligences and others less so.

netiquette: A set of norms for Internet-based communications. These norms clarify the messages sent by individuals and help to prevent misunderstandings.

newbies: Online students who are complete novices with technology usually taking their first ever online course. The extreme newbie is a student who is very unsophisticated with technology requiring help with very simple technological tasks such as sending an email.

online learning: *See* eLearning.

original response: A student's answer to the instructor's discussion prompt. This is different than a reply. Students reply to the original responses posted by their colleagues. An original response creates a new thread in a threaded discussion. Also known as an original posting or original message.

overposting: Posting an overwhelming number of messages by any individual, including an instructor, which leads others to pull back from the discussion.

pandemic proof: Courses taught via the Internet can be continued despite a pandemic disease or serious national or global event (terrorist attack such as 9/11 or severe weather such as a hurricane that devastates a region) that disrupts normal day-to-day activities.

paradigm: A perception of reality which is difficult to change. When the perception or understanding evolves this is called a paradigm shift.

pedagogy: Educational theory which may apply to: (a) All educational practices and activities, or (b) educational practices for children as the instructional population. The second definition, childhood educational practices is the one used in this book. This theory emphasizes that the teacher knows all that needs to be learned and the student is dependent on the teacher for all knowledge. (*See also* instructivism.)

plagiarism: Improper use of copyrighted materials without permission of the copyright holder.

podcast: Audio or video file, which can be downloaded to a handheld device such as an iPod. The file originates on the Internet but unlike streaming audio or video a live Internet connection is not required to replay the file once it is downloaded.

POP3 forwarding: Utility program allowing an email user to receive mail from a second email account in the Inbox of their first email account. For example, the user can receive their work email in their personal email account at home.

portal: A web page that leads into a web of other Internet sites. Also, may be the login page for an Internet site or course management system.

posting: Message placed on a threaded discussion board. This is different than an email message.

pragmatic dialogue: Messages which are topic directed and offer ideas and resources to others deepening the overall discussion.

procedural messages: Messages which explain how the curriculum or the lesson is to be carried out.

remedial learners: Students who are retaking a class or course or need developmental skills to be ready for the regular curriculum.

remote access: Program that allows the user to connect with the files, email accounts, and server in another location. For example, an instructor working at home could access files stored on a computer at their workplace.

reply posting: Answer to an original response. In a threaded discussion, a reply would appear under the original message and indented from the margin. There can be replies to replies, each one indented further from the margin indicating which message was being addressed and in what order.

retention: Student stability in enrollment in a course and in a program. Retention of first time online learners has been shown to be lower than retention of such students in traditional courses.

RSS: Stands for really simple syndication. An Internet user subscribes to have a website send updates by email, or RSS reader, whenever the site is updated. This update could be anything from breaking news from a news site or an alert that a new posting has been made to a blog.

rubric: A learning and grading tool, which explicitly defines all levels of achievement for specified characteristics of a student assignment or project.

scenario: Learning activities where students discuss an event, real or fictional, which occurred in the past.

Section 508: Part of the Vocational Rehabilitation Act (1998), which states that information technology must be made accessible to people with disabilities. It is unclear how or if this law applies specifically to online course management systems. (*See also* Americans with Disabilities Act.)

simulation: Learning activities where students work through a potential event.

smart phone: Internet-enabled cell phone that can be used to send email, work on files, and access PDA-enabled websites handhelds such as Blackberry.

social dialogue: Online discussions that build community by creating ties between the individuals. This type of conversation is encouraged in the Introductions forum and thereafter in a separate forum such as The Lounge. Social dialogues should, for the most part, be kept out of discussions about the course content.

social learning theory: An educational theory which states discourse between people is needed for deep learning to occur.

social networking: Web 2.0 sites featuring interaction with others as the primary purpose. Examples are MySpace and Facebook.

spam: Unsolicited junk mail. Free email accounts such as Hotmail and Yahoo mail receive a lot of spam.

streaming audio: Media available on the Internet that downloads while it is playing. If the computer does not have a fast enough connection or enough available memory, the audio playback will be garbled or stop and start. Streaming video does not have to fully download to the computer before beginning to play.

streaming video: Media available on the Internet that downloads while it is playing. If the computer does not have a fast enough connection or enough available memory, the video playback will be garbled or stop and start. Streaming video does not have to fully download to the computer before beginning to play.

subject matter experts (SME): Instructors, or course designers, who are degreed or have considerable successful work experience in their content area and are therefore qualified to teach at the college or university level. These individuals may lack pedagogical experience, on the ground teaching experience.

summative assessment: Evaluation of student learning that takes place at the end of a lesson or unit to determine student mastery of the skills or knowledge.

synchronous: Activities that occur at the same time or simultaneously. For example, a chat session requires everyone involved to be logged in at the same time. Synchronous activities can be inconvenient if learners are geographically disparate. (*See also* asynchronous.)

teachable moment: Separate mini-modules or insert boxes providing extra instruction with an unfamiliar tool or skill necessary to complete an assignment.

technical messages: Messages explaining how to do something such as attach a document to an email.

telecourse: A series of TV shows either broadcast or prerecorded and given to the student for the duration of the course often supplemented with print materials.

the window: The critical phase in any online course from course shell creation through the first week of the course. Students will make a determination about whether to continue in the course during this time period. This is also the time when a sense of community begins to form between the participants. Seventy percent of an instructor's time is expended during the window. (*See also* 70/30 rule.)

threaded discussion: A forum in a course management system where conversations can take place. The replies under each original message are indented. Subsequent replies to replies are further indented creating a stair-step effect. In this way the viewer can follow the conversation or thread of conversation. Each new, original posting begins a new thread in the forum.

time management: Efficient use of time, specifically as it relates to online teaching.

traditional learning: Physical classroom with a live teacher instructing the class. (Also known as face-to-face, f2f, campus-based, or bricks and mortar.)

Type A/Type B personalities: Personalities designated as Type A or Type B according to the personality definitions first identified by cardiologists Friedmann and Rosenman (1959). Type A learners tend to get to work on a module as soon as it opens and they finish assignments well before the due date. Type A learners are referred to as early birds. Type B learners are more laid-back in getting started and often use the pressure of a deadline to get them going on an assignment, submitting right at the last minute. Type B students are referred to as late risers.

universal design: Design of web pages or learning activities, which allow all learners regardless of their abilities or disabilities to fully participate.

visibility: Instructors should make themselves visible to students regularly, preferably daily. Being visible may be accomplished by posting messages or announcements, returning graded work, or emailing students from the course site.

vodcast: Stands for video-on-demand casting. Video and audio recording placed on the Internet for download or viewing. Similar to a podcast but with video as well as audio.

voice over Internet protocol (VoIP): A tool that uses existing Internet infrastructure to send and receive live audio. Anyone with an Internet and a headset with a microphone can place a VoIP call to anyone else. Essentially the Internet is used as a worldwide telephone service.

Voki: Software from a company called OddCast, which allows the user to record their own voice but uses an animated character which appears to be doing the speaking. This is much like an animated character in a movie.

Web 2.0: Internet tools created particularly with the idea of collaboration and interactivity in mind. These characteristics are what differentiate Web 2.0 from Web 1.0 technologies. Social networking sites are an example of a Web 2.0 tool.

webmail: Email accessed by using an Internet browser window. Some Internet providers have a Webmail option which allows the user to look at the email while on the Internet and later download the same messages into the email folders on their computer.

wi-fi: Also known as a hot spot. An Internet-enabled server broadcasting a signal widely, allowing anyone within range and a wireless network card to use the Internet. Some wi-fi servers require a password or other login information in order to use the server.

wiki: A web page that can be changed by anyone with access rights to the page. Wikis are good for collaborative projects. Wikis differ from blogs in that anyone with permission or rights can change the content of the page. Only the author of the blog can change the blog page. Others can add comments on a blog, but they cannot change the original material posted by the author. In a wiki, all those with access can change the original material infinitely.

WYSIWYG (pronounced *whizzy-wig*): Stands for what you see is what you get. This type of tool eliminates the need to write all the code to format the web page or message. The user can change font, font color, spacing, and so on, and everything appears as it will on the screen.

References

Abdal-Haqqs, I. (1998). *Constructivism in teacher education: Considerations for those who would like practice to theory.* (Report No. EDO-SP-97-8). Washington, DC: Office of Educational Research and Improvements. (ERIC Document Reproduction Service No. ED4266986.)

Allen, D. (2001). *Getting things done.* New York: Penguin Books.

Allen, I. E., & Seaman, J. (2007). *Online nation: Five years of growth in online learning.* Needham, MA: Sloan-C.

American Association of University Professors. (2002). *Sample distance education policy and contract language.* Special Committee on Distance Education and Intellectual Property Issues. Retrieved September 10, 2008 from http://www.aaup.org/AAUP/issues/DE/sampleDE.htm.

American Council on Education. (2000, September 11). *Fact sheet on higher education: Frequently asked questions about distance education.* Retrieved September 14, 2003 from ACE: http://www.acenet.edu/resources/fact-sheets/distance-education.pdf.

Anderson, L. W., & Krathwohl, D. (Eds.). (2001). *A taxonomy for learning, teaching, and assessing: A revision of Bloom's taxonomy of educational objectives.* New York: Longman.

Andrade, H. G. (2005). Teaching with rubrics: The good, the bad, and the ugly. *College Teaching, 53*(1), 27–30.

Baker, A. (2005). *ePortfolio tools and services: State of the art of ePortfolio technologies.* Abstract for Keynote at ePortfolio Forum Austria, 2005, also www.eportfolio.salzburgresearch.at.

Ballenger, B. (2007). *The curious researcher: A guide to writing research papers* (5th ed.). New York: Pearson Longman.

Barnes, M. (1980). *Questioning: The untapped resource.* ERIC document 1888555, Paper presented at the annual meeting of the American Educational Research Association, Boston, MA, April 7–11, 1980.

Berlyne, D. E. (2001). *Jean Piaget; The psychology of intelligence.* M. Piercy & D. E. Berlyne (Trans.). London: Routledge.

Bloom B. S. (1956). *Taxonomy of educational objectives, handbook I: The cognitive domain.* New York: David McKay Co. Inc.

Brooks, C. M., & Ammons, J. L. (2003). Free riding in group projects and the effects of timing, frequency, and specificity of criteria in peer assessments. *Journal of Education for Business, 78*(5), 268–272.

Bruner, J. (2007). Factors motivating and inhibiting faculty in offering their courses via distance education. *Online Journal of Distance Learning Administrators, 10*(2), 1–24.

Bruning, R. H., Schraw, G. J., Ronning, R. R. (1999). *Cognitive psychology and instruction* (3rd ed.). Upper Saddle River, NJ: Prentice-Hall, Inc.

Cavanaugh, J. (2005). Teaching online: A time comparison. *Online Journal of Distance Learning Administration, 8*(1).

Chamberlin, L. (2006a). *The digital abyss?* Retrieved October 4, 2008 from http:// infohighway.wordpress.com/2006/09/29/the-digital-abyss/.

Chamberlin, L. (2006b). *The icebreaker.* Retrieved October 5, 2008 from http:// infohighway.wordpress.com/2006/10/16/the-icebreaker/.

Chang, S., & Smith, R. (2008). Effectiveness of personal interaction in a learner-centered paradigm distance education class based on student satisfaction. *Journal of Research on Technology in Education, 40*(4), 407–426.

Chickering, A. W., & Ehrmann, S. C. (1996, October). Implementing the seven principles: Technology as a lever. *American Association of Higher Education Bulletin,* pp. 3–6. Retrieved October 1, 2008 from http://www.tltgroup.org/programs/ seven.html.

Chickering, A. W., & Gamson, Z. F. (1987). Seven principles for good practice in undergraduate education. *The Wingspread Journal, 9*(2). Racine, WI: The Johnson Foundation.

Chyung, S. (2007, Fall). Age and gender differences in online behavior, self-efficacy, and academic performance. *Quarterly Review of Distance Education, 8*(3), 213–222.

Clegg, P., & Heap, J. (2006). Facing the challenge of e-learning: Reflections on teaching evidence-based practice through online discussion groups. *Innovate, 2*(6).

Collison, G., Tinker, R., Elbaum, B., & Haavind, S. (2000). *Facilitating online learning: Effective strategies for moderators.* Madison, WI: Atwood Publishing, LLC.

Critical Thinking.org. (2008). Our concept of critical thinking. Retrieved September 30, 2008 from http://www.criticalthinking.org/page.cfm?PageID=411&Category ID=51.

Dede, C. (2006). *Technology-based and distance learning strategies. The condition of education in rural schools.* Washington, DC: Center for Rural Education, U.S. Department of Education.

Deenen, V. P. (2005). From message posting to learning dialogues: Factors affecting learner participation in asynchronous discussion. *Distance Education, 26*(1), 127–148.

Edmonds, C. D. (2004). Providing access to students with disabilities in online distance education: Legal and technical concerns for higher education. *The American Journal for Distance Education, 18*(1), 51–62.

Ehrmann, S. C., & Zuniga, R. E. (1997). *The Flashlight evaluation handbook, including the Flashlight Current Student Inventory,* Washington, DC: The TLT Group.

Fleming, N. (2006). *VARK: A guide to learning styles.* Accessed August 12, 2008 at http://www.vark-learn.com/english/index.asp.

Friedmann, M., & Rosenman, R. H. (1959). Association of specific overt behavior pattern with blood and cardiovascular findings. *Journal of the American Medical Association, 169,* 1286–1296.

Galagan, P. (2001). Mission e-possible: The Cisco e-learning story. *Training & Development, 55*(2), 46–56. (ERIC Document Reproduction Service No. EJ619225) Retrieved October 4, 2008, from ERIC database.

Gardner, H. (1983). *Frames of mind: The theory of multiple intelligences.* New York: Basic Books.

Gillies, R. M., & Ashman, A. F. (Eds.). (2003). *Co-operative learning: The social and intellectual outcomes of learning in groups.* London: Routledge Falmer.

Global Learning Objects Brokered Exchange. (2008). Retrieved August 18, 2008 from http://globe-info.org/en/.

Green, R. S., Eppler, M. A., Ironsmith, M., Wuensch, K. L. (2007). Review question formats and web-design usability in computer-assisted instruction. *British Journal of Educational Technology, 38*(4), 679–686.

Gupta, S., Eastman, J. K., & Swift, C. O. (2005). Creating an effective online learning environment: A shift in the pedagogical paradigm. *Academy of Educational Leadership Journal, 9*(3), 79–88.

Hall, B. (2000). *eLearning: Building competitive advantage through people and technology.* Retrieved September 14, 2003, from Forbes eLearning: http://www.forbes.com/special sections/elearning/e-01.htm.

Herman, C., & Kirkup, G. (2008, February). Learners in transition: The use of ePortfolios for women returners to science, engineering and technology. *Innovations in Education & Teaching International, 45*(1), 67–76.

Howard, J. R. (2002). Do college students participate more in discussion in traditional delivery courses or in interactive telecourses? A preliminary comparison. *The Journal of Higher Education, 73*(6), 764–780.

Karp, D., & Yoels, W. (1987). The college classroom: Some observations on the meanings of student participation. *Sociology and Social Research, 60,* 421–439.

Keeler, C. G., & Horney, M. (2007). Online course designs: Are special needs being met? The *American Journal of Distance Education, 21*(2), 61–75.

Keinan, G., & Koren, M. (2002). Teaming up type A's and B's: The effects of group composition on performance and satisfaction. *Applied Psychology: An International Review, 51*(3), 425–445.

Kim, K-J., & Bonk, C. J. (2006). The future of online teaching and learning: The survey says. *EduCause Quarterly, 29*(4), 22–30.

Knowles, M., Holton, E., & Swanson, R. (1988). *The adult learner.* Wolburn, MA: Butterworth-Heineman.

Lehmann, J. M. (2008). *Voice-over Internet protocol and student learning: Graduate student perception of learning when VoIP is used as one method of communication.* Saarbrucken, Germany: VDM-Verlag.

Lehmann, K. L. (2004). *How to be a great online teacher.* Lanham, MD: Rowman & Littlefield.

Lehmann, K. L. (2008). *Creating cooperative groups that work: The role of Type A/B personalities in forming cooperative groups.* Saarbrucken, Germany: VDM Verlag.

Loh-Ludher, L. (2007). The socioeconomic context of home-based learning by women in Malaysia. *Distance Education, 28*(2), 179–193.

Lokken, F., Womer, L., & Mullins, C. (2008). *2007 Distance education survey results: Tracking the impact of eLearning at community colleges.* Instructional Technology Council.

McLuhan, M. (1994). *Understanding media: The extensions of man.* Cambridge, MA: MIT Press.

McTighe, J., & Wiggins, G. (1999). *The understanding by design handbook.* Alexandria, VA: Association of Supervision and Curriculum Development.

Merriam-Webster Online. (2007). Retrieved on July 20, 2007, from http://www.m-w.com.

Motteram, G., & Forrester, G. (2005). Becoming an online distance learner: What can be learned from students' experiences of induction to distance programmes. *Distance Education, 26*(3), 281–298.

Nagel, L., Blignaut, A. S., & Cronjeacute, J. C. (2008). Read-only participants: A case for student communication in online classes. *Interactive Learning Environments.* Retrieved August 28, 2008 from http://www.informaworld.com/smpp/content~content=a792260223~db=all~order=pubdate.

National Center for Educational Statistics. (2004). *Digest of education statistics tables and figures.* Washington, DC: U.S. Department of Education, Institute of Education Sciences.

O'Quinn, L., & Corry, M. (2002). Factors that deter faculty from participating in distance education. *Online Journal of Distance Learning Administration, 5*(4), 1–16.

Pachnowski, L. M., & Jurczyk, J. P. (2003). Perceptions of faculty on the effect of distance learning technology on faculty preparation time. *Online Journal of Distance Learning Administration, 6*(3), 1–10.

Papastergiou, M. (2006). Course management systems as tools for the creation of online learning environments: Evaluation from a social constructivist perspective and implications for their design. *International Journal on E-Learning, 5*(4), 593–622.

Pellerin, C. (2007, July 18). *Pandemic preparation boosts readiness for other disasters.* America.gov Retrieved September 24, 2008 from http://www.america.gov/st/washfile-english/2007/July/20070718125554lcnirellep0.3902094.html.

Phillips, V. (1998). Virtual classrooms, real education. *Nation's Business, 86*(5), 41–44.

Polsani, P. R. (2003). The use and abuse of reusable learning objects. *Journal of Digital Information, 3*(4). Retrieved August 18, 2008 from http://jodi.tamu.edu/Articles/v03/i04/Polsani.

Prensky, M. (2001). Digital natives, digital immigrants: A new way to look at ourselves and our kids. *On the Horizon, 9*(5), 1–6. Retrieved June 19, 2008 from http://www.marcprensky.com/writing/Prensky%20-%20Digital%20Natives,%20D igital%20Immigrants%20-%20Part1.pdf.

Prensky, M. (2008). Turning on the lights. *Educational Leadership, 65*(6), 40–45.

Price, L. (2006). Gender differences and similarities in online courses: Challenging stereotypical views of women. *Journal of Computer Assisted Learning, 22*(5), 349–359.

Richardson, J., & Newby, T. (2006). The role of students' cognitive engagement in online learning. *American Journal of Distance Education, 20*(1), 23–37.

Royal, C. (2005). A meta-analysis of journal articles intersecting issues of Internet and gender. *Journal of Technical Writing and Communication, 35*(4), 403–429.

Shea, P. J. (2007). Bridges and barriers to teaching online college courses: A study of experienced online faculty in thirty-six colleges. *Journal of Asynchronous Learning Networks, 11*(2), 73–128.

Shea, P. J., Fredericksen, E. E., & Pickett, A. (2001). *Student satisfaction and reported learning in the SUNY learning network.* New York: The State University of New York.

Silver, H. F., & Hanson, J. R. (1996). *Learning styles and strengths.* Woodbridge, NJ: The Thoughtful Education Press.

Simba Information, Inc. (2007). Leading e-learning platform vendors to generate $660.8 million this year, capturing 48% of their market. *Corporate Training and Development Advisor, 12*(6), 1–4.

Simoncelli, A. P. (2005). *Designing online instruction for post-secondary students with learning disabilities.* Unpublished doctoral dissertation. Retrieved January 26, 2007 from ProQuest retrieval number AAT 3199763.

Stacey, E. (1999). Collaborative learning in an online environment. [Electronic version] *Journal of Distance Education, 14*(2). Retrieved July 5, 2004, from http://cade.athabascau.ca/vol14.2/stacey.html.

Stodel, E. J., Thompson, T. L., & MacDonald, C. J. (2006). Learners' perspectives on what is missing from online learning: Interpretations through the community of inquiry framework. *The International Review of Research in Open and Distance Learning, 7*(3). Retrieved October 4, 2008 from http://www.irrodl.org/index.php/irrodl/article/viewArticle/325/743.

Summerville, J., & Fischetti, J. (2007). The loophole generation. *Innovate: Journal of Online Education, 4*(2).

Sweeney, P. (2007). Web-based learning gains more converts. *Financial Executive, 23*(4), 18–21.

Tennessee Board of Regents. (2006). *TBR e-Learning wiki: Quality matters peer course review rubric.* Retrieved September 30, 2008 from http://eLearning-wiki.tbr.edu/QMannotated.

Tomlinson, C. A. (1999). *The differentiated classroom: Responding to the needs of all learners.* Alexandria, VA: Association of Supervision and Curriculum Development.

Tyler-Smith, K. (2006). Early attrition among first time eLearners: A review of factors that contribute to drop-out, withdrawal and non-completion rates of adult learners undertaking eLearning programmes. *Journal of Online Learning and Teaching.* 2(2), 73–85.

United Nations Educational Scientific and Cultural Organization. (2002). *Open and distance learning: Trends, policies, and strategy considerations.* Paris: UNESCO Division of Higher Education.

United States Access Board. (2008). *Section 508 homepage: Electronic and information technology, e-Learning.* Accessed Aug. 11, 2008 at http://www.access-board.gov/sec508/e-learning.htm.

United States Department of Health and Human Services. (2008). *Pandemic flu home.* Retrieved October 11, 2008 from http://pandemicflu.gov/.

Viscusi, S. (2008, August 26). *Survey: Two-thirds of colleges leveraging green technology.* TMCnet.com. Retrieved September 24, 2008 from http://green.tmcnet.com/topics/green/articles/38089-survey-two-thirds-colleges-leveraging-green-technology.htm.

Vygotsky, L. (1978). *Mind in society: The development of higher psychological processes.* M. Cole, V. John-Steiner, S. Scribner, & E. Souberman, (Eds.). Cambridge, MA: Harvard University Press.

Weiss, T. R. (2008, August 29). *New Orleans IT departments brace for Gustav.* ComputerWorld.com. Retrieved September 24, 2008 from http://www.computerworld.com/action/article.do?command=viewArticleBasic&taxonomyName=Disaster+Recovery&articleId=9113880&taxonomyId=151&pageNumber=1.

Wells, A. T. (2008, February 6). *A portrait of early Internet adopters: Why people first went online and why they stayed.* Pew/Internet and American Life Project. Retrieved October 11, 2008 from http://www.pewinternet.org/pdfs/PIP_Early_Adopters.pdf.

Wenger, E. (1999). *Communities of practice: Learning, meaning, and identity.* Cambridge University Press.

Wirt, J., Choy, S., Rooney, P., Provasnik, S., Sen, A., & Tobin, R. (2004). *The Condition of Education 2004 (NCES 2004-077).* U.S. Department of Education, National Center for Education Statistics. Washington, DC: U.S. Government Printing Office.

Woolfolk, A. (2004). *Educational psychology.* (3rd ed). Boston: Pearson.

Young, J. R. (2008, July 8). Gas prices drive students to online courses. *Chronicle of Higher Education.* Retrieved September 25, 2008 from http://chronicle.com/free/2008/07/3704n.htm.

Zandberg, I., & Lewis, L. (2008). *Technology-based distance education courses for public elementary and secondary school students: 2002–03 and 2004–05.* (NCES 2008–008). National Center for Education Statistics, Institute of Education Sciences, U.S. Department of Education. Washington, DC.

Index

ANN SNYDER
UWM HUMAN MOVEMENT SCIENCES ENDERIS HALL RM 411 2400
2400 E. HARTFORD AVENUE ENDERIS 411
MILWAUKEE, WISCONSIN 53201−0413
United States

Billing Address:
WENDY PRIBBANOW
UWM ALLIED HEALTH
ENDERIS HALL RM 411 2400 E. HARTFORD AVENUE
MILWAUKEE, WISCONSIN 53201−0413
United States

D2LrtgJXR/−1 of 1−/std−us/4464164 1S

Your order of October 5, 2009 (Order ID 002−5487851−9586660)

Qty.	Item
	IN THIS SHIPMENT
1	**Making the Move to eLearning: Putting Your Course Online** Kay Lehmann −−− Paperback (** P−3−G9B167 **) 1607090414 1607090414

Subtotal
Shipping & Handlir
Order Total
Paid via Visa
Balance due

This shipment completes your order.

Have feedback on how we packaged your order? Tell us at www.amazon.com/packaging.

http://www.amazon.com

For detailed information about this and other orders, please visit
Your Account. You can also print invoices, change your e-mail
address and payment settings, alter your communication
preferences, and much more – 24 hours a day – at
http://www.amazon.com/your-account.

Returns Are Easy!

Visit http://www.amazon.com/returns to return any item –
including gifts – in unopened or original condition within 30
days for a full refund (other restrictions apply). Please have
your order ID ready.

**Thanks for shopping at Amazon.com, and please
come again!**

Shipping Address:

ANN SNYDER
WM HUMAN MOVEMENT SCIENCES ENDERIS HALL RM 411 2400
2400 E. HARTFORD AVENUE ENDERIS 411
MILWAUKEE, WISCONSIN 53201-0413
United States

Item Price	Total
$28.59	$28.59

	$28.59
g	$2.49
	$31.08
	$31.08
	$0.00

millennials, 45, 213. *See also* digital
  natives/immigrants
mini-module, 63, 116, 240
module zero. *See* orientation
multiple intelligences, 19, 25–26, 28–
  30, 116, 160

National Center for Educational
  Statistics, 46, 90
navigation, 2, 39, 55, 85, 87, 89, 149,
  171–72, 179–80, 197
negative Nellies, 36, 107, 111, 119,
  133–34, 141, 143, 145–46, 150
netiquette, 141–42, 144, 166
newbie, 44–45, 53, 56, 70, 123, 148,
  165, 195–96
news. *See* announcement
nonvolunteer faculty, 36, 37

objectives. *See* outcomes
office hours, 79, 126, 180, 187, 213, 215
offline, how to work, 176, 189, 203
operating system, 32, 133, 191, 195,
  205–9, 215, 231
orientation, 195, 157, 172–73, 195
original response, 100, 106, 164,
  235–36
outcomes, 2, 13, 16, 38, 68–69, 75, 77,
  91–93, 95–97, 104–5, 108, 228, 230
overposting, 120, 144

pandemic proof, 3, 13
paradigm shift, 38, 58–59
participation, 52, 62, 76–77, 81, 93,
  100, 103, 105–6, 108, 120, 136, 140,
  144, 148, 158, 165–66, 168–71, 177,
  235–36. *See also* attendance
pedagogy learning theory, 5, 19, 24–25,
  31–32, 36–38, 46, 66, 136
peer review, 62, 79–80, 101, 185
performance tasks, 93, 97–98, 105. *See
  also* authentic assessment
Piaget, 20–21, 139
plagiarism, 82, 95, 101, 129, 213, 225.
  See also cheating; exams/quizzes

podcast, 13, 61, 87, 89, 218
policies, course or institution, 35, 37,
  57, 165, 168–69, 185, 188, 223, 225
portal, 12, 183
positive, 4, 16, 107–8, 110–11, 114–
  15, 123–24, 126, 128, 133, 140–
  41, 145, 196. *See also* sandwich
  method
precourse, 60, 141, 155–56, 161, 188,
  191, 203, 205, 211, 231
Price, 52–53
privacy online. *See* security online
proactive, 133, 152, 157–58, 172, 180,
  188, 190, 203–4, 208, 211, 224
program director, 5, 14, 41, 175, 213–
  15, 218, 222–23
prompt, discussion or assignment
  starter, 64, 77, 82–83, 96, 98, 100,
  113, 119, 140, 159–60, 163–64,
  168–69, 235

Q&A, 60, 117, 126, 145, 149, 158, 167,
  179, 196, 210, 231

radical truth, 1–2, 6
reflective teaching, 21, 27, 63, 83, 94,
  98–99, 105, 107, 109, 111, 179, 182,
  187, 194, 236–38
remedial learners, 55–56
remote access, 214–15
retention of students in online courses,
  114, 141
revision, 40, 63, 70, 90, 99, 105, 187
rubric, 64, 80–81, 83, 97, 99–101, 103–
  6, 108–10, 122, 144–48, 169, 185,
  193, 236–38

sandwich method, 107–8
scaffolding, 3, 21, 38, 63, 68, 79, 89,
  197, 238
scenario, 19, 23, 29, 61, 64, 83–84, 111,
  127, 145, 151, 163, 167, 170, 226,
  233, 236
screen reading software, 25–26, 56–57,
  65, 87–90, 136, 179